THE
INQUIRING MIND

Da Capo Press Reprints in

AMERICAN CONSTITUTIONAL AND LEGAL HISTORY

GENERAL EDITOR: LEONARD W. LEVY

Claremont Graduate School

THE
INQUIRING MIND

by
Zechariah Chafee, Jr.

DA CAPO PRESS • NEW YORK • 1974

Library of Congress Cataloging in Publication Data

Chafee, Zechariah, 1885-1957.
   The inquiring mind.

   (Da Capo Press reprints in American constitutional
and legal history)
   Reprint of the ed. published by Harcourt, Brace,
New York.
   1. Liberty of speech — United States — Addresses,
essays, lectures. 2. Labor laws and legislation —
United States — Addresses, essays, lectures. I. Title.
KF4772.A75C43   1974   342'.73'085   74-699
ISBN 0-306-70641-5

This Da Capo Press edition of *The Inquiring Mind* is an unabridged
reprint of the first edition published in New York in 1928.

Published by Da Capo Press, Inc.
A Subsidiary of Plenum Publishing Corporation
227 West 17th Street, New York, N.Y. 10011

186693

THE INQUIRING MIND

ZECHARIAH CHAFEE, Jr.

Author of
FREEDOM OF SPEECH

Contributor to
CIVILIZATION IN THE UNITED STATES
THE NEXT WAR

Editor of
CASES ON EQUITABLE RELIEF AGAINST TORTS
BRANNAN'S NEGOTIABLE INSTRUMENTS LAW ANNOTATED

THE INQUIRING MIND

BY

ZECHARIAH CHAFEE, Jr.

PROFESSOR OF LAW IN HARVARD UNIVERSITY

NEW YORK
HARCOURT, BRACE AND COMPANY

PRINTED IN THE U. S. A. BY
QUINN & BODEN COMPANY, INC
RAHWAY, N. J.

TO

THOMAS WILLIAM SALMON

TIRELESSLY EAGER TO CUT HIS WAY
THROUGH BAFFLING PROBLEMS
TO REACH ISOLATED AND PERPLEXED MINDS
AND BRING THEM INTO RENEWED COMMUNICATION
WITH THEIR FELLOW MEN
THIS BOOK IS DEDICATED WITH ENDURING AFFECTION
MANY OF ITS CONCLUSIONS ARE NOT HIS
BUT INTO ITS SPIRIT HAVE ENTERED
FIFTEEN YEARS OF FRIENDSHIP
WITH HIS INQUIRING MIND

Nicht die Wahrheit, in deren Besitz irgend ein Mensch ist oder zu sein vermeinet, sondern die aufrichtige Mühe, hinter die Wahrheit zu kommen, macht den Werth des Menschen. Denn nicht durch den Besitz, sondern durch die Nachforschung der Wahrheit erweitern sich seine Kräfte, worin allein seine immer wachsende Vollkommenheit bestehet. Der Besitz macht ruhig, träge, stolz. Wenn Gott in seiner Rechten alle Wahrheit und in seiner Linken den einzigen immer regen Trieb nach Wahrheit, obschon mit dem Zusatze, mich immer und ewig zu irren, verschlossen hielte, und spräche zu mir: ":Wahle!" Ich fiele ihm mit Demuth in seine Linke, und sagte: "Vater, gieb! die reine Wahrheit ist ja doch nur für Dich allein!"

Not the truth in any one's actual or supposed possession, but the sincere effort he has exerted to master the truth, makes the worth of the man. For not through the possession but through the pursuit of truth comes that widening of a man's powers by which alone is achieved his ever-growing perfection. Possession makes one stagnant, lazy, proud. If God held shut in His right hand the whole of truth, and in His left hand only ever-active striving after truth with the certainty of ever and always erring, and He said to me, "Choose!" I should humbly reach toward His left hand, saying, "Father, give me this! The pure truth is indeed for Thee alone!"

LESSING, *Eine Duplik*

PREFACE

THIS collection of essays on liberty and other constitutional problems was made possible by the courtesy of the periodicals in which most of the papers were originally printed, the *American Mercury*, the *New Republic*, the *Nation*, the *Independent*, the *Harvard Law Review*, the New York *Evening Post*, and the New York *World*. Thanks are due to all of these for permitting the use of the material. A few of the essays are here printed for the first time.

Expressions of opinion have not been altered in the process of revision, but a few errors of fact have been corrected and passages of temporary nature have been omitted or modified. In addition I have endeavored to supply in an initial footnote any facts which seem important as a background for the particular essay, for much that was fresh in the public mind when it was first printed may now need recalling.

These essays were written for the general reader and endeavor to avoid technicalities in the text, but footnote references to statutes, decisions, and other sources have been inserted for the convenience of those who wish to pursue further the inquiries suggested. My purpose has been to outline problems and state difficulties rather than furnish final solutions. I have played the part of the beater who stirs up the game for others to shoot at, and like him I must not complain if I am grazed by an occasional shot.

Most of the essays are attempts to ascertain the proper scope for liberty in various concrete situations. The theoretical and historical bases of liberty of discussion have been more fully examined in my book on *Freedom of Speech,* which applied the principles worked out in its opening chapter to events between 1917 and 1920. Much has happened during the seven years since that book went to press. Because recent free speech problems have not been systematically considered elsewhere, it may be useful to collect in one volume these contemporaneous reviews of successive judicial decisions. All the important cases in the United States Supreme Court have been included except those relating to searches and seizures, and several interesting cases in the state courts are also treated. In order to avoid repetition, I have occasionally inserted references to *Freedom of Speech* for material on the earlier history of some of the topics discussed. Aspects of the recent history of liberty of discussion which I have not had the opportunity to investigate are: the repeal in 1921 of the 1918 amendments to the Espionage Act; the operation of the laws governing the immigration and deportation of radical aliens, particularly the refusal of temporary visits to well-known foreigners like the Karolyis; the disbarment of several of the few lawyers who have been willing to represent radicals in the courts; and the action of some judges in punishing criticism of their decisions as contempt of court.

The essays on industrial relations are necessarily less complete than those on sedition laws. The alternative policy to sedition laws is fairly simple—toleration, an efficient police to put down violence, good arguments against revolution, and stimulating education. The alter-

native policy to our present methods of handling industrial disputes is still uncertain, and, whatever it is, it
must surely be complicated. For instance, the machinery
for satisfactory governmental arbitration, if that is the
way out, will have to be developed in detail after careful
investigation of the methods used in Australia, Canada,
and other countries. Such a task will require the work
of several men with special training and prolonged investigations abroad. These essays are chiefly concerned with
certain undesirable features of the present methods,
which indicate the need of a changed policy.

This book sometimes reaches the conclusion that an
unpopular group has been badly treated. That is no
reason for the assumption that the author shares the
beliefs of that group. An alienist who wants better insane
asylums is not necessarily a lunatic. William Lloyd Garrison was not a negro, and Gamaliel was not a Christian.
In the same way, the expression of doubts regarding certain aspects of the labor injunction does not involve un-
qualified support of the American Federation of Labor
or any other union by one who began active life among
employers. The essay on the Interchurch Steel Report
ought to make this plain. In order to avoid any misap-
prehensions that I am a socialist, a communist, an anarchist, an I.W.W., or an atheist, let me intrude my personal views and deny participation in the intellectual
views of all or any of these various groups. I have not
the slightest desire for a soviet government in the United
States, and I do not want Fascism here either. While I
think that there has been insufficient toleration for the
expression of arguments against private property, I remain sufficiently convinced of the value of property to

spend most of my time studying how the law can adequately protect it. My sympathies and all my interests and associations are with people who save, who manage and produce. But I want my side to fight fairly and wisely, and I regard some of the methods hereafter discussed for safeguarding the existing political and economic system as distinctly short-sighted or unfair fighting.

Z. CHAFEE, JR.

Cambridge, Massachusetts
February, 1928

CONTENTS

THE INQUIRING MIND

THE INQUIRING MIND[1]

I

KNOWLEDGE is not a series of propositions to be absorbed, but a series of problems to be solved. Or rather I should say, to be partly solved, for all the answers are incomplete and tentative. This view of life is in no way original, but it is frequently ignored. From the fact that reading, writing, and arithmetic are the bases of education and were long the only education for most persons, we have unfortunately been led to regard them as typical of *all* education. We feel that knowledge is something that has been settled by others and given us to learn, just as we learned the multiplication table.

Nevertheless, outside the field of such established facts as the three R's there lies a much vaster area, and with it citizens must acquaint themselves if democratic government is to manage our modern industrial civilization successfully. Knowledge of this vaster area cannot be obtained merely from what others tell us; it must come from what we find out ourselves by asking and answering questions. Therefore, the true type of education is not the certainty of the multiplication table, but the incomplete approximation of the square root of two, or better yet, the undiscoverable ratio between the circumference and

[1] First printed in *The American Mercury,* August, 1924. Copyright by the author. Originally part of an address delivered on the twentieth anniversary of the Sphinx society at Brown University, March 27, 1924.

3

the diameter of a circle. (How strange that such a common fact should be so complex!) Indeed, we may eventually come to take as our typical fact the square root of minus one, which, although we call it an imaginary quantity, forms a necessary element of many of the electrical calculations that make possible the ordinary operations of our daily lives. In school geometries the propositions are printed in large type and the originals are tucked away in the back in small print. Some day we shall realize that the propositions are far less important than the originals.

II

The fruitfulness of this method of constant inquiry is demonstrated by the experience of Darwin. His voyage around the world brought him into contact with many interesting facts which he recorded faithfully, but he was not content to rest with the acquisition of facts. He began to ask himself a question that he could not answer. Soon after his return to England he opened his notebook on the origin of species, in which he preserved all the information he could find for the sake of answering that one question. His method of using books he learned from Buckle, who used to jot down on the fly-leaf of every book he read references to passages in it which he thought might prove serviceable to him. "How do you know," Darwin asked, "which passages to select?" Buckle replied that he did not know, that a sort of instinct guided him. When the thinker has formulated his problem, the facts he meets are bound to shape themselves with regard to it, just as a magnet throws all the iron filings brought near it into one pattern.

Darwin asked himself one question, and spent the rest

of his life answering it. Pasteur propounded a succession of riddles, and his earlier problems offered little prospect that their solution would aid mankind. What relation to human happiness was there in his first riddle, the difference in the deflection of light through the crystals formed by tartaric and paratartaric acids, a difference which apparently concerns nobody? From this he passed to the even more useless problem of the possibility of spontaneous generation. Yet this led to the question of fermentation, and from the diseases of beverages he turned to explain those of animals and men. The possession of theoretical knowledge, indeed, seems almost sure to create opportunities for its practical use.

This progress from the theoretical to the practical was reversed in the riddles that beset Kepler, the forerunner of Newton. Finding himself financially prosperous, he decided to place some well-filled casks in his cellar. They must be made of wood, and wood was expensive. Hence a problem, quite independent of the pleasures of theory, but all-important to the economical head of a household: how to get the greatest cubical content of wine into the minimum amount of wood. Should the cask be apple-shaped, pear-shaped, or lemon-shaped? We can imagine him out in his orchard laying boards in various positions on temporary frames and then generalizing his results in mathematical formulae. They developed into his book on the measurement of casks, and became the foundation of infinitesimal calculus, the basis of all our pure and applied science today.

Einstein at five years old was, as he lay in his cot, given a compass by his father. The remembrance of the swinging needle remained with him, suggesting invisible forces, which later he was to explore in electromagnetic waves and gravitation. At twenty-two, struggling with poverty as a private tutor, a friend obtained for him a position as examiner of patents in the Swiss Patent Office. Instead of repining at this job as five years' enslavement, he made his experience in varied fields of invention interlock so widely with the solution of theoretical problems that before he left he published in quick succession the first series of his dissertations on the theory of relativity. To the inquiring mind, all experience is gathered into the solution of overmastering problems.

Nor need my illustrations be limited to the non-human sciences. Frederick William Maitland, the English legal historian, became interested in a German treatise on the political theories of the Middle Ages. What could be more alien to the twentieth century than medieval doctrines of the relation between the empire, the church, and the guilds? Yet Maitland's attitude was, "Today we study the day before yesterday, in order that yesterday may not paralyze today, and today may not paralyze tomorrow." He began to inquire into the nature of groups of human beings, incorporated and unincorporated. Is such a group merely an aggregation of human beings, or is it in itself a person? Facts accumulated in his mind, he cross-examined documents like a string of hostile witnesses, he talked about his problem, he wrote to America, to men he had never seen, for data about our corporations. And somehow the problem of the Middle Ages became the problem of the great unincorporated groups of today: the Roman Catholic Church; the trade unions —Chief Justice Taft's decision in the Coronado case on the possibility of suing the United Mine Workers of

America is just this question; the New Jersey corporation doing business in states where it owes none of its legal existence to the local legislature; the nature of that most powerful of groups, the state itself. Is the state only a sort of glorified public service company, as Maitland's followers would have it, that sells police protection and schooling to its citizens as a trolley company sells rides? Or is it, as the other side contends, a sort of ethical culture society to lead us onward and upward toward the light? Whichever of these two views we take of the state, whether it is an organization for specific business services to the community or an inspirer of souls, why does it haggle over the settlement of its contracts, impose double taxation, deny all responsibility when its mail-trucks run over us, refuse to be sued in its own courts, and in general fall far below the standards of fair dealing which it imposes upon every taxicab driver or keeper of a restaurant?

The old system of water-tight compartments into which knowledge was supposed to be divided, and each of which had to be entered separately, is breaking down. The late Jacques Loeb, whose vital personality was hard to explain by his own mechanistic doctrines, once remarked: "People ask me, 'Why are you studying mathematics? Why are you learning physics? Aren't you a physiologist?' And I say, 'I don't know.' Then, 'Aren't you a chemist?' or 'Aren't you a biologist?' I don't understand these questions. I am preoccupied with problems." Problems—the material for solving them must be drawn from every available source! No place, then, for jealousy between workers in sharply demarcated fields. As H. G. Wells says in *Joan and Peter*, "All good work is one."

III

It will probably be objected that all this is very well for the leaders of thought, but that few of us can hope to be ranked among them. What are the inquiries of the rest of us worth? On the contrary, I insist that this way of looking at life as a series of questions and answers is not for originators and specialists alone, but for every man and woman whose vision is not confined to the acquisition of a bare subsistence. Beyond the facts that immediately affect us are the problems of the world in which we find ourselves with no choice of our own, the solutions of which are bound to mold us in the end, however remote such problems seem. It has become a commonplace to remark, and yet it cannot be said too often or it will be forgotten, that a shot in Bosnia brought over a hundred thousand homes in this country into mourning. Financial disorganization in Central Europe means foreclosed mortgages in the Dakotas. The time has long since passed when Dr. Johnson could say that he would not give half a guinea to live under one form of government rather than another, because it was of no moment to the happiness of the individual. The government of these days can decide what we shall think or what we shall drink, allow sugar to go up and the dollar to go down, tax us out of the income we meant to devote to travel or the education of our children, force our boys—by imperceptible extensions of the present training-camps—to spend one or two of the best years of their lives in barracks learning the art of killing, then send them out to be shot by some nation we happen to dislike at the moment, and afterward dictate school-books to demonstrate how profitably they died.

Most of us are too busy contending with the effects of these obscure forces to probe long into their causes, but the undergraduates in our colleges have abundant leisure for acquiring an understanding of the obstacles to progress, and if they acquire it, may do much to remove those obstacles in after life. Instead, they allow the leisure available for such inquiries to be filched from them by those who want them to use it up in the drudgery of managerships and committee meetings—just the sort of tasks on which they will have to spend all their lives after they leave the campus.

Why is it that the average undergraduate allows himself to be lured into thus anticipating the Gradgrind monotony of his middle life and away from the pursuit of ideas, for which he now has opportunities that will never return? In large measure because such college activities seem a part of real life, while the reading and thinking that he is asked to do appear unrelated to his own experience and expectations. Once this supposed want of relationship is shown to be a falsity, once the solution of a given problem is proved to be as intimate an influence upon his life as the choice of a roommate, will not the natural human thirst for ideas assert itself? Learning, therefore, must be related to individual experience, but that experience may reach beyond the maintenance of bodily existence to the enjoyment of distant landscapes, of children at play, music, the converse of friends, the mind voyaging through strange seas of thought alone.

IV

A few illustrations will make clearer what I mean by the relationship between theory and our own experience, and the way in which the investigation of a problem draws in facts from several departments of knowledge.

The front page of every daily newspaper was occupied in 1924 by the senatorial committees investigating the oil scandal and the Department of Justice. It is the fashion in many quarters to regard such investigations as annoying interruptions to legislation—an attitude somewhat inconsistent with the usual sigh of relief when Congress adjourns without inflicting any more legislation upon us. But this attitude of hostility toward the committees was vigorously combated by an editorial in a newspaper that can hardly be called radical—the Boston *Transcript*. It insisted that the investigative function of a legislature is just as important as its law-making function. College undergraduates might well turn from their study of political science as an abstraction, and ascertain the limits of this investigative function. On what occasions did the British Parliament call Cabinet ministers to account? Is the punishment of impeachment a satisfactory remedy for official misconduct? What was the process in Parliament by which the removal of an official by impeachment became obsolete as too cumbersome, and was succeeded by the custom that he should resign on receiving a vote of want of confidence? What would happen to a British minister if he did not resign? Did the vote of the Senate calling for Denby's resignation mark the beginning of a similar process in this country? Is the separation of the executive from the legislature an essential incident of democracy, as Mr. Coolidge told the Filipinos? If so, why is it that England and France are not democracies?

Under Washington and under Taft, proposals were

nearly adopted for Cabinet officials to appear on the floor of Congress and answer questions. Should this be done? Would it be superior to investigating them long after they have acted? Does the great increase of federal powers in the last few years necessitate the creation of more definite channels through which the representatives of the people may get at the conduct of officials who have acquired so much control over our daily lives? In such inquiries, history and political science would interlock.

Another interesting group of problems arise from the decision of our government not to recognize the government of Russia, which, in turn, has refused to recognize us until we clean house. Adopted, as our decision has been, by a distinguished Secretary of State, the undergraduate must unquestioningly assume it to be based upon a valid reason. But let him inquire what that valid reason is. One day it is stated that the Russian government is so weak that it is about to fall. A few days later, the same person or newspaper worries for fear that it is so strong that any day the red flag may be seen fluttering over the White House. Either of these reasons may be sound, or neither, but not both. Then the inquirer might consider other reasons. The Bolshevik atrocities would open the way to an historical consideration of the recognition of the French Republic by Washington's Cabinet during the Reign of Terror. Then the undergraduate could turn to the general question of the effect of moral ideas upon recognition. He could recall our relations with a massacring Czar; he could ask whether our attitude toward the Huerta administration in Mexico marked a departure from our previous policy, and whether that departure was proper. The suggested reason for non-recognition, that the Soviets have sent money into this country to overthrow our government, would lead to an inquiry into the amount of American loans to Admiral Kolchak. The repudiation of debts would furnish an economic topic, involving a study of the repudiation of state debts in this country, and of the difference between debts that are recognized but not paid and those that are neither recognized nor paid. Thus, in time, after surveying political science, international law, economics, and history, our inquirer will doubtless find the valid reason that makes it impossible for us to follow the English course, so heartily endorsed by such conservative newspapers as the London *Spectator*.[2]

An inquirer interested in economics will find plenty of material at hand in the income tax. Loud complaints have been made that most of this tax has been paid by the citizens of a few states—New York, Pennsylvania, and Massachusetts—whose representation in Congress is small compared with that of the citizens of states wherein little or no income taxes are paid. The basis of this resentment is plain. Taxes ought not to be imposed by those who do not pay them, and it is natural to assume that the man who gets the tax bill and sends in his check to the collector is the man who pays the tax. But now we find that the persons who are loudest in making this complaint have been the most eager advocates of the Mellon plan for the reduction of high surtaxes, on the ground that the man who gets the bill for the surtax does

[2] The severance of relations between Great Britain and Russia in the summer of 1927 may give rise to additional inquiries as to the reasons and wisdom of the British decision.

not really pay it at all, but collects it from his poor customers! In advocating its abolition, he is consequently
acting for their advantage and from entirely disinterested
motives!

Now, this may be true; if so, let the investigating undergraduate prove it. He could show, for instance, how,
when the author of a very successful two-dollar novel,
such as *Main Street*, was obliged to pay a big surtax, he
shifted it to the reading public by increasing the price of
his novel, and selling it for more than another two-dollar
novel that had fallen stillborn from the press. Or he
might find even more telling examples for Mr. Mellon's
argument. But how can it be that the 50 per cent. surtax
is not paid by the man who pays it, when the total income taxes levied in New York, Pennsylvania, and Massachusetts are paid *entirely* by citizens of those three states?
If the poor pay the surtax, why don't they pay *all* income
taxes, and why do not the customers in the West and
South, who buy from those three states, pay a very large
share of the taxes imposed there? Either theory may be
right, or neither, but not both. An inquiry will show
which is. A widely diffused knowledge of the principles
of that very difficult subject, the shifting and incidence
of taxation, would make it possible for the American people to criticize Mr. Mellon's next proposal with much
greater discrimination.

I should like to go on with other problems: in history,
whether the American Revolution was really, as some
recent writers intimate, a combination of debtors and
smugglers against the prosperous and law-abiding, and
if so, how the participation of Franklin and Washington
is to be explained; in literature, how much misfortune

is necessary to stimulate an author to create without going so far as to kill him off; in classical studies, how far the conditions which brought about the flowering of Athenian culture are attainable in a modern factory city. But I hope that enough has been said to indicate the fruitfulness of the method of the inquiring mind.

V

Nor are such problems as these for undergraduates alone. The inquiring mind is not to be thrown aside with cap and gown, rolled up in a diploma with a ribbon of the appropriate color around it. Oxford was once said to be a place of such great learning because so much was brought there and so little taken away. The value of a man's education cannot be determined until we see what books he is reading ten years after he has been graduated. Dallas Lore Sharp has said that the student passing through college is like the wind blowing through the orchard; it carries away some of the fragrance and none of the fruit. Unless the college man has enrolled in a fifty-year course, in a continuing education, his four-year course has failed of its purpose. And if my view of the nature of education be sound, this means that he must continue to preoccupy himself all his life with problems.

There is, indeed, no reason for limiting such investigations to college graduates. A very large amount of reading is now carried on by other persons, especially in public libraries, as will appear from a visit to one of their reading-rooms any Sunday afternoon. Desultory reading is a desirable recreation and even when carried to excess is probably harmless, but so is solitaire. Much of the time now spent on books leaves no trace in the reader's

mind, because it is directed to no continuous purpose.
This energy and love of books could be profitably canal-
ized into the pursuit of the solution of problems related
to the life of our own time. Consider the value of such
an inquiring attitude to the citizen! By continually asking and answering questions, he may gradually approach
the qualities of that great teacher of whom it was said,[3]
"I sometimes think that the one and only prejudice he
had was a prejudice against his own results." He will
come to appreciate, too, the wisdom of De Tocqueville: [4]
"I am tempted to believe that what we call necessary
institutions are often no more than institutions to which
we have grown accustomed, and that in matters of social
constitution the field of possibilities is much more extensive than men living in their various societies are ready
to imagine." Whether this citizen call himself conservative or radical, he will certainly not be ranked among
those conservatives who, if they had been present on the
first day of creation, would have exclaimed, "Let us con-
serve Chaos!" nor yet among those radicals who account
it so much a virtue to be ahead of the procession that
they sometimes find that the line of march has been de-
flected into a side street behind them, and that they are
left stranded.

Only if there be an abundance of inquiring minds
among the people can the leaders who are striving to answer the riddles of the time meet a sympathetic response
from the masses whose support is essential to their success. The high-power broadcasting station would be futile

[3] Of Henry Sidgwick, by F. W. Maitland. See H. A. L. Fisher's
biographical sketch of Maitland, p. 8.
[4] *Recollections,* p. 101.

if it were not for the low-power receiving sets, and they must be tuned to it. Elaborate schemes such as Walter Lippmann's for developing public opinion through experts will be useless if the public refuse to ask questions about the material which the experts and leaders supply. The want of such responsive inquiring minds has caused some of our most conspicuous national failures of recent years. We have insisted on propositions, and refused to consider problems. Before the war we accepted freedom of thought as a venerable tradition, and neglected to exert ourselves to define its scope. Freedom came to mean in practice the liberty to do what everybody else did, but not to do anything different. We would not allow a man to be prevented from wearing his straw hat in July, but we saw no reason why he should be free from molestation if he wore it on a hot day in October. A conception of freedom which had been given no genuine content through general thinking quickly vanished with the advent of war, when free inquiry was most needed. We lapped up propositions like "the war to end war," and "an association of nations," without caring to ask what they meant, and we shrank from unpalatable problems like the secret treaties in the same spirit that a man avoids going to the dentist's for fear that a bad cavity may be discovered. Consequently, when we had obtained the victory, we did not know what to do with it, and we patched up a separate peace which made no provision to secure any of the things for which we had so eagerly fought. The Harding administration swept triumphantly into office with another set of propositions which acquired an unexpected significance at Teapot Dome—"government by the best minds," and "more business in government." If we neglect to exert ourselves to define by arduous inquiry what we really want and expect to get, we can at least be sure of getting something that we do not want at all.

To men of inquiring mind a main concern is the universities, for they are the principal centers of systematic investigation among us. The government of a university by its graduates has been accepted for many years as an indubitable good. Yet Graham Wallas, in *Our Social Heritage,* says of alumni control in England and America: "That expedient was devised from the mass meetings of resident teachers in the medieval universities, and has, I believe, now ceased to have any but bad effects. The alumnus, as such, has neither the knowledge and interest of the teacher, nor the knowledge and interest of a well-chosen representative of the community." Thus alumni control is still a problem for us to consider, though it is to be hoped that our eventual answer will be favorable to it. Certainly it is significant that the two most striking efforts of our time to transform colleges into real institutions of learning, Woodrow Wilson's at Princeton and Alexander Meiklejohn's at Amherst, both failed, and, despite the presence in each case of other factors, failed mainly because a large body of alumni did not want that kind of college. In the Harvard Law School the reform of Langdell, which revolutionized legal education, alienated permanently many influential graduates and could never have succeeded had not President Eliot supported the dean against both faculty and alumni.

VI

Not the least of the values of the preservation of the inquiring mind by the alumnus is that it renders him sym-

pathetic to theoretical research with no visible practical
value, to free investigation by the faculty and students
of his university, and to experimentation in its administration. If, on the other hand, he has allowed his idealism
to be worn away by the preoccupations of daily life, he
is likely to adopt toward the aspirations of thoughtful
and eager undergraduates the attitude described by Ro-
main Rolland: [5]

In the hostility, sullen or ridiculing, displayed by most
persons towards the dreams of the young, there enters in large
measure the bitter thought that they themselves were thus once
upon a time, that they too had these ambitions and did not
realize them. All those who have denied their souls, all those
who have had in them the possibility of achievement and have
not brought it to pass, accepting instead the safety of an easy
and honorable life, think: "Since I have not been able to do
what I dreamed of doing, why should they do it, these boys?
I do not want them to do it." How many Hedda Gablers among
mankind! What a sullen struggle to annihilate new and free
forces! What studiousness to kill them by silence, by irony,
by the wearing down of daily life, by discouragement—and by
some perfidious seduction, just at the right moment!

And so curious fears spring up among graduates that
the students are learning higher ideals than are practicable in the rough and tumble of actual existence. A powerful group of Harvard alumni in New York City objected to the work of Professor Davison in training the
Glee Club to sing songs of the first rank because its members would thus acquire a taste for a type of music which
they would not find after graduation!

[5] *Jean Christophe à Paris, la Foire sur la Place,* p. 226.

As one leaves youth behind, the problem of growing old well acquires unexpected importance. Our anticipations become transformed into responsibilities. There is less to look forward to, and more to lose by changes. Extensive experience of human meanness is disheartening. For many of us, our college stands out as one of the few spots of idealism in our lives, and we resent the slightest possibility of alteration there, lest that, too, be lost to us. Such a motive may account for the almost savage intensity with which alumni have at times opposed novel tendencies in teaching. But we cannot expect to live over our own lives in those of others, either our own children or the children of our contemporaries. All we can do is to assure to them the same opportunities which we possessed to live our lives, and enjoy the spectacle of the use they make of their freedom for continuous development. Meanwhile we must keep our ideas like our wardrobes constantly renewed, opening new lines of inquiry, so that to the last each day brings us new pleasures and new work.

There is much uneasiness abroad among alumni today over radical teachers. I believe that this springs largely from the view which I opposed at the opening of this article, that the multiplication table is the type of knowledge, and that a teacher is assumed to hand out chunks of doctrine to his students which they accept unquestioningly. Elderly gentlemen easily exaggerate the immaturity of the undergraduate. President Cutten of Colgate stated in an address that one had to "talk to the little ones in words of one syllable." An effective statement of this multiplication-table view may be quoted from President Elliott, president of railroads, not of a university: [6]

> In giving young people their physical nourishment we do not spread before them every kind of food and say, "Eat what you like whether it agrees with you or not." We know that the physical machine can absorb only a certain amount and that all else is waste and trash, with the result that bodies are poisoned and weakened. In giving them mental nourishment, why lay before young and impressionable men and women un-American doctrines and ideas that take mental time and energy from the study and consideration of the great fundamental and eternal truths, and fill the mind with unprofitable mental trash? . . . After they get into the real world it takes them considerable time to become convinced that certain laws controlling social and material affairs are as unchangeable as the law of gravitation, and some never learn it.

Without pausing to ask what these unchangeable laws are, or to recall that even the law of gravitation is not so firmly settled as it was before Einstein, I protest that this food analogy misses the duty of a teacher, and of every man of inquiring mind, who inevitably (whether paid to do so or not) feels it one of his highest tasks to stimulate the same sort of mind in those younger than himself, whether his students, his children, or his friends. It is the business of such a man, not to hand out rigid bodies of doctrine, whether Socialism, Home Market Club protectionism, or anything else, but to train those to whom he speaks to think for themselves. He is not the gentleman behind the quick-lunch counter that Mr. Elliott's criticism

[6] *Harvard Train, 1881:* Remarks of Howard Elliott at the fortieth anniversary of the Class of 1881 of Harvard (privately printed, 1921), pp. 10-12.

suggests. He is more like the leader of a group of miners going into partially opened country. He has been there before; he knows more than they do about the technique of exploration and detecting the metal they seek, but he cannot give them definite directions which will enable them to go to this or that spot and strike it rich. He can only tell them what he knows of the lay of the land and the proper methods of search, leaving it to them to explore and map out for themselves regions which he has never visited or rivers whose course he has erroneously conceived.

"GIVE YOUR MINDS SEA ROOM" [1]

IN the fundamental conflict of academic life, stadium *v.* studium, the underdog still gives a few barks. Now and again, even in the heart of the football season, some venturesome professor affirms the belief that a college is, after all, an educational institution. Let us not be content, however, to use these words unless they possess for us a concrete and vital meaning. As Lincoln urged in beginning his House Divided speech, "If we could first know where we are, and whither we are tending, we could better judge what to do and how to do it." Otherwise, those with different views of the object of a college will easily drag us vague people along with them.

They know perfectly well what they want. One influential group wants the colleges to be a chief source of recreation for the tired business man. They want seating capacity for thousands with abundance of end runs in autumn and home runs in spring. It is an understandable wish, bound to prevail if nothing more tangible be offered. What adult has not been stirred by such sights, even though he has voted to abolish intercollegiate athletics, just as few pacifists can help marking time to a military band? And when we come to the youth who long to participate in such achievements, the most fanatical lover of learning must pause before denouncing such desires as inappropriate to the years between eighteen and twenty-

[1] This paper is based on addresses delivered at Wooster College, Ohio State University, and Brown University.

two. If the scholarly critic be a historian, he will remember how baseball first became important in the Northern armies, and Wellington attributed Waterloo to the playing-fields of Eton.[2] If he rank chasing Greek roots above chasing tennis balls, he will find Pindar writing almost all his poems about athletes, and Socrates preferring them as companions to the professors of his day, the Sophists. In short, the ideal of making the human body in the years of its maximum power do the best of which it is capable will never be abandoned. It may, however, be absorbed as a duly proportioned part of some broader aim which will prevent some of the vigor of the students' minds from going into their feet.[3]

A less outspoken but even larger group of persons whose view of college is much more definite than ours consists of parents who send their children to college and youth who go there, not for learning, not for sport, but, as a great legal writer [4] used to say, "in order to maintain or improve their social status." A certain number of distasteful hours must be spent in the laboratory and the lecture hall because these are the vestibules to the University Club and the fashionable ballroom. Students dutifully associate with unpractical professors so that one day they may be among the right people at luncheon and bridge. A Boston alumnus of a small college declares that a Harvard A.B. is almost indispensable to conspicuous business success in that city. Of course, this has nothing to do with any merit in the intellectual training at Cam-

[2] However, Bertrand Russell says that "the British Empire is being lost there." *Selected Papers of Bertrand Russell* (The Modern Library), p. 166.
[3] "Sed vigor ingenii quondam velocis in alas inque pedes abiit." Ovid, *Metamorphoses,* VIII, 254, "The Flight of Daedalus."
[4] The late Albert M. Kales.

bridge, but comes from the acquaintances formed and the lure of the label conferred on Commencement. The same result would be attained if the Harvard College Faculty were completely abolished, at a considerable saving in salaries much to be desired by modern business efficiency.

With no other ideals than these, the college is bound to go into the discard along with the medieval monasteries and other richly endowed institutions which survived their usefulness. Already, the college is getting crushed between the upper millstone of the graduate schools, which under the persuasive advice of Mr. Abraham Flexner, none the less persuasive because he is possessed of the power of the purse, are beginning, as at Johns Hopkins and in the medical schools, to dispense with the A.B. degree, and the nether millstone of the junior colleges which, perhaps, might better be called senior high schools. A harsh and unrelenting future awaits the student's ideal of "college-bred, or a four years' loaf."

And yet, when we sneer at the conception of the college rolls as an unrevised version of the society column and the Directory of Directors, or feel that it should be more than a wholesome athletic club, what alternative purpose shall we offer to justify its existence? It is not enough for this purpose to seem satisfactory to us professors and our confederates, the high-school teachers. We must offer an ideal powerful enough to blast the snobbishness of the social aspirant and awaken in the boy or girl of eighteen the same enthusiastic desire to test his or her maturing mental powers as is now felt with respect to physical strength and skill. Taking our own valuation of the college as an educational institution, what do we really want?

A very tempting vision pictures a college full of students obtaining from learning the same intense fascination which it gives to us professors, who are willing to devote to it our whole lives. They would thrill like Browning's Grammarian over *"hoti* and the enclitic *de,"* or spend four years happily tracing the French sources of the Arthurian legend or reading interminable correspondence between colonial governors and London officials just before the Revolution—hundreds of Arrowsmiths, all absorbed in minute research through four concentrated years—after which they would go out into banks, railroads, mail-order houses, factories, and farms.

It will not work. The enthusiasm that intensive research requires in order to be fruitful, the ability, the patience, the isolation, are peculiar to scholars, and we can not expect to turn all our students into replicas of ourselves. It is better so, since we live in a world where not only ideas have to be mastered, but things and men as well. For that task, the main task of most college graduates, prolonged research would be of little use. And let us scholars frankly admit that some of the fascination we find in minute investigation is, in a sense, a hobby, not altogether different in nature from the appeal of chess— and cross-word puzzles. We have to be always on our guard against the lure of the unimportant, the creed that all facts are created equal. Though many of the most productive investigations have been purely theoretical at first—Pasteur is a great example—the wise investigator sooner or later, and here Pasteur may be cited again, harnesses himself to move forward the world at the same time that he gratifies his passion for research, much like the Connecticut Yankee at the Court of King Arthur, when he saw the hermit who bowed himself all day long and hitched him to a sewing-machine.

Most students will prefer other types of recreation than research. The most we professors can hope is to have them spend enough time on research to comprehend something of its method, to see why *we* love it, though they cannot share our devotion, and above all to realize its essential importance, to realize how much that amuses or serves or grips their lives was brought about by the patient, isolated, apparently useless labor of investigators. Gregor Mendel, in a monastery garden, observes the colors of sweet peas year by year. He publishes his results in an obscure periodical. Sixteen years after he is dead, scientists find out about him for the first time, and in consequence vastly improve wheat and cattle and perhaps human beings. Research is not the task of most college graduates, but if they possess an understanding of its value, theirs is often the power to make possible the material environment, the facilities for publication, the encouragement, the mental freedom, in which investigation can best flourish.

A much simpler plan to make undergraduates study would consist in convincing them that the information obtainable by hard work will be pecuniarily valuable to them in earning a livelihood. The trouble is that except for vocational subjects, like agriculture and engineering, or those needed for admission to a professional school, the college courses are obviously worth nothing in dollars and cents. All the information needed to get on in life was acquired by the student years before, when he learned to read advertisements, write business letters, and enough arithmetic not to be short-changed. Arguments that Latin and medieval history have a cash value do not deceive the wily sophomore. If he is urged to prepare himself directly for business while in college, he will turn from the useless courses offered by the Faculty to practical courses offered by student organizations in getting advertisements for a college paper or managing a great financial enterprise like a football team.

It is significant that the great benefactors of American education were not college graduates—Rockefeller, Carnegie, George F. Baker. Universities did not teach them how to make their money, only how to spend it. And indeed it is arguable that one real function of college is to teach the students how to spend money—no mean end, since economists have now emphasized unintelligent expenditure as one of the largest causes of waste, and insist that consumption must be as wisely managed in the future as production in the past. Within these walls, men and women may learn how to gain the durable satisfactions of life with their money and with what is more precious than money, their time. The great gift of modern machinery is leisure, and we hardly know what to do with it. "Getting and spending we lay waste our powers."

This, however, is but part of the real aim of college education. It will enlist the energy and enthusiasm of youth only when they realize that it possesses a direct relation to their lives, not as a preparation for money-making, but for the whole of life. Its function is to supply not so much knowledge as power, power to understand the universe and the social order in which they exist, that in which they exist now and the different social order of a quarter century hence when they will be in the lead. They must not regard the principles of today as eternal truths. Life is an adventure with new experiences and contests beyond every turn on the road. Woodrow Wilson endeavored to galvanize the colleges of his day by representing them as training-grounds for citizenship. They are this and more. The student must find here the methods and the power to enable him to be at home not only in political life, but also in more intimate human relationships, in art, scenery, and the far-flung stars, in the spiritual and religious values of his world. Here he can gain the strength and intelligence to play an efficient and understanding part in his time. Above all, he must know that his time will not be our time. He must acquire the will to march on.

And so I urge undergraduates: Give your minds sea room, pushing out into the open ocean of thought whither your teachers have longed to set your course and theirs, but all too often have been obliged instead to drag you like barges along the placid canals of knowledge where the tow-path is worn deep by their repeated journeys. And when you have finished college and gone into the outside world, keep alert against the impulse always to hug the coasts charted out by those in your own occupation, to let yourselves be hemmed in by the barriers flung up by the terrific pressure of your daily tasks. Launch out ever and again into the troubled waters of unsettled questions, into the streams of thought of men far different from yourselves, toward the western islands of philosophy and poetry and art. Expect your happiness to come from the joy of intellectual work rather than from any praise by others. President Lowell has said, "You can do a thing or you can get the credit for it, but you can't have both." Now you look forward to great achievements

which will advance the world. Later will come the realiza-
tion that each man can accomplish only a little; but it is
of vast importance that he should do that little with all
his might. Be able to say without regret: "My dreams
have all come true to other men." [5]

This conception that colleges exist to create and encourage in their students the desire to fit themselves for
solving the new problems of their lives, although held by
most college presidents and professors, is bound to meet
opposition when they seek to put it into practice. A chief
obstacle is what may be described as the hickory limb
philosophy of education, because it is concisely expressed
in the old poem:

> "Mother dear, may I learn to swim?"
> "Yes, my darling daughter.
> Hang your clothes on a hickory limb;
> But don't go near the water."

According to this view, those in authority are to prevent
a youth from making a bad choice by protecting him
from influences which they consider harmful. This philosophy results from at least three emotions. The first
and strongest is fear. Men advocate the suppression of
forces they think bad because they distrust the strength
of the countervailing forces they think good. They want
to substitute force for argument because they are afraid
that their view of truth will not prevail if left to a fair
fight. "It is not faith that lights the fagot, but the lurking
doubt." When the choice between good and evil is to be
made by a child or a youth, there exists of course a real
danger that he will be too immature to reject evil if it is
presented to him completely unmasked, but the advocates

[5] Edwin Arlington Robinson, *Old Trails*.

of censorship come to deny that anybody is sufficiently mature to be trusted to make a wise choice. High school superintendents say that open discussion of controversial questions is all very well for college students. Mr. Coolidge when Vice President expressed great concern in the *Delineator* at the presence of radical teachers in the women's colleges. And others have a similar fear about professional schools, while legislators endeavor to safeguard full grown citizens from communistic books and speeches. Secondly, coupled with this disbelief by the advocates of suppression in the common sense of others, is a strong belief in their own superior power to discern the truth. The books forbidden to the Roman Catholic layman by the Index Expurgatorius may be read by cardinals and bishops.[6] Trust in ourselves tends to increase with distrust of others. The belief grows, that a few men—and the speaker naturally counts himself among their number—are so much wiser than the masses that they can safely regulate their views for them. Finally, the hickory limb philosophy is based on a longing for stability, that the world shall go on unchanged from what it was in the days of our youth.

Opposed to this attitude is the philosophy of the swimming hole, that youths must be thrown into life and can best master it by struggling with it, aided by the experience handed on to them by those who have gone through the same conflict.

If the stability desired by conservatives were possible, if the world could always remain the same, perhaps it would be best to teach college students only the principles underlying the existing order. But we have seen too many

6 *Codex Iuris Canonici* (1918), can. 1401.

changes in our own lives not to expect many more in
theirs. An old Maine man declared that all the evils of
his day could be traced to one fundamental mistake, the
adoption of the Australian ballot. He would have stopped
the clock years ago. It is just as hopeless for us to stop
it now. We are fond of saying how startled our grand-
fathers would have been by the progressive income tax,
the initiative and referendum, and votes for women, or
our grandmothers by flivvers and flappers. We forget that
the future may be equally shocking to us. The question
is whether students shall be trained to discuss these possible changes, however distasteful in the contemplation of
an older generation, and fully canvass their advantages
and disadvantages, or shall be left with bandaged eyes
to wander through novel situations equipped with no data
for choice except a strong love for the institutions of
today.

We live in a world of immense complexity. We may
have developed a situation too much for our powers of
control. We are like children in a speeding locomotive
who do not know one lever from another and who may not
be able to stop it. In four years an undergraduate cannot
be furnished with the explanations of all this complexity
even if they were known by his elders, but he can be
supplied with the desire and the method to find out as
much as possible for himself. The best that he can get
in college is not information but method and the spirit
of exploration, the spirit of the old monk Mendel, of
Darwin in his perfect brief autobiography, of Pasteur, of
Marshall, Hamilton, and Jefferson, men whom we admire,
not because they clung tenaciously to the old, but because, faced with new conditions, they searched and

planned to meet those conditions with new remedies and resources.

Not only must the student prepare for a complicated world where truth is hard to find, but for a world where the supposed truths of today may no longer hold good for tomorrow. The best kind of education I know was that received by Mark Twain and described in his *Life on the Mississippi*. After he had learned all the points and shoals from St. Louis to New Orleans, he found that many of them had changed. He had to learn them all over again and to be perpetually gathering information from which he could predict those changes.

The facts of life, tremendously uncertain in themselves, are in political, economic, and social matters made still more uncertain, because they necessarily come to us through the minds of other human beings, in newspapers and books. Consciously or unconsciously the writer is like the modern advertiser. He shapes what he says in a desired direction. For this too the student must train himself. He must learn to discount the bias of the source of any statement before assessing its value. Hence the usefulness of studying the enormous variation in two accounts of the same fact, the Pullman strike of 1894, the repeal of the Missouri Compromise, the closing days of July, 1914. And he must expect just the same sort of discrepancies in the versions presented to him of events in the future. Unless he be trained to discriminate true from false, he will either go through the world muddled, or else sink into unthinking acceptance of the editorials in the *New York Times* or the *New Republic* as the case may be.

In my statement of these needs and my vision of

the far-voyaging undergraduate I cannot reckon without those who fear to let him stray beyond the well-marked channels of the past. Some alumni, some trustees, some legislators, are appalled by the dangers of freedom. The growing influence of the desire to prescribe what shall and shall not be learned, with a corresponding restriction on the inquiring mind of youth, is strikingly illustrated by two recent movements in education.

The Tennessee law punishing any teacher in a university or school supported in whole or in part by public funds who shall be found "to teach any theory that denies the story of the divine creation of man as taught in the Bible, and to teach instead that man has descended from a lower order of animals," [7] was greeted as a mere joke when first proposed, but has been enforced in Tennessee and imitated in other states. Even if such legislation is

---

[7] Tenn. Laws, 1925, c. 27, was held constitutional by the Supreme Court of Tennessee in Scopes v. State, 289 S.W. 363 (1927), with one judge dissenting on the ground that the statute was uncertain in meaning. However, the judgment of the trial court was reversed because the fine of one hundred dollars assessed by the judge was unconstitutional since a fine in excess of fifty dollars must be assessed by the jury. The Attorney General dismissed the prosecution, following the recommendation in the opinion of the court. The statute was held valid not only under the Fourteenth Amendment to the U.S. Constitution, but also under the state constitution which provided: "It shall be the duty of the general assembly . . . to cherish literature and science," and "No preference shall ever be given by law to any religious establishment or mode of worship." See "The Constitutionality of the Tennessee Anti-Evolution Law," C. E. Carpenter, 6 Ore. L. Rev. 130, 61 Am. L. Rev. 276; "State Control of Public School Curriculum," C. J. Turck, 15 Ky. L. J. 277. The Supreme Court of the United States has invalidated state statutes limiting the instruction in private schools, infra, p. 99 n., but expressly said that the power of the legislature over public educational institutions might be wider.

Miss. Laws, 1926, c. 311, makes it unlawful in schools and universities supported by public funds to teach or select any text-book teaching that "mankind ascended or descended from the lower order of animals." Texas has eliminated such text-books by administrative action without a statute.

eventually held unconstitutional under the Fourteenth Amendment, which seems doubtful since the power of a state over its educational funds is very large, this will matter little since the purpose of such laws may easily be attained through decisions by state boards that teachers with evolutionary beliefs are incompetent. The courts can accomplish little for freedom of education until the controlling officials really believe in it. Nor will the issue be settled by a demonstration satisfactory to those in authority, that evolution is not yet conclusively proved. It is not for the legislature or the regents to decide scientific truths. Where scientists find difficulties, politicians are not likely to be infallible. Whether Bryan or Darwin was right, the truth can best be found if every one, teacher or text writer as well as preacher, be left free to present sincerely his own view and the alternative for the consideration of the student, leaving him to choose for himself. The youth brought up in blind ignorance of the evolutionary view and taught to regard every word of the Bible as unquestioned truth is all the more likely to lose his religion entirely when he is confronted, as he will be sooner or later, with the scientific evidence for the unity of all life. Much better to leave him free to arrive perhaps at the conception of organic life as the gradually unfolding creation of a Divine Thinker.

But let us not fling too many rocks at the South. We Northerners are equally ready to consider restrictions when teachers threaten our cherished principles, which happen to be in the fields of economics and politics. Far more serious than the anti-evolution statutes is the recent desire of state legislatures and patriotic organizations to regulate the teaching of American history. So far their efforts have been limited to the schools, but if they succeed there, sooner or later they will reach the colleges. The Oregon statute prohibits any text-book which "speaks slightingly of the founders of the republic, or of the men who preserved the union, or which belittles or undervalues their work." [8] The determination of historical truth is taken away from experts and placed in the hands of government officials, who are to apply the vague tests of "slightingly" and "undervalues" to facts dependent on obscure and conflicting testimony. Indeed, the most influential of this group disavow truth as their aim, and prefer what they call patriotism though based on falsehood. "I want our children taught that our forefathers were right and the British were wrong on this subject [taxation]." And another says, "Discussion of controversial subjects has no place in a history."

There will be controversies enough in the American history of the next quarter century. Will our citizens be fitted to meet them if they are carefully excluded from any attention in the schools? They are just the subjects which should be studied as a preparation for life—not indeed by memorizing a third-rate text-book, but by reading the arguments of the best men on both sides.

The effect of an unthinking worship of past statesmen and causes is unpreparedness for the making of history, in which every citizen must take his part at the ballot box and in the continuous discussion out of which public opinion is formed. The great fact to me in our history is that the men at the helm in crises were not superhuman beings with a unanimous purpose, but men with

[8] Oregon Laws, 1923, c. 39. See Bessie L. Pierce, Public Opinion and the Teaching of History in the United States, New York, 1926.

failings who disagreed bitterly among themselves, and yet frankly faced their shortcomings and differences and overcame them so as to bring new institutions into life. So must we. To picture the past as an heroic age unlike our own will produce in the student when once in politics either disgust at the supposed decline, which will make him shrink aside, or else cynicism and willingness to play the dirty game since nothing better seems possible. In either event he is liable to ignore the opportunities for idealism which the great men of the past displayed under circumstances not much unlike those in which he lives.

The teaching of the past is of little use unless it emphasizes its similarity to the present. The time when our forefathers lived seems long ago to us, but it did not seem long ago to them, and we must judge them as living in an up-to-date world, as ignorant as we of the future. Bertrand Russell remarked that in studying about Charles I, we often forget that he lived his entire life without realizing that he lost his head. We look at the past as if it were really as simple as it is presented in the books, and we imagine that we should unhesitatingly have chosen the side which later time has shown to be right. We assume that we would have been among the first to proclaim the innocence of Dreyfus, and do not see that for the men of his time the issue was clouded by the emotions and conflicting testimony which have made it so difficult for sincere men today to decide about the innocence of Sacco and Vanzetti.

Let us have enough faith in our institutions to believe that they can safely withstand voice and paper, and enough confidence in our students to trust them in the comparative maturity of college to face all the facts frankly and choose for themselves. It is their last chance to face them under guidance. If we hide them now, they will face them later, alone, without our help.

The public should beware of limiting the freedom of the teachers of youth. In any case their task loses its freshness all too easily. A recent *Atlantic* article [9] comments bitterly on the tendency of us professors to fall into dry rot. Say to us, "On this point you must not exercise your mind in the class room; here you must hide what you think when you make a speech or write a book," and you deprive us of the motive for action. To direct our teaching into specified channels may occasionally strengthen the existing order by inculcating unthinking loyalties among our students. It may secure more stability, but at the expense of that freedom of thought through which alone we and they can solve the problems of the future.

Historians tell us, writes Graham Wallas, that the great periods of intellectual activity are apt to coincide with the wide extension of a sense of personal liberty. Most men can explain this from their personal experience. There are some emotional states in which creative thought is impossible, and the chief among these is the sense of helpless humiliation and anger which is produced in a sensitive nature by the inability to oppose or avoid the "insolence of office."

Athens during the last quarter of the fifth century B.C. [he goes on] was not well governed; and if the British Empire had then existed, and if Athens had been brought within it, the administration of the city would undoubtedly have been improved in many important respects. But one does not like to

[9] G. Boas, "To a Young Man Bent on Entering the Professoriat," *Atlantic Monthly*, March, 1926.

imagine the effect on the intellectual output of the fifth century
B.C. if even the best of Mr. Rudyard Kipling's [English]
public-school [graduates] had stalked daily through the agora,
snubbing as he passed that intolerable bounder, Euripides, or
clearing out of his way the probably seditious group that were
gathered around Socrates.[10]

The tolerance I propose involves no mushy latitudina-
rianism. Willingness to hear all views does not mean that
we should, after hearing them, treat them all as of equal
value. Like St. Paul, we must prove all things, but then,
like him, hold fast that which is good. We must be slow
to impose our own standards of right and wrong upon
others, but rigorous in imposing them upon ourselves.
That was the strength of the Puritans, the merciless
steadfastness with which they held themselves to their
appointed task.

Let no one think that I am advocating merely a critical
and destructive attitude toward life in teacher and student
and citizen. There must be constant pulling down of the
old to build the new, but pulling down is useless without
rebuilding. The Inquiring Mind which I urge must be
joined with the Constructive Mind. In many ways the
period in which we live in this country resembles that in
England a century ago. Just as war and the reverberations of the Russian Revolution have shaken much that
we held precious, so war and the reverberations of the
French Revolution disturbed their old institutions. Some
men stood aghast and inactive; others prosecuted and
punished and suppressed the discontented and vociferous.
Yet there were not lacking men of a different mind who

[10] Graham Wallas, *The Great Society*, pp. 196-198.

realized that old ways had gone forever, and that their task was to build England anew. They were the builders —Jeremy Bentham, Sir Robert Peel, Thomas Babington Macaulay, Lord Shaftesbury, John Stuart Mill, and a host of less conspicuous helpers without whom little would have been accomplished. So in the United States, the undergraduates of today must be the builders of tomorrow.

FREEDOM OF SPEECH AND STATES' RIGHTS

GILBERT v. MINNESOTA [1]

DURING the early years of the American Revolution several states felt the need of protecting Congress and flag against the Tory wit who asserted that Martha Washington had a yellow tom-cat with thirteen black stripes around his tail, which suggested to her the design for the flag. Massachusetts accordingly passed a law fining any person who used expressions "in preaching or praying, or in public or private discourse or conversation, with an apparent design to discourage" people from sup-

[1] First printed in the *New Republic*, January 26, 1921.

The most important law for the control of opinion opposed to the war with Germany was the federal Espionage Act (U.S. Statutes, Act of June 15, 1917, c. 30, Title I, § 3; amended May 16, 1918, c. 75, § 1). The prosecutions under this statute and the series of Supreme Court decisions interpreting its penal clauses are fully discussed in my *Freedom of Speech*. Several states also enacted war-time sedition acts, which with the decisions are listed in Appendix V of the same book; their validity and desirability are considered on pages 110-113. It was not, however, till after the publication of *Freedom of Speech* that the constitutionality of this state legislation was passed upon by the United States Supreme Court. The only case is Gilbert v. Minnesota, 254 U.S. 325 (1920), which forms the subject of the present paper. The actual decision involved only the Minnesota statute, but the majority opinion necessarily upheld the power of other states to punish opposition to war, although the more sweeping terms of some state laws left additional questions unsettled. It is interesting to note that the Texas act was declared unconstitutional by the Court of Criminal Appeals of that state in *Ex parte* Meckel, 220 S.W. 81 (1920). Inasmuch as the fighting had long been over and state war-time prisoners had been already or were soon released by expiration of their terms or by pardons, the matter ceased to have further practical importance, whatever its consequences may be in another war.

porting independence. Virginia had a similar statute,
which came home to roost when that commonwealth denounced the Sedition Act of 1798 as a violation of freedom of speech. But state action was never used to curb
opposition to subsequent wars, until 1917. It remained
for our own day, when the doctrine of states' rights was
supposed to be on its last legs, to establish by the Supreme
Court decision in Gilbert v. Minnesota [2] that the weapons
which Massachusetts and Virginia used against the dis-
loyal remain sharp and active in the hands of modern state
governments and were not surrendered to the nation in
1787.

I

It is significant evidence of the altered attitudes of
Americans toward open discussion that during the recent
war eleven states and territories considered even the un-
precedented severity of the federal Espionage Act of 1917
an insufficient protection against pamphlets and oratory,
and supplemented it by drastic local legislation. Thus
Montana imposed a penalty of twenty years in prison for
various insults to the Constitution, the uniform, and the
flag, which were considered too trivial to be federal
crimes, until Congress in 1918 inserted the whole Montana law into the middle of the Espionage Act. Nothing
could show better the way state war legislation works than
the fate of Starr of Montana, as described by a United
States judge.[3] "He was in the hands of one of those too
common mobs, bent upon vindicating its peculiar standard of patriotism and its odd concept of respect for the
flag by compelling him to kiss the latter." In the excite-

[2] 254 U.S. 325 (1920).
[3] *Ex parte* Starr, 263 Federal Reporter 145 (1920).

ment of resisting their efforts, Starr said: "What is this thing anyway? Nothing but a piece of cotton with a little paint on it and some other marks in the corner there. I will not kiss that thing. It might be covered with microbes." The state authorities did absolutely nothing to the mob, but they had Starr convicted under the Montana Sedition Act for using language "calculated to bring the flag into contempt and disrepute," and sentenced him to the penitentiary for not less than ten nor more than twenty years at hard labor.

The right of the state to enact and enforce such legislation was vindicated by the Supreme Court in 1920 in the case of the Minnesota statute.[4] This was enacted right after we entered the war, before Congress passed either the Draft or Espionage Acts. It made it unlawful to advocate by writing, print, or public talking, "that men should not enlist in the military or naval forces of the United States or the state of Minnesota," or "that citizens of this state should not aid or assist the United States in prosecuting or carrying on war with the public enemies of the United States." Any violator could be arrested without warrant, fined $100 to $500, and imprisoned three months to a year. Those penalties, though enough to deter all but the most militant pacifists, are unusually light for a war statute; but in 1919 Minnesota, eager to be ready for our next war, substituted a far more sweeping law [5] of the Montana type, imposing the maximum penalty of twenty years in the penitentiary without which no American sedition statute can be thought up-to-date.

[4] Minn. Laws, 1917, c. 463. The decisions construing this statute are listed in *Freedom of Speech*, p. 400.
[5] Minn. Laws, 1919, c. 93.

The 1917 law, which alone concerns us, atoned for its want of severity by numerousness of prosecutions. On its face it seemed directed against the comparatively few men who urged prospective volunteers, "Don't enlist," and actually proposed resistance to the draft and other war laws. Not one such case appears among the eighteen prosecutions in the Minnesota Reports. The statute was used to reach a very different kind of language. These decisions, like the Espionage Act cases, pound home the truth so easily overlooked by high-minded advocates of a sedition law, that you never can tell from reading the law when enacted what sort of speeches and pamphlets will be suppressed by it six months later.

The courts held that this statute could be violated although not a single person was dissuaded from enlisting, without a word about enlisting, and even though the jury found and believed that the speaker had not the slightest intention of hindering enlistment or any other war service. It was enough for a conviction if "the natural and reasonable effect of the statements uttered was to deter those to whom they were made" from enlisting or giving aid in the war. Of course any discussion opposing our entry into the war would easily have this effect, and also—what was more objectionable to the ruling powers of Minnesota— any bitter criticism, even by a man who favored the war, directed against the actual war methods of the federal government and of the official and unofficial persons who managed the war activities of Minnesota.

It is impossible to understand the operation of this statute and of the vague test of guilt laid down by the courts without some mention of the Minnesota conditions which lay behind every prosecution and every verdict.

The presence of a large number of farmers of German birth was part of the trouble, but a still more important factor is summarized by an acute and trustworthy observer, John Lord O'Brian, who as Assistant to Attorney General Gregory directed the enforcement of the Espionage Act: [6]

The general condition in the grain-producing states was intensified by the traditional hostility of the farmer toward the commercial interests of the cities,—a phase of agrarian discontent usually summed up in the claim that the townsmen profited unjustly at the expense of the consumers. This steadily showed itself in many rural districts in a form of hostility toward state, county and local councils of defense, which, it was claimed, were usually dominated by business men, the boards of trade, commercial clubs, etc.

The situation described in the *Atlantic Monthly* under the title "Prussianizing Wisconsin" [7] was not peculiar to Wisconsin. Much resentment must have been caused in some parts of Minnesota by Liberty Bond committees who forced every one to file a complete inventory of his real and personal property, on the basis of which the committee, consisting partly of bankers, required him to buy bonds to an amount that necessitated his borrowing from these same bankers at an interest rate which from the very outset was considerably higher than that of the coupons on the bonds. The hostility caused by such methods evoked sharp comments, which those in control were not reluctant to silence.

Finally, the long-standing antagonism between farmers and business men had recently been crystallized by the

[6] 42 Rep. N.Y. St. Bar Ass'n. 297.
[7] By Charles D. Stewart, *Atlantic Monthly*, January, 1919.

formation of the Nonpartisan League. Whole counties were divided into Leaguers and opponents with no neutrals, and the belief of these opponents in the seditious nature of the League was so strong that almost any public discussion of the war by a League member would lead to his conviction by a jury, which, naturally enough, would not contain members of the League.

It followed from these conditions that practically every speech or pamphlet prosecuted, instead of dealing with enlistment, was an expression of this hostility to "big business" or an exposition of the economic views of the League in such sentences as: "This war was arbitrarily declared against the will of the people to protect the investments of Wall Street in the bonds of the Allies." "It is an insult to the American farmer to ask him to raise more grain and then take our boys and send them over there." One man was convicted for saying that he agreed with the speech which had just been delivered by Gilbert (quoted below), and another for discouraging women from knitting by the remark, "No soldier ever sees those socks." These convictions were sustained on appeal, but those that were reversed as erroneous after the armistice had an equally terrorizing effect during the war, and show how such a statute may be used to stifle personal liberty. One such conviction was for a criticism of the food at a training camp; another for a statement to a Red Cross committee which visited a farmer at his house to solicit funds, that the government which had got us into an unnecessary war could get us out of it, and ought to supply the Red Cross by direct taxation instead of always sending men to ask for money. In addition to those cases, an attempt was made to have the whole war program of the League declared criminal, but without success.

II

From this background, familiar to many of us in the pages of *Main Street,* the scene shifts to Washington. Gilbert, a Nonpartisan leader, was indicted and convicted for the following words in a speech:

We are going over to Europe to make the world safe for democracy, but I tell you we had better make America safe for democracy first. You say, What is the matter with our democracy? I tell you what is the matter with it: Have you had anything to say as to who should be President? Have you had anything to say as to who should be Governor of this state? Have you had anything to say as to whether we would go into this war? You know you have not. If this is such a great democracy, for Heaven's sake why should we not vote on conscription of men? We were stampeded into this war by newspaper rot to pull England's chestnuts out of the fire for her. I tell you if they conscripted wealth like they have conscripted men, this war would not last over forty-eight hours.

This language should be compared with the terms of the Minnesota statute as a demonstration of sedition-law construction. The conviction was sustained by the United States Supreme Court, the Chief Justice and Justice Brandeis dissenting. Justice McKenna delivered the opinion of the court, but Justice Holmes concurred only in the result and not in the reasons. The dissenting judges based their objections to the constitutionality of the statute on two distinct grounds. Chief Justice White was of the opinion that the subject matter of the statute, viz., interference with enlistment, is within the exclusive legislative power of Congress, when exerted, and that the action of Congress in passing the Espionage Act has occupied the whole field, leaving no room for state action.[8] Justice Brandeis took a somewhat similar position, and also held the statute a violation of freedom of speech.

(1) May a state constitutionally punish opposition to war, especially if Congress legislates on the subject? Justice McKenna answered that Congress alone can raise armies, but the states as well as the nation are intimately concerned in the outcome of the war. They must have power of coöperation against the enemies of all.

Whether to victory or defeat depends upon their morale, the spirit and determination that animates them—whether it is repellent and adverse or eager and militant; and to maintain it eager and militant against attempts at its debasement in aid of enemies of the United States, is a service of patriotism; and from the contention that it encroaches upon or usurps any power of Congress, there is an instinctive and immediate revolt.

Justice Brandeis, on the other hand, maintained that the nation alone can limit discussion about the army and war. Even though the majority deny that this is required by the Constitution, the stubborn fact remains that it is the only sound policy. The undesirability of state war statutes is far more important than their unconstitutionality. The federal government has exclusive control over enlistments and the sole responsibility for the conduct of a war. When it determines that a man should not enter the army without the fullest consideration from every

[8] Thus Justice White, who was a Confederate drummer boy, here supported national supremacy, while Justice Holmes, who fought in the Union army, upheld states' rights.

point of view of the consequences of his action, or when it decides to allow a fairly wide range of discussion to the opponents of a war either as a safety valve for discontent or for the sake of obtaining the advantage of their opinions, such national policies will be very seriously blocked if the various states see fit to run amuck and establish inconsistent limitations on discussion. These limitations will be enforced in the heated atmosphere of local fears and dissensions, and opinions will be suppressed which the nation thinks it wise to leave alone. If there is ever a time that the nation ought to act as a unit it is in war. It is strange indeed that a court which had lately decided that the regulation of workmen's compensation for accidents on vessels in a state harbor can not be entrusted by Congress to the state legislature, but must be uniformly fixed for the nation as a whole, should have allowed a state to limit war-time discussion in any way it pleased, regardless of the declared wishes of Congress.[9]

The injurious effects of state war laws upon a national policy toward such discussion are not a matter of conjecture. We know from Mr. O'Brian that the Minnesota policy was absolutely at variance with the national policy and proved a cause of real embarrassment and danger to the federal government:

Without entering into the discussion as to the loyalty or disloyalty of some of the early leaders of the Nonpartisan

[9] For comment on this inconsistency between Gilbert v. Minnesota and Knickerbocker Ice Co. v. Stewart, 253 U.S. 149 (1920), see the dissenting opinion of Brandeis, J., Washington v. Dawson Co., 264 U.S. 219, 235 (1924) ; E. M. Dodd, "The New Doctrine of the Supremacy of Admiralty over the Common Law," 21 Colum. L. Rev. 647, 665 (1921).

League, it would be unjust to question the patriotism or honesty of the great mass of its membership. . . . The Attorney General [Gregory] adhered to the policy that the Federal Law Department would insist upon the fundamental doctrine that guilt was personal and would not lend itself to proscribing any class of individuals as a class. . . . In the state of Minnesota, because of what was claimed to be either inadequate federal law or insufficient federal administration, state laws of a sweeping character were passed and enforced with severity. Whether justified or not in adopting this policy of repression, the result of its adoption increased discontent and the most serious cases of alleged interference with civil liberty were reported to the federal government from that state.

If the war had lasted another year with uncertain prospects of victory, the continuance of this Minnesota policy might easily have embittered great masses of farmers and seriously hampered the production of grain and other war essentials.

(2) The free-speech point in Gilbert *v.* Minnesota involves a preliminary question. Has the United States Supreme Court any power to reverse a state conviction because it unduly restricts freedom of speech? This power can not arise from the First Amendment, which limits only federal action. Since all the decisions in which the question had previously been raised held that there was no improper restriction in the particular facts, the Supreme Court had been willing to assume the existence of this power for the sake of argument. This continues to be Justice McKenna's position.[10] Justice Brandeis, however,

[10] Decisions in the Supreme Court subsequent to Gilbert *v.* Minnesota have definitely recognized the existence of this power. See the discussion in this book of the Gitlow case and of Syndicalism in the Supreme Court.

states very interesting reasons for the proposition that freedom to discuss national affairs is one of the "privileges or immunities" of citizens of the United States, which, under Article IV, Section 2, and the Fourteenth Amendment, no state can abridge:

The right of a citizen of the United States to take part, for his own or the country's benefit, in the making of federal laws and in the conduct of the government, necessarily includes the right to speak or write about them; to endeavor to make his own opinion concerning laws existing or contemplated prevail; and, to this end, to teach the truth as he sees it. Were this not so, "the right of the people to assemble for the purpose of petitioning Congress for a redress of grievances, or for anything else connected with the powers or duties of the national government" would be a right totally without substance. Full and free exercise of this right by the citizen is ordinarily also his duty; for its exercise is more important to the nation than it is to himself. Like the course of the heavenly bodies, harmony in national life is a resultant of the struggle between contending forces. In frank expression of conflicting opinion lies the greatest promise of wisdom in governmental action; and in suppression lies ordinarily the greatest peril.

And then he states the principles which ought to govern when suppression becomes necessary:

There are times when those charged with the responsibility of government, faced with clear and present danger, may conclude that suppression of divergent opinion is imperative; because the emergency does not permit reliance upon the slower conquest of error by truth. And in such emergencies the power to suppress exists. But the responsibility for the maintenance of the army and navy, for the conduct of war and for the preservation of government, both state and federal, from "malice domestic and foreign levy" rests upon Congress. . . . Congress, being charged with responsibility for those functions of government, must determine whether a paramount interest of the nation demands that free discussion in relation to them should be curtailed. No state may trench upon its province.

Justice Brandeis also suggests the possibility that liberty of speech is one type of "liberty" of which under another clause of the Fourteenth Amendment no person can be deprived without due process of law:

I have difficulty in believing that the liberty guaranteed by the Constitution, which has been held to protect against state denial the right of an employer to discriminate against a workman because he is a member of a trade union, the right of a business man to conduct a private employment agency, or to contract outside the state for insurance of his property, although the legislature deems it inimical to the public welfare, does not include liberty to teach, either in the privacy of the home or publicly, the doctrine of pacifism; so long, at least, as Congress has not declared that the public safety demands its suppression. I cannot believe that the liberty guaranteed by the Fourteenth Amendment includes only liberty to acquire and to enjoy property.

In view of the test of freedom of speech declared by the unanimous opinion of the Supreme Court in the Schenck case,[11] it would seem clear that Gilbert was improperly convicted, since the Minnesota statute requires no clear and present danger of interference with enlistment as a

[11] Schenck v. U.S., 249 U.S. 47 (1919), discussed in *Freedom of Speech*, 88 ff. But the application of the Schenck test to state legislation is seriously affected by the later Gitlow case, *infra*, p. 105.

basis of guilt, nor did his speech create such a danger. Nevertheless, the majority through Justice McKenna hold that even if freedom of speech can not be wiped out by state action, it can be limited, and that a limitation was proper in this case:

> Gilbert's speech had the purpose they [the words of the Minnesota statute] denounce. The nation was at war with Germany, armies were recruiting, and the speech was the discouragement of that—its purpose was necessarily the discouragement of that. It was not an advocacy of policies or a censure of actions that a citizen had a right to make. The war was flagrant; it had been declared by the power constituted by the Constitution to declare it, and in the manner provided for by the Constitution. It was not declared in aggression, but in defense, in defense of our national honor, in vindication of the "most sacred rights of our nation and our people."
>
> This was known to Gilbert for he was informed in affairs and the operations of the government, and every word that he uttered in denunciation of the war was false, was deliberate misrepresentation of the motives which impelled it, and the objects for which it was prosecuted. He could have had no purpose other than that of which he was charged. It would be a travesty on the constitutional privilege he invokes to assign him its protection.

I would ask the reader to turn back once more to the speech on which Justice McKenna is commenting. Few of us would regard Gilbert as a sound exponent of all the motives which led us into war, but how many American citizens two years after the armistice, knowing all they did about the dissensions at Versailles, about the British appropriation of Mesopotamian oil, about the defaulted interest on the American loans to our Allies, about the Republican National Convention of 1920, would have described that speech in the language of Justice Mc-Kenna? The experts on poison gas tell us that after the wind has swept it away from the levels of the battle-field, it still lurks for long in a few holes and crevices. Similar properties are apparently possessed by war emotion.

It was to be hoped, a hope doomed to disappointment, that Gilbert *v.* Minnesota would be the last decision of the Supreme Court on freedom of speech for some time to come. The test of "clear and present danger," announced by a unanimous court in the Schenck case, had since been more honored in the breach than in the observance, but as yet it had not been expressly rejected, and it still stood as a landmark to which we might hold fast in future. Nevertheless, even with this test, the war taught the lesson that final limits upon governmental power over discussion, though they have a real value for charging juries and setting aside verdicts, are of comparatively small service in the almost total absence from the national consciousness of any genuine belief in the usefulness of the open expression of unpopular ideas. President Wilson was a lover of Bagehot, but very little was seen during the Wilson administration of Bagehot's conviction of the value of toleration. Even tolerant officials administering the Espionage Act were continually hampered by the insistence of the people that conspicuous pro-Germans, pacifists, and socialists be prosecuted—otherwise they would be lynched. Those who still share Milton's confidence in the power of truth unguarded by sedition laws

—"Let her and Falsehood grapple; who ever knew Truth put to the worse, in a free and open encounter?"—can best prepare for the next emergency by spreading the principles of the *Areopagitica* and Mill's *Liberty of Thought* through the minds of the American people.

THE "MILWAUKEE LEADER" CASE [1]

No decision of the United States Supreme Court has gone so far in sustaining governmental powers over the press as its opinion on March 7, 1921, in United States ex rel. Milwaukee Social Democratic Publishing Co. v. Burleson,[2] which upheld the ex-Postmaster General's order of October, 1917, denying second-class mailing rates to Victor Berger's *Milwaukee Leader*. Although the case arose under the Espionage Act, its most important effect will probably be in extending the power of the Postmaster General to penalize discussion in time of peace.

The precise point decided may best be understood from a brief statement of the post-office statutes. Congress has specified certain matter as non-mailable, for example, obscene literature, lottery prospectuses, and prize-fight films. Sending such matter is a crime, and the Postmaster General may exclude the offensive document from the mails by an administrative order issued without a jury trial and virtually uncontrolled by the courts. His decision that a letter or circular or issue of a magazine falls within a class forbidden by Congress will not be judicially reversed unless it is "clearly wrong." This has long been

[1] First printed in the *Nation*, March 23, 1921. For further discussion of the control of the mails in war, see *Freedom of Speech*, 46 ff., pp. 106-109. Berger's exclusion from Congress is discussed, *ibid.*, pp. 315-332.

[2] 255 U.S. 407, affirming 258 Fed. 282 (D.C. App., 1919).

55

settled law. The Espionage Act of 1917 [3] merely added a new kind of non-mailable matter, unlawful opposition to war.

The important feature of the *Milwaukee Leader* case is that while the statutes made only those particular issues of the newspaper non-mailable which actually were found to violate law, Mr. Burleson claimed the right to penalize subsequent issues of the same newspaper however innocent in character. For this purpose he made use of an entirely distinct post-office statute. The Mail Classification Act of 1879 provides four classes of post-office rates for different kinds of mail.[4] Second-class rates are granted to periodicals which "must regularly be issued at stated intervals" and published "for the dissemination of information of a public character." Since these rates are from eight to fifteen times lower than the third-class rate for other printed matter, it is clear that the refusal of a second-class permit to a newspaper denies it any profitable use of the mails and places it at the mercy of competitors who enjoy the lower rates. The Postmaster General may withhold or revoke the permit if he finds that the publication does not fulfill the requirements of the Classification Act, for instance, that a newspaper has missed several issues, or that successive numbers of Frank Meriwether stories do not constitute a periodical.

These powers are wide but unquestioned. Mr. Burleson went much further. Although the Classification Act nowhere said that the existence of non-mailable matter in past issues forfeits second-class rates for future issues,

[3] U.S. Act of June 15, 1917, c. 30, Title XII, § 1; now U.S. Code (1925) Title 18, § 343.
[4] Act of Mar. 3, 1879, c. 180, § 14; now U.S. Code (1925), Title 39, § 226.

he held that because the *Milwaukee Leader* had frequently violated the Espionage Act, its second-class permit should henceforth be revoked. His right to do this is sustained by a majority of the Supreme Court speaking through Justice Clarke, Justices Brandeis and Holmes dissenting.

The court's finding that the *Leader* had been violating the Espionage Act before its suppression emphasizes the bad tendency of what was said, with no questioning as to its clear and present danger. "Articles denounced the draft law as unconstitutional, arbitrary, and oppressive, *with the implied counsel* [italics mine] that it should not be respected or obeyed." Soldiers in France were represented as becoming insane, and conveyed from the front in long trains of closed cars. (Dr. Thomas W. Salmon in the *American Legion Weekly* for January 28, 1921, reports over 7,000 insane veterans in the United States.) "The Food Control law was denounced as 'Kaiserizing America' "—the same law denounced by Chief Justice White only a week before the *Milwaukee Leader* decision.[5] As usual, the bad intention of the writers, although an essential element of the crime, was inferred from the bad tendency. "These publications," says Justice Clarke, "were not designed to secure amendment or repeal of the laws denounced in them as arbitrary and oppressive, but to create hostility to, and to encourage violation of, them."

All this may be conceded without affecting the main issue—if the Postmaster General decides that a newspaper has published non-mailable matter in past issues, may he revoke its second-class permit for all future issues?

[5] In U.S. *v.* Cohen Grocery Co., 255 U.S. 81 (1921). For the use of this statute against the coal strike of 1919, see *infra*, p. 204.

Nothing in the statutes expressly gives him this drastic power. In the *Masses* case, Mr. Burleson contended that when one issue was barred from the mails, the magazine ceased to be a "regularly issued" periodical under the Classification Act.[6] This was obviously unsound, for the statutory requirement refers, not to the propriety of the reading matter, but to its intended and actual appearance at stated intervals. The *Masses* was issued even when it could not be mailed. Justice Clarke adopts different reasoning, that the second-class rates are granted on the assumption that the periodical will continue to conform to law, both to the requirements of the Classification Act and to prohibitions against printing non-mailable articles. A newspaper which has published such objectionable matter in several issues may reasonably be expected to continue violating the law. It would not be possible, he says, for the government to maintain a reader in every newspaper office in the country to approve every issue in advance. Consequently, an offending newspaper must have its permit revoked until it submits satisfactory evidence of its repentance. "Government is a practical institution, adapted to the practical conduct of public affairs."

There is force in this reasoning, and indeed most strong exercises of executive power are justified from the official point of view by the need of thorough enforcement of law. On the other hand our Constitution, with its Bill of Rights, recognizes the necessity for some sacrifice of administrative efficiency in order to prevent wrongs to individuals—hence it prohibits unreasonable searches

[6] Bulletins of the Department of Justice on the Administration of War Statutes, No. 26. See *Freedom of Speech*, 46 ff.

and seizures and guarantees trial by jury—and in order to maintain other purposes of society such as the discovery and dissemination of truth on public questions. Moreover, Justice Brandeis shows that it is practicable to exclude illegal matter without a revocation of second-class rates, for there is more opportunity to inspect this class of mail than any other. It is the only kind which has to be submitted to the local postmaster for examination before it is mailed. And however desirable the Postmaster General may consider the powers claimed in this case, the dissenting judges hold that Congress did not see fit to grant them.

The correctness of this decision is far less important than its consequences. It is nowise limited to war cases, and enables the Postmaster General to suppress any newspaper with a few articles which are unmailable on any ground.[7] Thus without any jury, without any court, for it is rarely possible to say he is clearly wrong, he can punish by extinction a periodical which ventures to discuss problems of sex and family life which he considers obscene

---

[7] In December, 1919, more than a year after the Armistice, Mr. Burleson denied the petition of the *New York Call* for restitution of the second-class mail privilege, which had been revoked in November, 1917, for violation of the Espionage Act. The Supreme Court of the District of Columbia granted a writ of mandamus, requiring the Postmaster General to restore the privilege, but this order was reversed by the Court of Appeals. Burleson *v.* U.S. *ex rel.* Workingmen's Co-op. Pub. Ass'n., 274 Fed. 749 (1921). The refusal of relief was based in part on another statute making non-mailable "matter of a character tending to incite arson, murder, or assassination."

An important decision of the Supreme Court since the *Milwaukee Leader* case, Leach *v.* Carlile, 258 U.S. 138 (1922), shows another almost unlimited power of the Postmaster General over freedom of communication. If he decides that a business is fraudulent because in his opinion its wares do not fulfill the promises of the advertisements, he can forbid the delivery of any mail to it, including letters. According to the majority opinion by Justice Clarke, this fraud order may not be reversed by a court "where it is fairly arrived at and has sub-

though many others think them valuable. The wide
powers exercised by the government in war prosecutions
have been defended on the ground that the control over
speech was in the hands of a jury, which was all that the
founders meant by freedom of speech. This decision gives
no such chance for the expression of public opinion on
the value of the periodical. Moreover, prosecutions come
after the opinions and facts presented have reached the
public, while a censorship may prevent the public from
learning them at all. And the Postmaster General's powers
are vague. They are like the law in Restoration France
which allowed the government to suppress any journal,
"if the spirit resulting from a succession of articles would
be of a nature to cause injury to the public peace and
the stability of constitutional institutions." Such a law is
utterly foreign to the tradition of English-speaking freedom.

Finally, if the Postmaster General is to possess these
vast powers over opinion, his selection becomes a matter
of great importance. Such powers can only be properly
exercised by a man of judicial temper and training, con-

stantial evidence to support it, so that it cannot be justly said to be
palpably wrong and therefore arbitrary." Justice Holmes in his dissenting opinion (in which Justice Brandeis concurred) denied the
power of Congress to authorize any one to determine in advance, on
such grounds as were involved in the case, that certain words shall
not be uttered and that no letters should be sent to a person. "Even
those who interpret the [First] Amendment most strictly agree that
it was intended to prevent previous restraints." Congress is not acting
here for the safety of the nation. "The question is only whether it
may make possible irreparable wrongs and the ruin of a business" in
the hope of preventing some cases of private swindling, which is
usually accomplished without the aid of the post-office. If the Postmaster General's finding of fraud is incorrect, the business is nevertheless smashed by a fraud order since it is a crime to send sealed
letters otherwise than by mail, while merchandise, books and periodicals may be sent by express when excluded from the post-office.

fident of the value of freedom of thought. Such qualities can hardly be said to have distinguished Mr. Burleson. Will they be considered in the appointments of his successors? [8]

[8] Mr. Burleson's immediate successor, Mr. Hays, restored both the *Leader* and the *Call* to the second-class mail privilege.

THE RAND SCHOOL CASE [1]

IMAGINE a private educational institution in New York City, ostensibly giving technical instruction in chemistry, but actually teaching assassination. Suppose theoretical courses in The Morality of Tyrannicide, and The History of Political Killing from Jael and Sisera to Serajevo. Suppose practical courses in Clockwork and Time Fuses, or The Comparative Merits of Dynamite and TNT. Visualize its graduates going forth fanatical and expert bomb-makers, as eager for a victim as a law-school graduate for his first client. Its managers and teachers could be prosecuted for past instruction under the Criminal Anarchy Act,[2] but must the government wait until the pernicious doctrines have been absorbed by immature minds? Should it not have power as soon as the aims of the school are ascertained, before a single lecture is delivered, to padlock the doors of this nursery of assassination?

It is only by conjuring up some such lurid picture that you can understand the attitude of the supporters of the New York 1921 legislation for the suppression of sedition in schools. The two statutes were based on the recommendations of a legislative Committee for the Investigation of Seditious Activities, usually named for its chairman, Senator Lusk. One law was aimed at those

[1] First printed in the *New Republic*, Sept. 27, 1922. The earlier activities of the Lusk Committee and its raid upon the Rand School are discussed in *Freedom of Speech*, Chapter VI.
[2] N.Y. Laws, 1902, c. 371. See "The Gitlow Case," *infra*, p. 101.

wolves in sheep's clothing, revolutionary teachers in the public schools, and directs the expulsion of any teacher who had advocated "a form of government other than the government of the United States or of this state." [3] This statute was perhaps not open to attack in the courts, but a vigorous contest over its enforcement was waged within the public school system. The validity of the other statute, directed at private schools, was the issue in the Rand School case.

The provisions of this act [4] were simple. First, private education was brought within reach of the state broom. Nobody might conduct "any school, institute, class or course of instruction in any subjects whatever" without a license from the regents of the state education board (legally entitled the University of the State of New York). The only exceptions were public schools, institutions—such as ordinary colleges—incorporated by the regents and thus already under their supervision, schools maintained by a religious denomination recognized as such in 1921—like the Roman Catholic parochial schools —and classes teaching the rituals of fraternal orders. The application for a license must be made according to rules prescribed by the regents, and must state "the nature and extent and purpose of the instruction to be given."

Secondly, the state broom swept clean. "No license shall be granted . . . by the regents . . . where it shall appear that the instruction proposed to be given includes the teaching of the doctrine that organized governments shall be overthrown by force, violence or unlawful means,"

[3] N.Y. Laws, 1921, c. 666; repealed by Laws, 1923, c. 798.
[4] N.Y. Laws, 1921, c. 667; repealed by Laws, 1923, c. 799.

or that the institution is to be conducted in a fraudulent manner. A license already granted must be revoked by the regents if the prohibited doctrines are taught. A licensed school or class was subject to visits by the regents or their employees.

What happened to a school which went ahead without a license? Every teacher and officer was liable to one hundred dollars fine and sixty days in prison. What was much more effective, the Attorney General might stop the unlicensed teaching at once by an injunction.

Those who would condemn this statute unreservedly should first ask themselves this question: "Do I want young people to be deliberately and systematically taught that the government of the United States ought to be forcibly overthrown?" Most sober-minded persons will answer by an emphatic "No." The real difference of opinion among such persons arises because many of them will continue their reply, "No; but though violent revolutionary instruction is an evil, yet the danger of it is far less menacing to our society than the dangers created by the methods enacted in this statute for ferreting out such instruction." It is for that reason that the Lusk laws were opposed by such conservative bodies as the Association of the Bar of the City of New York, vetoed by Governor Alfred Smith the year before their final enactment, and denounced by Bertrand Russell, a lifelong enemy of force and violence. In his little book, *Free Thought and Official Propaganda*,[5] he states that education has become one of the chief obstacles to intelligence, and turns for an example to the Lusk laws, "not because America is any worse than other countries, but because

[5] Watts & Co., London (1922), pp. 21-31.

it is the most modern, showing the dangers that are growing rather than those that are diminishing." The growing danger he finds exemplified by these laws is that resulting from the monopoly of power in the hands of a single organization, whether the church or a federation of trusts or the state. Through a monopoly of education the officials of the state can in time prevent the young from hearing any doctrine which they dislike.

We have before us, therefore, not a contest in which the state or radicalism—according to the point of view—has all the argument on its side, but a question of balancing two evils, violent ideas against a censorship. The New York Legislature and Governor Miller had pronounced the censorship the smaller evil of the two, but the Rand School case was to decide whether the people of New York did not conclusively prefer to run the risk of dangerous teaching when they adopted the free speech clause in their constitution.

The Rand School for Social Science is a Socialist and labor college maintained by the American Socialist Society at 7 East Fifteenth Street, near Fifth Avenue. It was established in 1906 and has over 5,000 registered students. Its work is announced by its director as falling into two parts, opportunities for the general public to study Socialism, and systematic training to render Socialists more efficient workers for the Socialist party, trade unions, and coöperative societies. It also maintains a large public library and reading room, and a book-store, doing a large mail-order business chiefly in material on social and labor questions. None of its activities had previously been held illegal, although its owner, the American Socialist Society, was convicted under the Espionage Act for publishing Nearing's *The Great Madness,* a matter unconnected with the school except that Nearing was a principal member of the teaching staff.[6]

The litigation now discussed was only one stage in a running fight between the school and the Lusk Committee. The school was one of the objects of the series of spectacular raids conducted by the committee in 1919. The number of radicals on its teaching staff, the revolutionary character of some of the books and pamphlets on sale in its store, and the incendiary nature of letters seized from its files without much attempt to learn whether they were addressed to the school by extremists or actually written by its officers on school business, alarmed the committee, which issued startling reports to the press about this hive of revolutionists, and induced the Attorney General to start proceedings to cancel the school's charter. However, the school had broken no law, and when Samuel Untermyer came forward as its counsel the suit was promptly dropped. Some new legislation was necessary to reach the institution, and the licensing statute recommended by the Lusk Committee would abolish the Rand School if actually teaching what the committee charged, and at all events make possible its supervision by the state. The school refused to apply for a license, and the Attorney General, assisted by the principal lawyer of the committee, asked for an injunction to stop its teaching.

The school suffered defeat in the first phase of the litigation, for the injunction was granted by the Appellate Division, which is the next to the highest New York

[6] U.S. *v.* Am. Socialist Soc., 252 Fed. 223, 260 Fed. 885; Bulletins of the Department of Justice on the Interpretation of War Statutes, Nos. 129, 192, 198.

court.[7] Judge Merrell wrote the majority opinion with three judges concurring; Judge Greenbaum dissented. The question whether the Rand School was entitled to a license was not raised. The case decided only that the school must apply for a license, since the statute was constitutional. Four important points were raised for judicial settlement.

1. Although the statute literally required a license for instruction "in any subjects whatever," which would bring under state control classes in swimming or sewing, and in handicrafts like bricklaying or typesetting, the court limits it to the ordinary subjects of school curricula.

2. Even so, all teaching of academic subjects is brought under state supervision and visitation, and such an extensive regulation of one of the oldest and most important human activities is a deprivation of liberty and property in violation of the Fourteenth Amendment to the United States Constitution and the corresponding New York provision, unless it may reasonably be interpreted to serve some public purpose so as to fall within the police power and be considered due process of law.

In the past much social legislation restricting private enterprise had been held unconstitutional under these clauses, to the indignation of Socialists, labor leaders, and even such a staunch individualist as Theodore Roosevelt. The class rooms of the Rand School must have frequently echoed to denunciations of Ives v. Railway Co.,[8] invalidating the first New York Workmen's Compensa-

[7] People v. Am. Socialist Soc., 202 N.Y. App. Div. 640 (1922).
[8] 201 N.Y. 271 (1911).

tion Act, *Re* Jacobs,[9] denying the state power to forbid the manufacture of cigars in crowded tenements, and Lochner *v.* New York,[10] upsetting the ten-hour day in bakeshops. It was amusing, therefore, to find the Rand School, a Socialist institution, striving on the authority of these very cases to limit governmental control over a private activity. After the school's foot was pinched by state regulation, its teachers may have understood better the irritation which other kinds of business feel under government regulation. And the emphasis placed by the school in this litigation upon the value of private initiative in education might cause some qualms about the coming epoch when education and everything else will be operated solely by a bureaucratic state.

The Appellate Division took a broader view of the police power than the old cases just stated and held that the public safety is menaced by revolutionary schools as well as by exposed buzz-saws and dirty barber shops. They are grounds for prosecution, and so is advocacy of bloody rebellion under the Criminal Anarchy Act. But the state does not rest content with prosecution in the case of dirty barber shops. It inspects and closes them unless they will conform to administrative regulation. The legislature adopted the same policy, that an ounce of prevention is worth a pound of cure, in the case of private schools. The court saw no reason for a distinction.

3. Sound as the court's interpretation of the police power seems, this power is restricted by another clause of the New York Constitution, Art. I, sect. 8:

[9] 98 N.Y. 98 (1885).
[10] 198 U.S. 45 (1905).

Every citizen may freely speak, write and publish his sentiments on all subjects, being responsible for the abuse of that
right; and no law shall be passed to restrain or abridge the
liberty of speech or of the press.

Here is a difference between schools and barber shops,
which may well take schools outside the legitimate field
of state licensing. A school is engaged in the production of
ideas and of intelligence, which are bound to suffer from
bureaucratic supervision. An official may be trusted to
recognize dirt or discriminate between dangerous and
harmless machinery. He cannot be trusted to discriminate
between dangerous and harmless ideas. Human nature has
too strong a tendency to regard what one dislikes or dis-
agrees with as a menace to the social order.

It may be objected that advocacy of the overthrow of
organized government by violence is so plain that anybody can spot it at sight. The facts prove just the contrary.[11] Judge George W. Anderson ruled that the Communist party did not profess that doctrine. Secretary of
Labor Wilson ruled that it did, but that the Communist
Labor party did not. Attorney General Palmer ruled that
both parties were promulgating it, and his secret service
agents helped several state prosecutors to land the two
types of Communists in prison for long terms. When such
sharp differences of opinion are exhibited by those in
high authority about programs of social reconstruction,
the task of determining whether a Rand School course on

[11] See Swinburne Hale, "The Force and Violence Joker," *New Republic,* Jan. 21, 1920; *Freedom of Speech,* 213 ff. The various rulings
on Communists are discussed with references in *Freedom of Speech,*
243 ff., pp. 250, 256-262. Judge Anderson's opinion in Colyer *v.* Skeffington, 265 Fed. 17 (1920), was reversed on this point in Skeffington
v. Katzeff, 277 Fed. 129 (C.C.A., 1922).

modern radical movements involves a bare intellectual interest in these programs, or approval, or exhortation to the students to put the principles studied into practice, is too delicate for any subordinate state official to decide. The Appellate Division did not discuss the free-speech clause at all. The following passage indicates that they thought the question was settled when it was previously decided that advocacy of violent revolution could be punished under the Criminal Anarchy Act of 1902:

> The legislature has as much right to enact a salutary statute to prevent the promulgation of doctrines inimical to our form of government, the putting into effect of which would lead to the conviction of those who had adopted said doctrines under existing penal law, as to punish those who were guilty of violating such penal laws. A state has as much right to guard against the commission of an offense against its laws as to inflict punishment upon the offender after it shall have been committed.

This reasoning would equally justify a statute establishing a censor for newspapers with power to exclude any passages which in his opinion would if published be held criminal by a hypothetical jury. It gives no consideration to the fundamental difference between punishment by a jury and censorship by an official.

Even Blackstone, the upholder of the powers that be, declared: "The liberty of the press . . . consists in laying no *previous restraints* upon publication." And his view was wholeheartedly adopted by an important New York decision (Brandreth *v.* Lance),[12] not cited in the

[12] 8 Paige 24 (1839). The doctrine of this case, that the injunction of defamatory writing violates liberty of speech, appears still to be law in New York, Marlin Fire Arms Co. *v.* Shields, 171 N.Y. 384

Rand case, which declares that such a power of preventive justice "can not safely be entrusted to any tribunal consistently with the principles of a free government." A jury is none too well fitted to pass on the injurious nature of opinions, but at least it consists of twelve men who represent the general views and the common sense of the community and often appreciate the motives of the speaker or writer whose punishment is sought. A censor, on the contrary, is a single individual with a professionalized and partisan point of view. His interest lies in perpetuating the power of the group which employs him, and any bitter criticism of that group smacks to him of incitement to bloody revolution.

It may be that even a censorship is constitutional under circumstances of extreme danger, as when a newspaper proposes to publish the sailings of transports. Did similar circumstances exist to justify the New York licensing statute? Again, a censorship of motion pictures has been upheld; they are somewhat different from books or speeches. Does a school, because of the systematic character of its utterances and the immaturity of many of the listeners—this last is hardly true of the Rand School— also fall into a peculiar category? These are some questions which, it was hoped, would be answered in the Court of Appeals.

4. Even if a censorship of schools is constitutional, the censor must act according to "due process of law," and

(1902). The courts have been insistent on the application of the free-speech guarantee to the one class of cases where no social interest in the spread of truth is infringed. See R. Pound's comment in 29 *Harv. L. Rev.* 640, 648.

this is almost always held to require notice and a hearing before decision. Although this statute provided a hearing before a license is revoked, it said nothing at all about the procedure when a school applied for a license, and the Appellate Division construed this silence to mean that the regents might refuse a license without a hearing. It considered the defect to be cured by the school's right to a review of the regents' decision by a court, for the school would be heard in court, but inasmuch as the court had no greater power to reverse the regents than to set aside the verdict of a jury, this right was worth very little. In other words, a school might have been driven out of existence by officials who acted on their own whimsical interpretation of its catalogue or on the reports of the Lusk Committee, and the school would have had no opportunity to present its case unless the regents' decision was outrageously wrong.

The Rand School case was not ended by this decision of the Appellate Division in June, 1922. At the time it was hoped that a fuller consideration of the issue of freedom of speech might be secured in the Court of Appeals and that the issues of due process of law might eventually be carried to the United States Supreme Court. Should it have been finally decided by the courts that the School must apply for a license, the question whether the license could properly be withheld still remained to be fought out. While the appeal was pending, Governor Miller, who signed the Lusk bills, was defeated in November, 1922, by Governor Smith, who had in his previous term vetoed them in a stinging message for violating freedom of speech. Smith's return to office was followed by the repeal of the Lusk legislation,[13] and the proceedings against the Rand School automatically lapsed. The cause of liberal education was won, not in the courts but at the polls.

[13] See notes 3 and 4, *supra*.

THE CALIFORNIA I.W.W. INJUNCTION [1]

FOR a hundred years after the Sedition Act of 1798, political and economic discussion among citizens of the United States was unrestrained by law, although occasional alarm was felt at the possibility that the open statement of extreme radical views might lead to violent acts. The Espionage Act showed that men can be punished in this country for what they say as well as for what they do, and within three years after its passage thirty-one states had made sedition in time of peace a serious crime.[2] More than half these states adopted an almost uniform statute, which created the new crime of criminal syndicalism and was directed mainly against the Industrial Workers of the World.

WHAT IS CRIMINAL SYNDICALISM?

Thus the California statute [3] begins by defining criminal syndicalism as:

Any doctrine or precept advocating, teaching or aiding and abetting the commission of crime, sabotage (which word is

[1] First printed in the *New Republic*, Sept. 19, 1923. The original case was People *ex rel.* Webb *v.* I.W.W., Superior Court, Sacramento County, C.C.P. 1707 (unreported). The main source for the article was a typewritten copy of the record, which has been verified as far as possible from the printed sources cited in note 7, *infra*.

[2] A list of references to these statutes and many judicial decisions construing them is given in Appendix V of the author's *Freedom of Speech.*

[3] Cal. Laws, 1919, c. 188. Several decisions construing this statute are listed in *Freedom of Speech*, 405; and many more have subse-

hereby defined as meaning willful and malicious physical
damage or injury to physical property), or unlawful acts of
force and violence or unlawful methods of terrorism as a means
of accomplishing a change in industrial ownership or control,
or effecting any political change.

Imprisonment from one to fourteen years may be inflicted upon any person who advocates, teaches, or aids
and abets criminal syndicalism; who willfully attempts to
justify it; who publishes or circulates any written or
printed matter advocating or advising it; who organizes,
assists in organizing, or knowingly becomes a member of
any group organized to advocate it (without necessarily
urging this doctrine himself); or who commits any act
advocated by this doctrine with intent to effect a change
in industrial ownership or any political change.

Although these Criminal Syndicalism Acts soon became
a dead letter in most states, not so in California. At least
thirty-two [4] cases have gone to appellate courts, in which
at least one hundred and twenty-five persons were prosecuted under this statute. One prosecution has been used
to bring on another. When some I.W.W.'s were on trial
and Miss Anita Whitney was produced as a witness for
the defense to describe the aims of the organization, she
was rejected because, not being a member, she had no

quently been printed in the California reports. Examples showing the
evidence of the criminal objects of the I.W.W. admitted at trials are:
P. v. McClennegen, 195 Cal. 445 (1925); P. v. Roe, 209 Pac. 381
(1922); P. v. LaRue, 216 Pac. 627 (1923); P. v. Flanagan, 223 Pac.
1014 (1924); P. v. Wagner, 225 Pac. 464 (1924)—the last two before
Judge Busick. An interesting prosecution for mailing defense circulars
widely, some of which reached men later drawn as jurors, is P. v.
Connors, 233 Pac. 362 (1924), 246 Pac. 1072 (1926). See also "Criminal Syndicalism in the Supreme Court," infra.

[4] Seventeen was the number before the Busick injunction; fifteen
more appeals have since been decided.

expert knowledge. Consequently, other I.W.W.'s had to
be brought in as witnesses. As soon as these left the
court room after testifying, they were arrested on the
ground that they had admitted being members of the
proscribed organization, and they were also tried and
convicted.[5]

BREAKING UP THE I.W.W.

Nevertheless, the results secured by the criminal law
proved unsatisfactory to the prosecuting officials. The
Defense Committee said that "jurors are refusing to
convict" on the evidence of "the self-confessed criminals
whom the prosecutions have been in the habit of using as
their chief witnesses." (Compare the nature of the affidavits mentioned hereafter.) However this might be, the
Attorney General eventually adopted a very different
method from trial by jury for breaking up the I.W.W.
in California.

On July 16, 1923, he applied to the Superior Court in
Sacramento County for an injunction against the Industrial Workers of the World, and various specified
committees, officers, and members of the organization.

[5] See People v. Casdorf, 212 Pac. 237 (1922) ; People v. LaRue, 216
Pac. 627 (1923) ; P. v. Johansen, 226 Pac. 634 (1924). In the first
case the district attorney is said to have declared in the presence of
the jurors that all witnesses admitting they were paid-up members of
the I.W.W. would be arrested, and this was done when they left the
court room; their convictions were affirmed in the second case. In the
last case men in Alameda County were subpenaed to appear as witnesses in a trial in Sacramento County, where they had not previously
been. After they had testified that they were members of the I.W.W.,
they were arrested and convicted for being members of a criminal
syndicalist organization in Sacramento County. The court, in affirming their convictions, said that although they came into the county in-
voluntarily they might have severed their connection with the I.W.W.
before coming.

The same day Judge Charles O. Busick granted a restraining order in the terms requested by the Attorney General. Such an order is a preliminary injunction, to remain in force for only a few days until a hearing can be held; it is issued when the judge is convinced by affidavits of an emergency so serious that he must forbid the defendants at once instead of waiting for them to present their reasons against an injunction. When the hearing is held the judge may dissolve the injunction as unwarranted, but in this case Judge Busick on August 23, after the defendants had stated their objections, turned the restraining order into a temporary injunction, which was to last until the whole evidence of both sides had been given. Then, if he were satisfied of the merits of the state's case, the injunction would be made permanent. The defendants, however, contended that the judge's conduct of previous criminal trials showed prejudice against the I.W.W. If they had established this contention, the case would have been transferred to another judge, who might have taken a different view from Judge Busick and dissolved the injunction forthwith. If this course failed, the defendants announced their intention to appeal from the injunction, and if necessary to carry the case to the Supreme Court of the United States.[6]

[6] Apparently no transfer to another judge was made and no appeal was taken. A member of the I.W.W. was adjudged in contempt of court for violating the injunction by procuring new members, fined, and imprisoned to work out his fine in default of payment. He then brought *habeas corpus* to secure his release on the grounds that the injunction was invalid and that the affidavits charging contempt were insufficient. Relief was refused. *In re* Wood, 194 Cal. 49 (1924). In this proceeding the Supreme Court decided only that the injunction was a legitimate exercise of equitable jurisdiction and was not void. Whether the trial court erred in granting it was a question with which the Supreme Court was not concerned, as it would have been upon an appeal from the injunction. The opinion also stated that the allegation,

The terms of the restraining order, and substantially of the temporary injunction,[7] were as follows:

> It is further ordered, that the defendants, . . . and each of them, their and each of their servants, agents, solicitors, attorneys, and all others acting in aid or assistance of the defendants, or each of them, do absolutely desist and refrain from further conspiring with each other to carry out, and from carrying out, or attempting to carry out, their conspiracy to injure, destroy and damage property in the state of California and to take over and assume possession of the industries and properties in said state as well as the government thereof; and from knowingly circulating, selling, distributing and displaying books, pamphlets, papers or other written or printed matter advocating, teaching or suggesting criminal syndicalism, sabotage or the destruction of property for the purpose of taking over the industries and properties of all employers, or otherwise, and from advocating, by word of mouth or writing, the necessity, propriety and expediency of criminal syndicalism or sabotage, direct action, willful damage or injury to physical property and bodily injury to person or persons, and from justifying or attempting to justify, criminal syndicalism, the commission or attempt to commit crime, sabotage, violence or unlawful methods of terrorism with the intent to approve, ad-

that property owned by the state of California itself would be injured by the defendants, might be indefinite, uncertain, or otherwise defective, but that this question, also, was not open to consideration on *habeas corpus*. The injunction must be obeyed by the defendants until reversed on appeal, even if erroneously issued. This decision was adversely criticized by Professor H. W. Ballantine, 98 *Central L.J.* 5.

State *ex rel.* Lindsley *v.* Grady, 114 Wash. 692 (1921) also denied *habeas corpus*. A similar injunction in Kansas was sustained on appeal. State *ex rel.* Hopkins *v.* I.W.W., 113 Kansas 347 (1923).

[7] The temporary injunction will be found in *In re* Wood, 194 Cal. 49, 52. It has very slight differences from the restraining order, which was taken from the typewritten copy of the record (note 1, *supra*), and corresponds to the wording of 'the order given in *Law and Labor*, October, 1923, where extracts from the opinion of Judge Busick are also given.

vocate or further the doctrine of criminal syndicalism, as said terms "Criminal Syndicalism" and "Sabotage" are defined in [the Criminal Syndicalism Act of California], and from organizing or aiding or assisting to organize or extend or increase any society, assemblage or association of persons which teaches, advocates, aids and abets criminal syndicalism or the duty, necessity or propriety of committing crime, sabotage, violence or any unlawful method of terrorism as a means of accomplishing a change in industrial ownership or control, or effecting any political change, and from doing any acts to carry out the doctrines, theories and acts of criminal syndicalism and from in any manner whatsoever conspiring or confederating together for the carrying out of said purposes, or either thereof, until the further order of this court.

The Sacramento injunction combined two significant legal tendencies of recent years, governmental suppression of radical discussion and organizations, and governmental use of the injunction instead of criminal prosecutions to maintain "law and order."

THE I.W.W. THRIVES ON PERSECUTION

The first tendency, which was sketched in my opening paragraph, raises the familiar problem of the desirability of using force against opinions. Such a policy of coercion is especially questionable as applied to the I.W.W. The organization thrives on discontent, and persecution is the best way to increase discontent. Carleton Parker showed this before the Syndicalist Acts were passed.[8] Professor D. D. Lescohier of Wisconsin, whose interest-

[8] "The I.W.W.," *Atlantic Monthly*, November, 1917, reprinted in his *The Casual Laborer* and Other Essays, New York, 1920.

ing first-hand observations of "The I.W.W. in the Wheat Lands" were published in the August, 1923, *Harper's,* reached the same conclusions:

They are a social tragedy rather than a social menace. . . . The nation cannot avoid what the I.W.W. stands for by forcible suppression of the organization, and it should not try. It can avoid revolutionary organizations among the workers only by removing the economic and social disadvantages that are the source of revolutionary discontent.

It is a mistake to spend energy in a mosquito-killing campaign which might be used in draining the swamps where the insects breed. The I.W.W. is largely recruited from migratory laborers who wander haphazard from one seasonal crop to another. Much of the evil might be cured if large groups of laborers could be systematically organized and transported by rail to the place where such a seasonal crop is to be gathered. They might even be induced to alternate this temporary agricultural work with labor in city factories. In this connection, the practice of the Canadian government in transporting workers from industrial England to the wheat harvest is worthy of study.

ADVANTAGES AND DISADVANTAGES OF AN INJUNCTION

The second legal tendency noted above, the use of the injunction instead of the criminal law, is much more far-reaching in its possibilities of harm. Let us assume, though the defendants vigorously denied it, that the I.W.W. intended to do all the acts prohibited by this injunction. Nevertheless, any violence they might commit might be and ought to be severely punished under the ordinary Penal Code, and the Criminal Syndicalism Act contains sweeping provisions for the punishment of speech and writing short of action. How then did it happen that the Attorney General resorted to an injunction?

Courts of equity have no power to prevent crimes as such. They exist primarily to protect individual rights and not the state. B's factory is sending smoke into A's house. A gets an injunction forbidding B to continue the nuisance. If B disobeys, the court will order him imprisoned for contempt until he stops the smoke. The state is not a party to the proceeding.

However, the state may also get into equity as a property-owner. If B's factory is sending its smoke into the State House, the state may get an injunction just as A can, and it is immaterial that B's nuisance is also a criminal violation of a smoke ordinance. What is still more important, a defendant may be injuring the public at large in a manner analogous to a private nuisance. Suppose B's smoke contains poisonous fumes which are endangering the lives of the neighbors. Then the state may obtain an injunction, not only as a property-owner, but also as the guardian of the health and general welfare of its citizens. On the same principle, in a California case [9] cited by the Attorney General as a precedent for his I.W.W. injunction, one of his predecessors in office had mine-owners prohibited from casting large quantities of débris into a river, so as to obstruct the navigation and water supply of a district. This injunctive power has been extended by statute to objectionable establishments like

[9] People *v.* Gold Run Ditch, 66 Cal. 155 (1884).

disorderly houses or illegal saloons, which constitute a plague-spot like the poison-spreading factory.

Such equitable proceedings have advantages over the criminal law. They avoid juries, which are reluctant to impose punishment for these minor offenses. An injunction may be obtained on proof by a preponderance of the evidence; conviction requires proof beyond a reasonable doubt. And it is often desirable to get rid of a clearly illegal establishment by direct suppression of the thing itself without the crude and round-about method of imprisoning the human beings who operate it. Yet there are obvious disadvantages, which until the last few years have rendered courts very reluctant to extend this injunctive power against public nuisances, especially in the absence of express legislative authority. If the defendant seriously disputes the illegality of his conduct and thus is liable to disobey the decree, he will be imprisoned for conduct which, unless it is criminal, constitutes no cause at all for his confinement. He and his sympathizers in the community will reflect that he is in jail without a jury trial and at the will of a single judge, who both passed on the facts and determined the duration of confinement, and from whose decision the right of appeal is very limited. Lawyers may distinguish contempt from conviction, but the man himself sees little difference. The prison fare is the same in both cases, the prison walls are equally thick. If a judge may, by the simple process of calling any crime a public nuisance, throw into jail any person whom he considers to have violated his injunction, trial by jury for crimes becomes a virtual nullity.

THE ALLEGED CASE AGAINST THE I.W.W.

The complaint in the California case declared that the
I.W.W. existed to teach criminal syndicalism, and was
attempting "thereby to fan flames of discontent among
all laboring men and women and all employees" in the
state; that the defendants were conspiring to advocate
sabotage and crime, and the breaking of employment
contracts, for the purpose of accomplishing a political
and economic revolution in the state and nation; that
they aimed at taking over the control of all industries
and governments and "destroying all civilization as it
now exists"; that many members had come into California during the two months preceding and conspired to
cause a stoppage of work in the farms, mines, oil fields,
and lumber industries of the state by syndicalism and
sabotage; that if their purposes were accomplished, the
health, lives, and property of the people would be endan-
gered, and the production of the necessaries of life would
be injured and decreased.

Aside from the allegations that the state was interested
as a property owner, because its revenues from taxes
would be diminished by these prospective injuries to its
citizens' property, a ground obviously too remote for an
injunction, the state's case must rest on the existence of
a public nuisance by virtue of the threats summarized in
the preceding paragraph. Yet the situation was entirely
different from the recognized public nuisances like poisonous factories and illegal saloons. There was nothing
you could put your finger on as a plague spot, only a
vague congeries of prospective violations of the Criminal
Syndicalism Act, which ought to have been dealt with, if

at all, under that statute by the criminal proceedings which the legislature authorized, and not by an injunction without trial by jury, which it did not authorize.

And whether or not the suit presented any ground for equitable action after all the evidence had been heard, the granting of an injunction at the very outset of the proceedings was improper. A temporary injunction may properly be issued to preserve the status quo during the trial of a case; this restraining order attempted to change the status quo by driving out of existence an organization which, whatever its merits, had been going on for years. If it be said that such an injunction may sometimes alter the status quo if its continuance during the suit would work outrageous irreparable injury to the plaintiff, no evidence was offered in this case to show that the situation with respect to the I.W.W. in California was any different from what it had been during the previous five years without fatal damage to lives and property

The affidavits (on which a restraining order must be based) were only three in number. One, by a former deputy sheriff, merely stated the prevalence of incendiary fires in his neighborhood in 1917, without mentioning the I.W.W. The other two were by W. E. Townsend and Elbert Coutts, former members of the I.W.W., on whom the state was accustomed to rely in I.W.W. prosecutions.[10]

10 "They were also witnesses in several of the [seven] cases above cited, if not in all of them." Seawell, J., in P. v. McClennegen, 195 Cal. 455 (1925).
"Elbert Coutts and W. E. Townsend, former members of the I.W.W., and whose testimony has been received in every criminal syndicalism case which this court has been called upon to review in the past three or four years, testified in the instant case, going over practically the same ground that they had at previous trials." Hart, J., in P. v. Wright, 226 Pac. 953 (1924), also referring to Davis, the

Aside from the suspicion which must always rest upon such professional witnesses, almost everything they said related to acts of sabotage (including the incendiary fires) in 1917 and 1918, and the contents of I.W.W. pamphlets which had been long in circulation. The only statement that indicated the possibility of especial danger in the immediate future was a single paragraph at the end of the seven-page affidavit of Townsend, a Los Angeles policeman and thrice a former member of the I.W.W., who stated on the witness-stand in another I.W.W. case that he "had never told the truth before in his life," "admitted participation in numberless atrocious offenses," and was judicially characterized as showing himself to have been "one of the most reprehensible characters thinkable." [11] Townsend now said that in 1922 he was

deputy sheriff, as testifying about the incendiary fires in two or three criminal cases. (I find him in three.)

I have found Coutts mentioned as a chief witness for the state as to the criminal activities of the I.W.W. (not of the particular defendants involved) in ten appellate opinions, and Townsend similarly mentioned in eight. Townsend's sanity was unsuccessfully questioned by the defense in P. v. LaRue, 216 Pac. 631 (1923) and P. v. Cox, 226 Pac. 17 (1924). Another state witness, Arada, not a former I.W.W., appears by name in seven appellate cases. As one reads the testimony of these professional witnesses, he finds himself becoming very familiar with a few destructive events attributed to the I.W.W., which took place before the enactment of the Criminal Syndicalism Act and yet recur as evidence against the I.W.W. in case after case.

I do not recall any appellate opinion in which the defendants were charged by witnesses with themselves committing or participating in the destruction of property or personal injuries, or even with directly inciting such acts in speeches. Their offense was either distributing the usual revolutionary documents of the I.W.W., or being organizers or members of the association which issued such documents and other members of which were said to have committed or incited destructive acts. The wording of the documents became milder after the statute was passed, but the state met this by evidence that members of the I.W.W. had said this was camouflage.

[11] Plummer, J., in P. v. Cox, 226 Pac. 17 (1924), continuing: "It is unfortunate that any one confessedly guilty of so many despicable crimes must be used as a witness; but competency and character are

asked by several unnamed members to join an "Inner Circle . . . composed of trusted and desperate characters who would bind themselves under oath to assassinate jurists, prosecuting officers and others who were opposing the defendant organization . . . with the idea and purpose of so terrorizing officials and the public that they will cease to oppose the activities of the defendant organization, and cease to oppose its plans to take over all private property and overthrow the government."

There seemed to be no reason why the existing state of affairs should not have been left alone until the suit was finished.

WORKING THE INJUNCTION OVERTIME

In conclusion, two points must be emphasized. First, aside from the validity of any particular injunction in these governmental suits, we are making a very grave mistake in allowing prosecuting officials to employ courts of equity in place of criminal courts. It is true that the criminal law has broken down in this country. The police will not or cannot arrest, the rules of evidence furnish countless technical obstructions, juries refuse to convict, new trials are readily granted. The prosecutor turns with relief from this uncertainty to the automatic, hair-trigger

separate and distinct terms. A witness may be competent and yet of such unspeakably degraded character as to be unworthy of belief, hence his testimony . . . may be . . . given such weight as [the jury] may deem it entitled to under all the circumstances. It is not for the court to close the door of reformation and say that a witness who has never told the truth up to a certain period of time, may not thereafter mend his ways and speak words conformable to the facts. . . . It may be, that if the I.W.W. organization is a criminal conspiracy in its essential fundamental principles, doctrines and advocacies, no other kind or character of testimony or no other kind or character of witnesses may be had from its membership."

action of a judicial restraining order. Once more, as in
our failure to attack the causes of the I.W.W., we are
evading the issue. Instead of setting ourselves diligently
to reorganize the administration of criminal justice, we
shrink from the difficult task and try to make the injunction do the same job of maintaining order in industrial
disputes. Sooner or later we shall pay the price. In a jury
trial, the responsibility is distributed. It does not all fall
on the judge. The accused is convicted by men from the
street, not very different from himself except in their
freedom from crime. The jury takes up the slack, as it
were. In a court of equity, there is nothing to take up
the slack. The judiciary, the most delicate part of our
political machinery, is subjected to a terrific strain, when
it is made to do unaided, and in highly controversial
cases, work fitted for the rougher mechanism of the
criminal law.

Finally, the efficiency of the governmental injunction
in maintaining the normal processes of life during industrial disputes does not necessarily make it desirable. The
natural wish of those in authority to make the government strong enough to meet the needs of the moment with
rapidity may lead them to obtain efficiency by an undue
sacrifice of freedom. Law and order are good, but they
shade by imperceptible gradations into the order that
"reigns in Warsaw." Experience has proved it wise that
the public should have a fairly direct share in those
functions of government that intimately affect the life of
the average man; for instance, taxation, which may only
be initiated by the branch of the legislature closest to
the people, and punishment, which must be inflicted by a
jury. The delays and uncertainties incident to such popu-

lar participation in government render men of action impatient. Charles I wanted taxes without Parliament, and the Star Chamber was instituted to suppress crime without a jury. The increased efficiency thereby secured was not adequately appreciated by the people at large. The use of the injunction to put men in prison without a jury trial for reasons that seem insufficient to a considerable body of their fellow citizens is liable to produce a resentment that may eventually sweep away some judicial powers that had better be preserved along with what can be spared.

Instead of these get-peace-quick methods, let us tighten up the machinery of criminal justice to punish violent acts with all the swiftness and sureness of which the jury system is capable; rely on reforms and carefully considered economic adjustments to eradicate large strikes and the revolutionary spirit; and keep courts of equity for the tasks for which they have been developed by long experience. An equity judge ought not to be turned into a super-policeman.

COMPULSORY CONFESSIONS [1]

RECENT plans for limiting the powers of the United States Supreme Court face the vigorous objection that the court's ability to insure protection to personal liberty as guaranteed by the Constitution would be seriously curtailed. In reply, attention is called to the rarity of decisions upholding personal liberty in comparison with those guarding property. This may be due to the relative infrequency of appeals to the court for enforcement of the guarantees of personal liberty rather than to any superior regard for property rights, although the whittling away of freedom of speech in the Espionage Act cases is not reassuring. At all events, a refreshing attitude was displayed in 1924 by the opinion in Ziang Sung Wan v. United States,[2] in which the unanimous court, speaking through Mr. Justice Brandeis, protected a lone Chinaman against the District of Columbia police, who had arrested him in February, 1919, for three murders at the Chinese Educational Mission in Washington.

Apart from the questions of law involved, the opinion is valuable for the powerful light which it casts upon the working of the so-called "third degree." (The "first degree" is the arrest, the "second degree" the taking of the prisoner to a place of confinement.) The charge that the police in our cities extort information from persons

[1] First printed in the *New Republic*, November 12, 1924.
[2] 266 U.S. 1 (1924); reprinted in the same issue of the *New Republic*.

accused of crime by protracted questioning combined with deprivation of food and sleep is frequently made, but the truth is naturally hard to discover. The few prisoners who venture to report the practice are accused of gross exaggeration and too often lack a reputation for veracity. The officials concerned are silent, or minimize and defend the process.

Thus, at the 1910 meeting of the International Association of Chiefs of Police,[3] Chief Corriston, of Minneapolis, said:

The "third degree" as understood by the public, is a very different thing from the "third degree" as known by a police official. . . . This body of men should by every means in their power refute the sensational idea the public has of the so-called "third degree." . . . In making an investigation as to who is responsible for committing an offense, it is often necessary to have several talks with the persons suspected, and their statements as to their whereabouts and conduct at the time in question are important links in unraveling a mystery. These investigations by the police have no doubt cleared the record of many an innocent suspect. The object is to ascertain the truth, not, as the public seems to think, fasten the commission of a crime upon some one—whether guilty or innocent.

And Major Sylvester, of Washington, President of the Association, said:

Volunteer confessions and admissions made after a prisoner has been cautioned that what he states may be used against him, are all that there is to the so-called "third degree."

Fortunately, we are not altogether without reliable information on the details of the practice. A paper on

[3] These extracts are taken from John H. Wigmore, *Treatise on Evidence,* 2d. ed., II § 851.

"Methods of Obtaining Confessions and Information from Persons Accused of Crime," presented by B. O. Chisolm and H. H. Hart to the American Prison Association and published by the Russell Sage Foundation in March, 1922, summarizes the answers to questionnaires sent to prosecuting attorneys and chiefs of police in the larger cities of the United States. We also have a few accounts of the process by judges,[4] but none has approached Judge Brandeis's opinion in fullness of detail:[5]

Wan was held in the hotel room without formal arrest, *incomunicado*. But he was not left alone. Every moment of the day, and of the night, at least one member of the police force was on guard inside his room. Three ordinary policemen were assigned to this duty. Each served eight hours, the shifts beginning at midnight, at eight in the morning, and at four in the afternoon. Morning, afternoon and evening (and at least on one occasion after midnight), the prisoner was visited by the superintendent of police and/or one or more of the detectives. The sole purpose of these visits was to interrogate him. Regardless of Wan's wishes and protest, his condition of health or the hour, they engaged him in conversation. He was subjected to persistent, lengthy and repeated cross-examination. Sometimes it was subtle, sometimes severe. Always the examination was conducted with a view to entrapping Wan into a confession of his own guilt and/or that of his brother. Whenever these visitors entered the room, the guard was stationed outside the closed door.

On the eighth day, the accusatory questioning took a more excruciating form. A detective was in attendance throughout the day. In the evening, Wan was taken from Hotel Dewey to the Mission. There, continuously for ten hours, this sick

[4] E.g., People *v*. Vinci, 295 Ill. 419 (1920).
[5] Ziang Sung Wan *v*. U.S., 266 U.S. 1, 11 (1924).

man was led from floor to floor minutely to examine and re-examine the scene of the triple murder and every object connected with it, to give explanations, and to answer questions. The places where the dead men were discovered; the revolver with which presumably the murder was committed, the blood stains and the finger prints thereon; the bullet holes in the walls; the discharged cartridges found upon the floor; the clothes of the murdered men; the blood stains on the floor and the stairs; a bloody handkerchief; the coat and pillow which had been found covering the dead men's faces; photographs, taken by the police, of the men as they lay dead; the doors and windows through which the murderer might have entered or made his escape; photostat copies of writings, by means of which it was sought to prove that Wan was implicated in a forgery incident to the murder—all these were shown him. Every supposed fact ascertained by the detectives in the course of their investigation was related to him. Concerning every object, every incident detailed, he was, in the presence of a stenographer, plied with questions by the superintendent of police and the detectives. By these he was engaged in argument—sometimes separately, sometimes in joint attack. The process of interrogation became ever more insistent. It passed at times from inquiry into command. From seven o'clock in the evening until five o'clock in the morning the questioning continued. Before it was concluded, Li, who was again in attendance, had left the Mission about midnight, worn out by the long hours. The superintendent of police had returned to his home, apparently exhausted. One of the detectives had fallen asleep. To Wan, not a moment of sleep was allowed.

On the ninth day, at twenty minutes past five in the morning, Wan was taken from the Mission to the station house and placed formally under arrest. There, the interrogation was promptly resumed. Again the detectives were in attendance, day and evening, plying their questions, pointing out alleged contradictions, arguing with the prisoner, and urging him to confess, lest his brother be deemed guilty of the crime. Still the statements secured failed to satisfy the detectives' craving for evidence. On the tenth day, Wan was "bundled up," was again taken to the Mission, was again questioned there for hours; and there "the whole thing was again talked of and enacted." On the eleventh day, a formal interrogation of Wan was conducted at the station house by the detectives in the presence of a stenographer. On the twelfth day, the verbatim typewritten report of the interrogation (which occupies twelve pages of the printed record) was read to Wan, in his cell at the jail. There, he signed the report and initialed each page. On the thirteenth day, for the first time, Wan was visited by the chief medical officer of the jail, in the performance of his duties. This experienced physician and surgeon testified, without contradiction, to the condition of the prisoner:

"[He] found . . . [Wan] lying in a bunk in the cell, very weak, very much exhausted, very much emaciated; he complained of abdominal pain, which was rather intense. He told witness, and witness afterwards saw, that he vomited if he attempted to take food; . . . witness thought he was very seriously ill; . . . concluded he was suffering from spastic colitis. . . . The result . . . would be almost constant pain. . . . Witness knows defendant was in bed at least a month after his treatment was prescribed. From witness's observation and medical experience, judging from the defendant's emaciation and history he gave witness, and his condition generally, would say that when witness saw the defendant on February 13 he had been ill for a matter of weeks. . . . He told me he had been talked to all one night and had not received any medical attention, and had been in constant pain all of this time and had been unable to eat for days, and considering all those facts I came to the conclusion that he was so exhausted that he was really desperate—he told me also that he had signed a confession."

The extreme methods Justice Brandeis describes may be exceptional and contrary to the custom in most cities, but it is disturbing to find them used, not in a remote frontier town, but in the capital of the nation.

This brings us to the legal problem—should the courts endeavor to check this method of investigation into crime where no actual violence is used, by excluding confessions thus obtained from the evidence submitted by the prosecution against the prisoner? That this question is not always answered by reputable and thoughtful men in the affirmative, is shown by the fact that the Chinaman's confession in the case under discussion was admitted by both the trial court and the Court of Appeals of the District of Columbia, and by the well-considered opinion of John H. Wigmore,[6] that "the attempts, legislative and judicial, to exclude confessions obtained by police questioning of persons arrested and in seclusion represent simply a misguided solution of the problem."

The contrary opinion of the Ziang Sung Wan case, that such confessions should be excluded, does not rest upon any clause of the Constitution, but upon a well-established principle of the common law, originating in England where there is no written constitution, that confessions secured by improper methods must not be used as evidence against a person on trial for crime. The test of this impropriety is commonly phrased as the extraction of the confession by threats of harm or by promises of benefit, such as a pardon or light sentence. This test may fairly be criticized as wooden, and it is more rational to require that the threat or promise should have placed the prisoner in a situation where an untrue statement of guilt

---

[6] *Treatise on Evidence,* 2d ed., II § 851.

became more desirable to him than the alternative courses of silence or a truthful avowal of innocence. Historically, the courts have gone very far in excluding confessions, influenced at the start by the harshness of the old criminal law, which forbade the prisoner to be represented by a lawyer or to testify on his own behalf and denied him the power to compel witnesses to testify for him. Since he now possesses all these privileges, adherence today to the old confession precedents causes too much mercy, and some decisions in the Supreme Court itself seem over-lenient, in cases where no such compulsion was used as that employed against Ziang Sung Wan.

To what extent should the old confession rule be retained in the criminal courts of the future? This problem involves the Constitution, for although, as already stated, the rule excluding confessions was established by the common law independently of any constitutional clause, yet in so far as the confession was obtained by fear or other compulsion, the common-law rule overlaps the requirement of the federal and state constitutions that no man shall be compelled to incriminate himself. Thus the question of obtaining compulsory information about the crime from the prisoner in preliminary investigations before trial is intimately connected with the question whether he should be obliged to take the stand during the trial. It may be urged that we ought to abolish or greatly modify both the common law and constitutional provisions which prevent the government from obtaining information about a crime from the person who often knows most about it, and who is, in many cases where the law now protects him, guilty. For instance, the evidence offered against Ziang Sung Wan in addition to his confessions, which is stated by the Court of Appeals of the District of Columbia,[7] makes it possible that he was justly convicted.[8] Why, then, regardless of his guilt, should the conviction be set aside? Certainly the rules against compulsion can no longer be retained merely from mercifulness or the feeling that it is hard on a guilty man that he should be condemned by his own words. What more rational grounds exist for forbidding compulsion at the present day?

The most obvious reason is the danger that confessions of guilt obtained through intolerable pressure will be false. Wigmore gives an impressive list of cases where this has happened.[9] Of late years, psychologists have shown that even without any serious pressure, love of notoriety or other pathological causes lead innocent persons to profess guilt. This danger may be exaggerated, but it must at least be considered.

Secondly, if prosecuting officials are given free rein to establish their case against a prisoner from his own lips, they will be tempted to rely almost exclusively upon this dubious kind of evidence instead of exerting themselves to build up a strong case by searching laboriously for independent proof such as documents, eye-witnesses of the crime, and persons who by their testimony may furnish good circumstantial evidence against the prisoner. Prosecuting officials and the police are comparatively few in

[7] 289 Fed. 908 (1923).
[8] After his confessions were excluded, two subsequent juries disagreed as to his guilt. The district attorney stated to the judge that it would be impossible to find a jury which would declare the defendant either innocent or guilty. The accused was thereupon released, seven years after his arrest, *New York Times,* February 10, May 14, June 17, 1926.
[9] *Op. cit.* note 6, II § 867.

COMPULSORY CONFESSIONS   97

number in this country in proportion to their tasks. They are terribly rushed, and like most human beings, are inclined to take the line of least resistance. To extort a confession will often seem the easiest way to convict. Once sanction is given to one kind of brutality, others will easily follow. Fitzjames Stephen, the historian of English criminal law, concludes that the French law by admitting compulsory statements of the accused before trial often brings about a poorer case for the prosecution than in the English courts, where the proof is ordinarily confined to objective evidence.

This objection, however, applies much less forcibly to the compulsory testimony of the accused in the criminal trial itself, after the prosecution has built up its case by objective evidence; yet in all the states in this country but one and in the federal courts, if the accused stays off the stand, neither the prosecuting attorney nor the judge may argue to the jury that this fact is any indication of guilt, although such an inference is only common sense. Comment on this fact ought to be allowed, as it is now in England and New Jersey. If prosecuting officials and police knew that this pressure could be exerted to obtain the prisoner's story of the crime at the trial, where he is safeguarded by the presence of the judge and his counsel, they would be less tempted to get it from him before the trial in seclusion by such methods as the "third degree."

Finally, even if confessions extorted by grilling were usually true and furnished satisfactory proof of guilt, the use of such a method should be rejected because of its injurious effect upon the public. If a government is to retain the devotion and confidence of the people, it must not violate their sense of decency. Inquisitorial methods are bound to leak out, perhaps in exaggerated form. The men who are convicted thereby are believed by a considerable number of persons to be innocent. It is not enough that the people should get justice; they must believe that they are getting justice. They will not so believe if conduct of the police like that in the Ziang Sung Wan case is a frequent occurrence.

The Supreme Court's opinion forcibly proves the need of a thoroughgoing investigation of the extent to which the "third degree" prevails in American cities, and a careful consideration of the circumstances under which interrogation of the accused by government officials should be permitted, if at all. Such an inquiry may lead us to change the law so that a prisoner may be forced to take the stand at his trial. Perhaps even an examination before trial might be permitted if conducted by a responsible magistrate, in the presence of the prisoner's counsel who should abstain from vexatious interference but be on hand to furnish proper protection. If interrogation before trial really is essential to the proper discovery of crime, as the defenders of the "third degree" insist, the practice should be expressly recognized by the law and surrounded by proper safeguards, and not allowed to go on illegally in a place where the prisoner is isolated from impartial officials, family, friends, and legal advisers, with no one to inform him of his rights or report brutalities.

THE GITLOW CASE[1]

ATTORNEY GENERAL PALMER, in laying a large quantity of revolutionary material before a committee of Congressmen, warned them, "It is not good reading late at night when you are at home in your own house. It gives you the creeps a little." No one need fear similar terrors from the Left Wing Manifesto, for publishing which Benjamin Gitlow's conviction was sustained by the Supreme Court

186693

[1] First printed in the *New Republic*, July 1, 1925.

Most free speech cases in the Supreme Court of the United States before 1925 involved limitations on the power of Congress under the First Amendment to the Constitution, which has no concern with state legislation. However, in Gilbert *v.* Minnesota (*supra*, p. 49), the court assumed for purposes of argument that liberty to speak and write might be one of the kinds of "liberty" of which under the Fourteenth Amendment no state could deprive any person without due process of law; in other words, which could not be curtailed by an arbitrary statute. During the interval between this decision and the Gitlow case, this interpretation of "liberty" was strengthened by Meyer *v.* Nebraska, 262 U.S. 390 (1923); Bartels *v.* Iowa, *ibid.* 404; which held it to include liberty of teaching, so that a state could not constitutionally forbid a private religious school to instruct young children in a foreign language by the kind of statute which was adopted by several states during the late war. Justice McReynolds wrote the majority opinion. Justices Holmes and Sutherland dissented, on the ground that the statutes might be considered reasonable. Just a week before the Gitlow case the court in the Oregon School case, Pierce *v.* Society of Sisters, 268 U.S. 510 (1925), invalidated a law making it illegal for parents to send their children to private schools, and construed "liberty" to include the right of parents to direct the upbringing of their children. While in both these cases the schools were deprived of property in the form of tuition fees, the decisions cleared the ground for a decision that liberty of thought without any property is protected under the Fourteenth Amendment. (It will be observed that neither school case bore on the power of the state to regulate teaching in public schools and universities, e.g. by anti-evolution laws.)

State peace-time sedition laws, discussed in *Freedom of Speech*, Chapter IV, became very common after the war, and were with a few exceptions held constitutional by state courts (see the list of statutes

99

of the United States in 1925.[2] After twenty pages of somniferous type telling the recent history of the world, it reaches its first incendiary passage: "Strikes are developing which verge on revolutionary action, and in which the suggestion of proletarian dictatorship is apparent, the strike-workers trying to usurp functions of municipal government as in Seattle and Winnipeg. The mass struggle of the proletariat is coming into being." And then fourteen pages more about destroying the bourgeois parliamentary state, with repeated exhortations to "mass strikes," "mass action," "expropriation of the bourgeoisie," and establishing "the dictatorship of the proletariat," until at last it winds up by prophesying "a revolutionary struggle against Capitalism" that may last for tens of years before "the final act of conquest of power."

Any agitator who read these thirty-four pages to a mob would not stir them to violence, except possibly against himself. This Manifesto would disperse them faster than the Riot Act. It is best described by recalling the Mouse in *Alice in Wonderland* reading about the Norman Conquest to dry off the Dodo and the Lory. " 'Ahem,' said the Mouse with an important air, 'are you all ready? This is the driest thing I know.' "

and decisions, Appendix V). On the California statute, see "The California I.W.W. Injunction," *supra*, p. 74, and "Criminal Syndicalism in the Supreme Court," *infra*, p. 119. The New York statute, passed long before the war and discussed in *Freedom of Speech*, pp. 187, 188, was not construed by appellate courts until 1921 in the Gitlow prosecution discussed in this paper.

[2] Gitlow *v.* New York, 268 U.S. 652 (1925). The state decisions affirming conviction are: People *v.* Gitlow, 111 N.Y. Misc. 641 (1920) ; 195 N.Y. App. Div. 773 (1921) ; 234 N.Y. 132, 539 (1922). Accounts of the original trial are found in the daily press. The decision of City Magistrate McAdoo holding Gitlow and his associates for the grand jury is reprinted in *Sedition, Hearing before the Committee on the Judiciary, House of Representatives* (Washington, 1920), p. 155.

It is one more illustration of the irony of suppression that the numerous judges who considered the fugitive publication of this dull document in its entirety so objectionable that it merited five years in the penitentiary, have thoughtfully winnowed out all the extremist passages and reprinted them in their opinions, so that they are permanently accessible to incipient revolutionists in brief and readable form at any lawyer's office.

In 1919 the Left Wing broke away from the Socialist party with this manifesto, printed in the *Revolutionary Age,* of which Gitlow was business manager. The Lusk Committee (which itself published the manifesto in full in its Report)[3] had Gitlow and others prosecuted for publishing it. A New York statute,[4] enacted in 1902 after McKinley's assassination, and a dead letter ever since, was revived for this purpose. This statute punished any advocacy of criminal anarchy, which was defined as "the doctrine that organized government should be overthrown by force or violence, or by assassination of the executive head or of any of the executive officials of government, or by any unlawful means."

[3] *Revolutionary Radicalism. . . . Report of the Joint Legislative Committee Investigating Seditious Activities . . .* (Albany, 1920), in four volumes, at page 706 of Vol. I. See also Vol. II, p. 1322, which lists the names of the managing council of the *Revolutionary Age,* all of whom were indicted. Of these, Gitlow, Ignaz Mizher, Harry M. Winitzky, and Jim Larkin, the Irish labor leader, were convicted and imprisoned; the convictions of Isaac E. Ferguson and Charles E. Ruthenberg were reversed by the New York Court of Appeals because they were not proved responsible for the publication of the Left Wing Manifesto, 199 N.Y. App. Div. 642 (1922), 234 N.Y. 159 (1925), Hogan, J., dissenting. The other four members, including John Reed, were never apprehended.

[4] N.Y. Penal Law, §§ 160-166. Besides the cases in notes 2 and 3, see Von Gerichten *v.* Seitz, 94 N.Y. App. Div. 130 (1904), holding it libelous to call a man an "anarchist," and *Re* Lithuanian Workers' Lit. Society, 196 *ibid.* 262 (1921), refusing a charter to a Socialist society.

Gitlow was convicted in January, 1920, and sentenced to hard labor from five to ten years, of which he served almost three. His conviction was upheld by the Appellate Division, by the Court of Appeals, Pound and Cardozo dissenting, and by the Supreme Court of the United States, Holmes and Brandeis dissenting.[5]

In the Court of Appeals the constitutionality [6] of the Criminal Anarchy Act was upheld, but the main question on which the court split was its construction. This, after all, is not a wholly distinct issue, for a statute means what the judges say it means, and one judicial interpretation of a sedition law might give enough scope for political discussion to satisfy a liberal like John Stuart Mill, while another conceivable interpretation might limit speech and press with great rigidity. Consequently, the constitutional guarantees restrict not only legislative action but also judicial construction of what the legislature has done. It is also a serious restraint upon open discussion if speakers and writers are liable to find themselves subsequently held guilty of violating a sedition law which does not seem at the time applicable to what they are saying. When Gitlow published his manifesto, the Criminal Anarchy Act was generally supposed to punish anarchy, but the majority applied it to communism, which is at the opposite pole of political thought. They held that communism,

[5] See note 2 for references. In the Court of Appeals majority opinions were filed by Crane, J., and Hiscock, Ch. J.

[6] The free-speech clause of the New York Constitution reads: "Every citizen may freely speak, write, and publish his sentiments, on all subjects, being responsible for the abuse of that right; and no law shall be passed, to restrain, or abridge the liberty of speech, or of the press." It is uncertain whether the liberty of speech protected under the Fourteenth Amendment would be stated in this form or in the different phraseology of the First Amendment; but the difference in wording has not been regarded by the courts as material.

which would bring all the activities of citizens under the
control of the state, was not "a condition which could be
fairly regarded as an organized government," and that to
urge the achievement of such a régime through mass
strikes was to advocate the overthrow of organized government by "unlawful means." Judge Pound's dissent,
while strongly disapproving the defendant's aims, insisted
that organized government need not be representative or
constitutional, but "is the political power in the state
whose commands the community is bound to obey and is
the antithesis of government without such political power
which is the unorganized or anarchistic state." Since Gitlow had urged the dictatorship of the proletariat and not
anarchism, he was not within the terms of this statute.

Although the defendant may be the worst of men; although
Left Wing socialism is a menace to organized government; the
rights of the best of men are secure only as the rights of the
vilest and most abhorrent are protected.

In the United States Supreme Court the only question
was the constitutionality of the Criminal Anarchy Act as
thus construed by the state courts. Unlike the Espionage
Act free speech decisions, the case did not come up under
the First Amendment, which restricts only Congress, but
under the Fourteenth: ". . . Nor shall any state deprive
any person of . . . liberty . . . without due process of
law," that is, by arbitrary and unreasonable legislation.
In several cases the court had carefully refrained from
deciding whether "liberty" protects liberty of speech as
well as liberty of the person and of contracts, but the recent holding that liberty to teach a foreign language in

private schools was within the Fourteenth Amendment [7]
naturally led the way to the unanimous statement of the
court in the Gitlow case that "we may and do assume
that freedom of speech and of the press . . . are among
the fundamental personal rights and 'liberties' protected
. . . from impairment by the states."

The majority of the court, however, held, through Mr.
Justice Sanford, that this statute did not wrongfully im-
pair Gitlow's liberty of speech. The New York courts had
expressly repudiated the test laid down by the Supreme
Court in a leading Espionage Act case [8] that words were
punishable only when their nature and the surrounding
circumstances created "a clear and present danger" of
wrongful acts, and there was no evidence of such danger
in this case. Consequently Gitlow's counsel contended
that he had been punished merely for doctrines and words
because of their supposed bad tendency to result at a
remote time in acts. This bad-tendency test is an English
eighteenth-century doctrine, wholly at variance with any
true freedom of discussion, because it permits the government to go outside its proper field of acts, present or
probable, into the field of ideas, and to condemn them
by the judgment of a judge or jury, who, human nature
being what it is, consider a doctrine they dislike as so
liable to cause harm some day that it had better be
nipped in the bud. The danger test, on the other hand,
leaves the doctrine to be proved or disproved by argument and the course of events. It avoids the risk of sup-

[7] See note 1, *supra.*
[8] Schenck *v.* U.S. 249 U.S. 47 (1919). The interpretation of free
speech in this case was repudiated in P. *v.* Gitlow, 195 N.Y. App. Div.
at 790.

pressing disagreeable truths, so long as there is no immediate risk of unlawful acts.

Justice Sanford virtually adopts the bad-tendency test. The words "tend" and "tending" are as frequent in his opinion as in an English charge during the prosecution of a reformer in the French Revolutionary Wars. As for the "clear and present danger" test, he declares that it merely served to decide how far the Espionage Act, which dealt primarily with acts, should be interpreted to extend to words. He rejects it altogether as a test of the constitutionality of a statute expressly directed against words of incitement which the legislature considers dangerous. Thus words may be punished for their bad nature regardless of the court's opinion that there is no danger of bad acts. The injudicious choice of language becomes a crime.

A single revolutionary spark may kindle a fire that, smoldering for a time, may burst into sweeping and destructive conflagration. It cannot be said that the state is acting arbitrarily . . . when . . . it seeks to extinguish the spark without waiting until it has enkindled the flame or blazed into the conflagration.

The trouble is that in extinguishing the spark we cause much damage that might be avoided if the spark were left to go out by itself. There is no better way to increase discontent than to impose severe sentences for acts which the accused and his friends do not consider criminal at all.

Justice Holmes's brief dissent stands by the danger test, which cannot apply to suppress this manifesto concerned with an uprising in some vague future. To the

majority view that it is punishable for the bad nature of
the words, he replies:

It is said that this manifesto was more than a theory, that
it was an incitement. Every idea is an incitement. It offers
itself for belief, and, if believed, it is acted on unless some
other belief outweighs it, or some failure of energy stifles the
movement at its birth. The only difference between the expression of an opinion and an incitement in the narrower sense
is the speaker's enthusiasm for the result. Eloquence may set
fire to reason. But whatever may be thought of the redundant
discourse before us, it had no chance of starting a present
conflagration.

A profit and loss account of the Gitlow case shows one
new gain, the possibility of federal protection against
state suppression. A more liberal court may prevent a
checker-board nation, with ultra-conservative states into
which moderately radical Americans come at peril of imprisonment for sedition. Not much can be hoped today.
Such extreme laws as the Tennessee evolution statute
may be invalidated, but the intolerance of the California
Syndicalism Act will not be checked by Mr. Justice Sanford. State freedom must be secured through state legislatures and state governors like Alfred E. Smith, who
pardoned Gitlow and his associates and stopped further
Anarchy Act prosecutions.[9]

The losses are much clearer. Without the danger test,
freedom of speech means little more than the right to say
what a considerable number of citizens regard as sound,
which consequently is not likely to be prosecuted. For

[9] Gitlow was pardoned by Governor Smith soon after the decision
of the U.S. Supreme Court.

novel and unpopular ideas, where alone it is really needed, it seems no longer to exist as a legal right.

We have also lost vision and courage. The Left Wing Manifesto is a tepid hash of the Communist Manifesto of Marx and Engels, which has been the program of influential parliamentary groups in every Continental country for over half a century. The terror which these dull and rusty phrases has caused our prosecutors and judges would render them the laughing-stock of European conservatives. The real danger in this country is not a conflagration but dry rot, "the slow smokeless burning of decay." The ballot-box is not likely to be overthrown by force, but if non-voting goes on increasing, it may become as meaningless as the Electoral College. The clash of ideas is to be welcomed, not feared, even if it occasionally involves the intemperate exhortations of a manifesto. We may wisely ponder the comment of Junius, after the English sedition prosecutions, "The mass of the people is inert. The country has lost its passions."

The victories of liberty of speech must be won in the mind before they are won in the courts. In that battlefield of reason we possess new and powerful weapons, the dissenting opinions of Justices Holmes and Brandeis. Out of this long series of legal defeats have come a group of arguments for toleration that may fitly stand beside the *Areopagitica* and Mill's *Liberty*. The majority opinions determined the cases, but these dissenting opinions will determine the minds of the future.

THE BIMBA CASE [1]

IT is a striking indication of the changed attitude toward discussion since the war that public authorities in an enlightened state like Massachusetts in the second quarter of the twentieth century should have used the utterances which Bimba was said to have made as the basis for an arrest and a revival of the obsolete offense of blasphemy. Even though he was acquitted in the District Court on the blasphemy charge and was eventually released from the charge of anarchy, the significant fact still remains that the prosecution was brought.

Religious disputes seemed the actuating motive of the case, which apparently arose out of a factional fight between the clerical and anti-clerical groups among the Lithuanians. The anarchy charge, on which he was con-

[1] First printed in the New York *World*, March 4, 1926. The facts are taken from the current files of the Boston *Herald* and the *New York Times*.

This paper was written during the trial in the District Court at Brockton, Mass., from February 24 to March 2, 1926, of Anthony Bimba, the young Lithuanian editor of a Brooklyn Communist newspaper, for a speech in his native language at a meeting of Lithuanians at Montello. The indictment charged, first, violation of the Massachusetts Anarchy Act, and secondly, blasphemy under an old statute. The judge was C. Carroll King, a Unitarian, and the case was tried without a jury. The decision was given March 2, 1926. Although the blasphemy charge attracted much more attention, the defendant was acquitted on this ground but convicted on the sedition charge. So far as I have been able to ascertain, this was the only prosecution under the Anarchy Act from its enactment in 1919 until the disturbances of August, 1927, at the time of the execution of Sacco and Vanzetti (see *infra*, p. 152). Bimba was fined one hundred dollars and appealed, seeking a jury trial in the Superior Court, but the district attorney entered a *nolle prosequi*, which brought the prosecution to an end.

victed in the District Court, received much less attention from the witnesses, although this crime, like sedition generally, may easily be applied to any unpopular political doctrines unless the court defines the offense with a strictness uncommon in sedition trials of the last decade.

The Massachusetts Anarchy Act of 1919 [2] punishes with a maximum of three years' imprisonment or $1,000 fine, or both, "whoever by speech or . . . document. . . advocates, advises, counsels or incites assault upon any public official, or the killing of any person, or the unlawful destruction of real or personal property, or the overthrow by force or violence of the government of the Commonwealth." Bimba was charged with committing this crime by saying in Lithuanian: "Here we are organizing Lithuanians among Lithuanians, the Poles among the Polish, and the Jews among the Jews, and so forth, to overthrow the American capitalistic government by revolution in the same way that they did in Russia, and to establish the same kind of government that they now have in Russia. Workers are out of employment. They are being persecuted here in America, and now is the time to organize. We don't believe in the ballot, we don't believe in any form of government but the soviet form, and we shall establish the soviet form of government here. The red flag shall fly on the Capitol at Washington, and there will also be one on the Lithuanian hall in Brockton." [3]

[2] Now Mass. Gen. Laws, 1921, c. 264, § 11.
[3] The translations are taken from the bill of particulars of the prosecution as printed in the Boston *Herald,* February 19, 1926. The testimony at the trial was conflicting as to how far Bimba used the language charged.

Regarding the sedition charge, the District judge found that some of Bimba's hearers were out to "get" him; that is, to ask him ques-

Just when this revolution was scheduled to come off did not appear. No marked desire for haste was exhibited. The "clear and present danger" of unlawful acts, which the United States Supreme Court had suggested as the basis for interference with speech, hardly existed here. And nobody was urged to do anything. The "force and violence" required by the statute were not contained in any glowing exhortations to bombs and bayonets, but had to be inferred by cold logic from the word "revolution" and the reference to Russia. And if these words were dangerous when fleetingly spoken in a little-known language in a small hall in Brockton, what must have been the public peril created by the Boston *Herald,* which reprinted them in full in English on its front page, where they incited a hundred thousand readers to the overthrow of the government of the Commonwealth!

The blasphemy statute is much more precise. "Whoever willfully blasphemes the holy name of God by denying, cursing or contumeliously reproaching God, his creation, government or final judging of the world, or by cursing or contumeliously reproaching Jesus Christ or the Holy Ghost, or by cursing or contumeliously reproaching or exposing to contempt and ridicule, the holy word of God contained in the holy scriptures, shall be punished by imprisonment in jail for not more than one

---

tions that would lead him to make expressions which would bring him into trouble. He found that the substance of Bimba's reply to a part of this heckling was that the red flag would wave over Washington and over Kovno. "As a net result, I believe that Bimba did bring himself within the part of the statute forbidding counseling but not within the part forbidding inciting. Considering the rather heavy penalties prescribed it may seem that the penalty [$100] I shall impose is meager, but we are at peace, war passions are not inflamed, and radical activities are on the wane." *New York Times,* March 3, 1926.

The sensible action of the district attorney in quashing the prosecution in the Superior Court nullified the effect of the conviction below.

year or by a fine of not more than three hundred dollars,
and may also be bound to good behavior." [4]

The present form of this statute dates substantially
from 1782, although the offender might also then be punished "by sitting in the pillory, by whipping, or by sitting
on the gallows with a rope about the neck." Older laws
had more sweeping definitions of blasphemy. The first
statute, of 1646, imposed the death penalty. Soldiers in
camp, by a law of 1675, need only have their tongues
bored by a hot iron. It does not appear whether the
provocation was considered greater or whether capital
punishment would remove too many fighting-men.

The last prosecution for blasphemy in Massachusetts
was in 1834, against Kneeland, an editor, for willfully
denying the existence of God. His conviction was affirmed
by the Supreme Judicial Court,[5] and he served two
months in jail. Although Kneeland had attacked the liberal churchmen, William Ellery Channing, leader of the
Unitarians, headed a petition for pardon with one hundred and sixty-seven other signers, which had such an
effect in educating the public mind that Channing's biographer predicted, "There will never in all probability be
another prosecution for atheism in Massachusetts." In
other states also blasphemy became a dead offense until
after the World War. The only reported case during the
last thirty years in the whole United States was in 1921,
in Maine,[6] where the law is the same as in Massachusetts.

After ninety years of disuse, the Massachusetts statute

[4] Mass. Gen. Laws, 1921, c. 272, § 36.
[5] 20 Pick. 206 (1838).
[6] State v. Mockus, 120 Me. 84 (1921). This also involved a Lithuanian meeting, at Rumford Falls in 1919. Mockus had previously been
sentenced by the City Court of Waterbury, Conn., in 1916, to ten days
in jail, but on appeal the jury disagreed, and he was not retried.
Whipple, *The Story of Civil Liberty in the United States*, p. 269.

was revived to charge Bimba with these words: "People have built churches for the last two thousand years. We have sweated under Christian rule for two thousand years, and what have we got? The government is in control of the priests and bishops, clerics and capitalists. They tell us there is a God. Where is He? There is no such thing. There still are fools enough who believe in God. The priests say there is a soul. Why, I have a sole, but that sole is in my shoe. Referring to Christ, the priests also tell that He is a God. Why, He is no more a God than you or I. He was just a plain man."

The guarantee of religious freedom in the United States Constitution applies only to Congress, so that the validity of this statute involves only the Massachusetts Declaration of Rights. This guarantees that no one shall be restrained, in his person, liberty, or estate, "for his religious profession or sentiments; provided he doth not disturb the public peace, or obstruct others in their religious worship." Another article declares that "the liberty of the press . . . ought not to be restrained," but this, if taken literally, would not apply to oral statements.

These clauses were held not to be violated by the blasphemy statute in the Kneeland case, and the Maine court held likewise in the more recent Mockus case.[7]

Bimba's only hope on constitutional grounds was to persuade the court to overrule the Kneeland case because the reasons that seemed satisfactory in 1838 no longer held good. Thus Chief Justice Shaw thought the freedom-of-speech clause intended merely to prevent the enactment of license laws or other direct restraints upon publication in advance, but did not limit the power of the

[7] *Supra,* notes 5 and 6.

state to punish utterances after they were made. Some of
the recent cases in the United States Supreme Court take
the sounder position that the free-speech guarantees prevent the punishment of words, unless they are so objectionable as to fall outside the protection of the Constitution. As for the religious-freedom clause, one judge, at
least, in the Kneeland case considered that it applied to
all expressions of opinion concerning religion, even if
atheistical; but the court agreed that it did not protect
"willfully" denying God where the purpose of the speaker
was not the discovery of truth but to calumniate and dis-
parage the Supreme Being and to destroy the veneration
due to Him.

It seems clear today that such a delicate judicial investigation into the mind of the speaker is liable to be
swayed by the attitude of the judge or jury on the doctrines expressed. A man with bad views is easily conceived to have a bad purpose. Once admit this distinction,
and the constitutional guarantee loses most of its force.

Further, Shaw's argument that punishing blasphemy
preserves the sanction of oaths has no validity now that
the law has been changed so as to permit atheists to testify on affirmation. His view that the repression of attacks
on Christianity is "essential to the peace and safety of
society" is just a roundabout way to make heterodoxy
a crime.

Those of us who feel strongly that faith in the teach-
ings of Christ means a better world must still recognize
that others deplore the evils of superstition, and concede
that the value of Christianity is one of the very questions
which ought to be freely debated, instead of being assumed by the courts as valid for the purpose of punishing

the contrary-minded. Finally, the argument of the old Massachusetts judges that blasphemy has a tendency to disturb the public peace varies in validity according to the circumstances in which the utterances are made. Disorder ought not to be assumed as certain. It is time enough for the police to interfere when it is actually threatened. In Bimba's meeting none took place. And a moderate risk of trouble should be run because of the countervailing importance of open discussion. A speaker ought not to be readily suppressed because his opponents will use violence. It is they who should be punished, not he.

Of course, there must come a point where utterances become so distasteful to the great majority of persons that their delivery in public will not be permitted. The words described in the Blasphemy Act go much beyond this, and that statute hardly seems necessary to prevent such language, since it is covered by another statute against cursing and swearing or by the common law of public nuisances.

Fortunately the constitutionality of the Blasphemy Act was not reaffirmed in the Bimba case, since the District judge refused to decide the point. Bimba escaped imprisonment as a freethinker because a bad motive in denying God was not established by the prosecution.[8] Even so, the continued presence of the law on the statute-books is

---

[8] Judge King said: "I don't hold that his statements as to his personal religion played any particular part, nor that it was intended to persuade any among his audience to become atheists. I am content to leave it that he declared his personal belief in a way allowed under the Kneeland decision."

In 1927 Warren W. Williams was prosecuted in Suffolk County for selling a blasphemous book and sentenced by the lower court to six months in jail; he appealed, and in the Superior Court the jury disagreed, October 28, 1927.

a real danger, and it ought to be immediately repealed. Clerical influence is likely to become an increasingly grave issue in this country, and vigorous attacks upon it may often be thought to fall within the definition of blasphemy. Those arrested need not always be Lithuanians. The statute enacted by the Puritans may some day be used against their descendants by the church which the Puritans most feared. Nor should the adherents of true religion oppose its repeal in the belief that it lends strength to their faith. The wind of the spirit bloweth where it listeth, and a devotion created by outside compulsion is worthless.

The most important aspect of this trial lay in its revelation of the attitude of the community toward open discussion.[9] Bimba's supporters were denied any effective opportunity to raise funds for his defense. Hall after hall in Boston, Brockton, and Worcester was denied to them, either by the owners, or, if they were willing, by the municipal authorities. The Mayor of Boston publicly commended his subordinates for forbidding Scott Nearing to speak on behalf of Bimba in a hall dedicated to the memory of Thomas Paine, of all persons.

In Boston the municipal authorities forbade the use of halls by a palpable subterfuge.[10] The Mayor has no

[9] The late Rev. Samuel McChord Crothers was a notable exception, and would have followed the example of Channing in protesting against a penalty for blasphemy, if Bimba had been convicted on that charge. Dr. Crothers' support of free speech when it was most unpopular was not the least of his many public services. In the spring of 1920 he urged tolerance despite the prevailing alarm over the "red menace"; and in 1925 he spoke against Mayor Curley's censorship of Boston meetings, arguing that no race had better reason to refrain from suppression than the Irish who have suffered from it so much in the past.

[10] See the further discussion of this topic in the subsequent paper on "The Freedom of the City."

power to prohibit a meeting because of its purpose. This would be a censorship, to which even Chief Justice Shaw objected. But the license of any hall may be revoked because of insufficient fire protection or structural strength, and a threat of such revocation is issued by the Mayor to any hall which permits a meeting that he considers objectionable. A sharp-eyed inspector can so easily find a defective fire escape or badly lighted corridor that no hall owner dares to run the risk of losing all his business for a year for the sake of one unpopular meeting.

The previous Mayor, Curley, used to be solicitous about the danger from fire to persons attending Ku Klux and birth-control meetings, while his successor, Nichols, having been put into office by respectable Republicans, worried about the safety of radicals. Neither of them showed any similar anxiety about building conditions in halls where meetings on his own side were held, although it would seem much more important to protect one's friends from fire and collapsing floors rather than one's enemies.

Outdoor meetings for Bimba on Boston Common were similarly forbidden, so that "any manifestations of lawlessness," as the Mayor put it, were thoroughly checked. In short, Bimba's guilt was assumed in advance of his conviction, and any attempt to secure his cause an adequate presentation, in or out of court, was regarded as an attack on our institutions.

In the light of these facts, what happened to Bimba is of little importance. It was not he who was on trial, but the Commonwealth of Massachusetts.

CRIMINAL SYNDICALISM IN THE SUPREME COURT

WHEN the Supreme Court in the Gitlow case [1] declared that freedom of speech may be protected against state laws by the Fourteenth Amendment, it created the hope that even though it had sustained the New York Anarchy Act, it might set aside convictions under the more sweeping Criminal Syndicalism Acts described in a previous article.[2] Important test-cases on the constitutionality of such statutes were decided on May 16, 1927.

The first of these was brought against the California law by Miss Anita Whitney.[3] She was a woman nearing sixty, a Wellesley graduate long distinguished in philanthropic work. She joined the Socialist Party, and in 1919 when her "local" participated in the Left Wing secession at Chicago, she became a temporary member of the new Communist Labor Party and went as a delegate to a convention at Oakland in November for organizing a California branch. Attorney General Palmer's raids on Communists had not yet occurred to warn the hundred delegates that they were engaging in an outlawed enterprise.

[1] *Supra,* p. 103. Walter H. Pollak of the New York Bar, who shared the oral argument for Gitlow before the Supreme Court, also argued the Whitney case.
[2] *Supra,* p. 74.
[3] Whitney *v.* California, 274 United States Reports 357. The opinion of the California Court of Appeals, First District, is in 207 Pac. 698 (1922). The facts are taken from the opinion of Justice Sanford and the pardon statement of Governor Young, which was reprinted in the *New Republic,* August 10, 1927.

If they were conscious of conspiring for the violent over-throw of the government, they took a strange way of going about it. The convention was openly held, reporters were present, and its deliberations were described in the next issues of the press. Miss Whitney vigorously sup-ported a resolution that the new state party should aim to capture political power through the ballot. The con-vention voted this down, and adopted in its place the Chicago program of the national party, which in terms resembling Gitlow's Left Wing Manifesto [4] urged the seizure of power by revolutionary industrial unionism and great strikes and commended the example of the I.W.W. "Notwithstanding her defeat," says the Governor of California, "Miss Whitney, as was perhaps natural, remained throughout the day of the convention, and, in fact, attended one or two committee meetings during the subsequent month. This, as far as the evidence discloses, marks the extent of her association with the Communist Labor Party, for membership in which she was after-wards convicted."

A special agent of the federal government who exam-ined Miss Whitney's entire correspondence informed the Governor:

Neither in all of the letters from and to her and about her, nor in the investigations covering her activities, does there appear a single line or word tending to show that she ever advocated a violation of any law.

Nearly three weeks after the convention Miss Whitney was arrested as she was leaving a meeting of Oakland club women where she had been speaking on the condi-

[4] *Supra*, p. 99.

tion of the American negro. In January, 1920, she was tried under the recent Criminal Syndicalism Act, for teaching, advocating, and justifying violence; for herself committing acts of violence; and also under this clause:

Any person who . . . organizes or assists in organizing, or is or knowingly becomes a member of, any organization, society, group or assemblage of persons organized or assembled to advocate, teach or aid and abet criminal syndicalism . . . is guilty of a felony. . . .

Miss Whitney's defense was greatly hampered by the sudden death of her able counsel during the trial. As against more than twenty witnesses for the prosecution, she was almost the sole witness for the defense, and her direct testimony occupies only three pages of the thousand-page transcript. A very large part of the evidence against her, which in the Governor's opinion had most effect upon the jury, had to do, not with the Communist Labor Party which Miss Whitney had joined, but with the I.W.W., with which she was never connected. The testimony was largely composed of a recital of atrocities committed in California by the I.W.W., occurring years before the Oakland convention, and the reading of incendiary and blasphemous I.W.W. songs. This evidence was admitted because of a brief endorsement of the I.W.W., not by the state Communist Labor Party, but by the national convention at Chicago, which she had not attended, but whose program had been adopted by the California party. On her part, Miss Whitney testified she was then a member of the Communist Labor Party, and that it was not her intention it should be an instrument of terrorism or violence, and not her purpose nor that of the state convention to violate any known law. Although the jury disagreed on the charges that she had herself taught, advocated, and committed violence, she was convicted of organizing and joining an association believed by the jury to be prohibited by the statute. For this crime she was sentenced to San Quentin Prison for a term of one to fourteen years. Only two others of the hundred delegates to the convention were convicted, and these were found guilty, not merely of membership in the Communist Labor Party, but also of themselves advocating or aiding violence.

Thus in the case of Anita Whitney the Supreme Court had before it a conviction for guilt by association [5] and nothing more. The court held that such guilt was enough to keep her outside the shelter given to "liberty" by the Fourteenth Amendment. Justice Sanford, who spoke for the majority, discussed four points.

(1) To the argument that she could not properly be convicted merely for attending the convention and lacking a "prophetic" understanding of the unlawful purpose it would be given without her intention and against her will, he replied that her original membership in the national party, her failure to protest or withdraw from the convention, and her subsequent activities were evidence which the jury could weigh in determining her knowledge of the illegality of the organization.[6]

[5] For discussion of guilt by association, see *Freedom of Speech,* p. 262 ff.

[6] It is not certain whether *"knowingly* becomes a member" in the California Criminal Syndicalism Act means that the accused must merely know he is enrolled in the organization, or that he must also know of the corporate purposes which are made illegal by the statute. The first construction is, of course, much more harsh. The California Supreme Court has in several cases refused to decide the question. The state Court of Appeals, Third District, has held knowledge of the

(2) The Syndicalism Act is not unconstitutional for vagueness and uncertainty of definition. As applied here, it "required of the defendant no 'prophetic' understanding of its meaning." It "meets the essential requirement, that a penal statute be sufficiently explicit to inform those who are subject to it what conduct on their part will render them liable to its penalties, and be couched in terms that are not so vague that men of common intelligence must necessarily guess at its meaning and differ as to its application." Does it have any bearing, one ventures to ask, that Secretary of Labor Wilson did differ as to the application of similar words in the deportation statute, and held they did not include this same Communist Labor Party? [7]

(3) It is no objection that the statute does not punish men who advocate violence as a means of opposing changes in industrial ownership or government, besides those who wish it to accomplish such changes. A law need not cover the whole field of possible abuses, and there is "nothing indicating any ground to apprehend that those desiring to maintain existing industrial and political conditions did or would advocate such methods."

(4) The Syndicalism Act as applied in this case is not invalid as a restraint of the rights of free speech, assembly, and association. The Constitution does not confer an unrestricted and unbridled license giving immunity for every possible use of language. Those who themselves advocate crime may be punished. By enacting this law

illegal purposes essential to guilt, and this seems to be Justice Sanford's view, but it is doubtful if the juries in several cases received any such impression from the instructions of the trial judges, which permitted convictions for conscious membership in the I.W.W. and nothing more.

[7] *Supra*, p. 69.

the state legislature has declared that to be knowingly a member of an association for advocating crimes as described involves such danger to the public peace and the security of the state, that membership should also be punished in the exercise of its police power. That determination must be given just weight, and the statute may not be declared unconstitutional unless it is arbitrary or unreasonable.

The essence of the offense denounced by the act is the combining with others in an association for the accomplishment of the desired ends through the advocacy and use of criminal and unlawful methods. It partakes of the nature of a criminal conspiracy. That such united and joint action involves even greater danger to the public peace and security than the isolated utterances and acts of individuals, is clear. We cannot hold that, as here applied, the act is an unreasonable or arbitrary exercise of the police power of the state, unwarrantably infringing any right of free speech, assembly or association, or that those persons are protected from punishment by the due process clause who abuse such rights by joining and furthering an organization thus menacing the peace and welfare of the state.

Justice Brandeis filed a concurring opinion, in which Justice Holmes joined. He was obligated to sustain the conviction because the constitutional issue had not been presented fully enough at the trial to bring the case within the Supreme Court's limited power of review in state criminal cases; but he disagreed sharply with the reasoning of the majority on freedom of speech and its application to the Syndicalism Act. The crime of membership in a society which this statute created is, he pointed out, very unlike the old felony of conspiracy, which requires an act by at least one of the group approaching successful accomplishment of a serious crime which must be intended by all the conspirators. On the other hand the new statute punishes a person for a step in preparation which, if it threatens the public order at all, does so only remotely. "The novelty in the prohibition introduced is that the statute aims, not at the practice of criminal syndicalism, nor even directly at the preaching of it, but at association with those who propose to preach it."

He agrees with Justice Sanford that the fundamental rights of free speech and assembly are not in their nature absolute, but demands a less vague test of the extent to which they may be restricted. The particular restriction proposed must in his opinion be necessary in order to save the state from destruction or from serious injury, political, economic, or moral, and this necessity does not exist unless speech would produce, or is intended to produce, a clear and present danger of such evils. This has been settled by the Schenck case, Justice Brandeis insists, in spite of the previous attempt of Justice Sanford in the Gitlow case to limit the application of the clear and present danger test to Congressional war statutes. While the legislature must decide in the first instance what is necessary, its decision is no more final when it denies liberty of speech than in the many cases where statutes have denied liberty of contract and been overthrown by the Supreme Court. In the end that court must decide whether there was a clear and present danger. True, it has not yet fixed the detailed rules for so deciding, but to reach sound conclusions on these matters, we must bear in mind why a state is ordinarily denied the power to prohibit the dissemination of social, economic, and political doctrine which a vast majority of its citizens believe to be false and fraught with evil consequence.

Justice Brandeis then states the reasons for the traditional American policy of freedom of speech guaranteed by the Constitution, which he and Justice Holmes have been endeavoring to protect against the assaults of sedition laws and prosecutions encouraged by those who have been most eloquent in their appeals to the Constitution, even while they strove to reduce to a nullity one of its most vital clauses. These professed patriots are its most dangerous enemies, while among the strongest conservators of Americanism must be counted the author of the following words:

> Those who won our independence believed that the final end of the state was to make men free to develop their faculties; and that in its government the deliberative forces should prevail over the arbitrary. They valued liberty both as an end and as a means. They believed liberty to be the secret of happiness and courage to be the secret of liberty. They believed that freedom to think as you will and to speak as you think are means indispensable to the discovery and spread of political truth; that without free speech and assembly discussion would be futile; that with them, discussion affords ordinarily adequate protection against the dissemination of noxious doctrine; that the greatest menace to freedom is an inert people; that public discussion is a political duty; and that this should be a fundamental principle of the American government. They recognized the risks to which all human institutions are subject. But they knew that order cannot be secured merely through fear of punishment for its infraction; that it is hazardous to discourage thought, hope, and imagination; that fear breeds repression; that repression breeds hate;

that hate menaces stable government; that the path of safety lies in the opportunity to discuss freely supposed grievances and proposed remedies; and that the fitting remedy for evil counsels is good ones. Believing in the power of reason as applied through public discussion, they eschewed silence coerced by law—the argument of force in its worst form. Recognizing the occasional tyrannies of governing majorities, they amended the Constitution so that free speech and assembly should be guaranteed.

If the words put into the Constitution by our forefathers are to mean anything, the danger arising from speech must not be checked by law unless it is imminent danger. Fear alone cannot justify suppression.

Those who won our independence by revolution were not cowards. They did not fear political change. They did not exalt order at the cost of liberty. To courageous, self-reliant men, with confidence in the power of free and fearless reasoning applied through the processes of popular government, no danger flowing from speech can be deemed clear and present, unless the incidence of the evil apprehended is so imminent that it may befall before there is opportunity for full discussion. If there be time to expose through discussion the falsehood and fallacies, to avert the evil by the processes of education, the remedy to be applied is more speech, not enforced silence. Only an emergency can justify repression. Such must be the rule if authority is to be reconciled with freedom. Such, in my opinion, is the command of the Constitution. It is, therefore, always open to Americans to challenge a law abridging free speech and assembly by showing that there was no emergency justifying it.

Moreover, even imminent danger cannot justify a prohibition of the functions essential to effective democracy unless the evil apprehended is relatively serious.

Prohibition of free speech and assembly is a measure so stringent that it would be inappropriate as the means for averting a relatively trivial harm to society. A police measure may be unconstitutional merely because the remedy, although effective as means of protection, is unduly harsh or oppressive. . . . Among freemen, the deterrents ordinarily to be applied to prevent crime are education and punishment for violations of the law, not abridgment of the rights of free speech and assembly.

After this statement of the theoretical reasons for maintaining the clear and present danger test, Justice Brandeis outlines the practical method for its application in a free speech trial.

Whenever the fundamental rights of free speech and assembly are alleged to have been invaded, it must remain open to a defendant to present the issue whether there actually did exist at the time a clear danger; whether the danger, if any, was imminent; and whether the evil apprehended was one so substantial as to justify the stringent restriction interposed by the legislature. . . . Whether, in 1919, when Miss Whitney did the things complained of, there was in California such clear and present danger of serious evil, might have been made the important issue in the case. She might have required that the issue be determined either by the court or the jury.

No such specific issue was raised by her, merely a general objection to the statute under the Fourteenth Amendment. Thus she lost the opportunity to secure an acquittal on this issue, and Justice Brandeis does not now feel able to decide it in her favor, since there was evidence on which the jury might have found that such a danger existed. He does not find such evidence in the mere fact of organizing the Communist Labor Party, for he thinks that "assembling with a political party, formed to advocate the desirability of a proletarian revolution by mass action at some date necessarily far in the future," is a right protected by the Fourteenth Amendment. What determines his decision against setting aside the conviction is the testimony about the I.W.W., which tended to establish a conspiracy on their part to commit present serious crimes and to show that such a conspiracy would be furthered by the activity of the Communist Labor Party, of which Miss Whitney was a member. His opinion of the truth and weight of this testimony was immaterial, especially as the court's power to review the evidence in a state criminal case is narrowly confined to the constitutional issues.

Although the Supreme Court did not release Miss Whitney, freedom of speech profited by her resort to this tribunal, not only from the moral effect of the minority opinion but also from certain modifications made by Justice Sanford in the position he took in the Gitlow case.[8] There his opinion seemed to indicate that the state legislature was a final judge of the danger of the overthrow of the government, but in the Whitney case he stated that the statutory limitation of speech and assembly must not be arbitrary, unreasonable, or unwarrantable. Thus he approached somewhat Justice Brandeis' view of the limited powers of the state legislatures, although he did not reëstablish the clear and present danger test as the standard of what was arbitrary, etc., but left this matter open for future definition. At least his opinion makes it

[8] *Supra,* p. 105. See 41 *Harv. L. Rev.* 527.

plain that some sedition convictions may be set aside under the Fourteenth Amendment.

And this result was actually reached in another opinion filed by him the same day on behalf of a unanimous court. In Fiske v. Kansas [9] an I.W.W. organizer had been convicted under the Kansas statute, which is much like that in California, for advocating criminal syndicalism orally and through the distribution of printed matter, and for obtaining new members. The only evidence in the indictment or at the trial to show the unlawful purposes of the I.W.W. was the preamble to its constitution, which did not mention violence but urged a struggle between the working class and the employing class without peace until the workers take possession of the earth and the machinery of production and abolish the wage system; and that, "instead of the conservative motto, 'A fair day's wages for a fair day's work,' we must inscribe on our banner the revolutionary watchword, 'Abolition of the wage system.' " The defendant testified at the trial that he had not advocated crime, sabotage, or other unlawful acts, and did not believe in criminal syndicalism or know it was supported by the society. The state court upheld his conviction, saying that although there was no expressed suggestion of crime in the preamble, the jury could read a sinister meaning between the lines and need not accept the defendant's testimony as a candid and accurate statement.

The Supreme Court set aside the conviction because a federal right had been denied "as the result of a finding shown by the record to be without evidence to support

[9] 274 United States Reports 380; in the state court, 117 Kan. 69 (1924).

it." There was no suggestion in the testimony that any but lawful methods were to be used to accomplish the purposes of the I.W.W. Thus applied, the Kansas Syndicalism Act was "an arbitrary and unreasonable exercise of the police power of the state, unwarrantably infringing the liberty of the defendant."

The great importance of Fiske v. Kansas may easily be overlooked. The opinion contains no ringing phrases and does not even use the words, "freedom of speech and assembly." It might be assumed that the court did nothing more than declare that a man cannot be convicted for a crime which is neither charged nor proved. Yet the decision necessarily goes much further. The Supreme Court of the United States would not and could not set aside a state conviction for murder where the indictment and the evidence failed to show the necessary intent to kill. The defendant's liberty may be unjustly taken away in such a case, but the court has no general power to review all state criminal trials, nor does it want them to crowd its calendar. Fiske was heard and released because he was deprived of liberty of speech under a statute which, though constitutional in itself, had been construed to punish utterances which were now held to be immune under the United States Constitution. In Fiske v. Kansas the Supreme Court for the first time made freedom of speech mean something.

Brief mention may be made of a third decision on May 16, 1927, Burns v. United States,[10] in which a conviction was sustained, Justice Butler writing the majority opinion and Justice Brandeis dissenting. This case did not arise under the Fourteenth Amendment like the other two

[10] 274 United States Reports 328.

cases, but under the First. Congress in 1920 provided that if any offense should be committed in the Yosemite National Park not prohibited by a law of the United States, it should be subject to the same punishment as the laws of California prescribed for a like offense. Though the framers of this legislation may not have had the California Criminal Syndicalism Act in mind, Congress was virtually enacting such a law for the Yosemite. Burns was convicted in a United States District Court in 1923. He was a member of the I.W.W., and an organizer. It was not alleged that he himself advocated violence or sabotage, but documents distributed by him contained the I.W.W. preamble, which seems over-emphasized by Justice Butler in view of the Fiske case. The court in the Burns case relied chiefly on additional evidence that other members of the organization urged sabotage, so that the offense was guilt by association. In this case, coming from a lower United States court, the Supreme Court's power of review was much wider than in the other two cases, which came from state courts, and was not limited to constitutional issues. The chief question on which the judges differed was whether the definition of sabotage by the trial judge was not so wide as to lead the jury to find the I.W.W. criminal for reasons not specified in the statute. The importance of the decision lies in its indication that a nation-wide federal peacetime sedition law in terms as broad as the California Syndicalism Act would probably be held by the Supreme Court, as now constituted, not to violate the First Amendment.[11]

---

[11] Even so, such a federal statute might possibly be invalid for lack of affirmative power in Congress to punish peace-time sedition with-

Proceeding in chronological order, we return to the case of Miss Whitney. The majority of the Supreme Court was against her, but the minority was in fact victorious. Within a few months she was pardoned by Governor C. C. Young of California, who in his statement of the reasons for his action repeatedly refers to the opinion of Justice Brandeis. The Governor approves his view that clear and present danger should be the vital issue of fact, and decides this issue in the Whitney case on the evidence before himself at the time of the pardon.

The Communist Labor Party has practically disappeared, not only in California, but also in other states where no criminal syndicalism law existed. It was a visionary attempt to plant a European radicalism upon an American soil, where it simply could not thrive. I am unable to learn of any activities of this party, in California at least, or possibly in America, which ever rendered it a danger to the state or a menace to our institutions. I am satisfied that, in the light of our present knowledge, no charge of criminal syndicalism would be now brought against its members.

After a full review of Miss Whitney's life and the trial, as to which he emphasizes her counsel's death and the misleading effect of the I.W.W. evidence, he sums up his impressive statement with a succession of reasons for the pardon, ending:

. . . because her imprisonment might easily serve a harmful purpose by reviving the waning spirits of radicals through making her a martyr; because, whatever may be thought as to

out express authorization in the Constitution; or because sedition is not punishable unless it fulfills the constitutional definition of treason. However, these objections are unlikely to prevail if the First Amendment does not restrain Congress. See *Freedom of Speech*, pp. 199-207.

"the folly of her misdirected sympathies," Miss Whitney, lifelong friend of the unfortunate, is not in any true sense a "criminal," and to condemn her, at sixty years of age, to a felon's cell is an action which is absolutely unthinkable.

It is to be hoped that less conspicuous victims of the California Syndicalism Act than Miss Whitney will submit the records of their trials to Governor Young and that the Fiske decision will make possible a review by the Supreme Court of other convictions based solely on the I.W.W. preamble.[12]

These three cases induce the following reflections:

First, there is still a possibility that the constitutional line between permissible and punishable utterances will be fixed at the point where a clear and present danger of injurious acts is created. This test, though not automatic, is much more practicable than any other which has been authoritatively suggested.

Second, the easy acceptance by legislatures and courts of guilt by association should cause anxiety to others besides supporters of freedom of speech. When such elastic extensions of the crime of conspiracy become habitual, they may be applied to more than radical agitators. Business men may some day find the Sherman Anti-Trust Law amended to punish innocent shareholders of monopolistic corporations, and high-minded persons who join a society for the repeal of the Eighteenth Amendment may be convicted on testimony that the officers occasionally said nullification of prohibition with the aid of bootleggers was the quickest way to secure its disappearance.

Thirdly, Miss Whitney's conviction shows the great danger of criminal syndicalism laws; while they seem at

[12] See 41 *Harv. L. Rev.* 528, note 20.

first sight to apply to thoroughly vicious persons, they can easily be interpreted by juries in times of excitement to include peaceable advocates of industrial or political change.

Finally, the ultimate disposition of her case emphasizes the truth that the only branch of the government which has done much since 1917 to preserve freedom of speech is the Executive. Legislatures have hastily enacted sedition laws with sheep-like imitativeness. Three courts refused to release Miss Whitney, and the judicial record shows many other instances where severe sentences were imposed and sustained against persons who urged no lawbreaking. There are few majority opinions setting forth the importance of open discussion. Contrast the action of executives. Smith of New York vetoed the Lusk bills in a strong message and pardoned all those convicted through the efforts of the Lusk Committee. Hunt of Arizona would not sign a sweeping sedition law. Small of Illinois pardoned William Bross Lloyd in reliance on a dissenting opinion in the state court. Young of California pardoned Miss Whitney in reliance on a dissenting opinion by Justice Brandeis. Presidents Harding and Coolidge released all the war prisoners who had not served out their terms. Would that it were possible to add a greater name to this list, and that we might read in the official biography of Woodrow Wilson the statesmanlike reasons for vetoing the two Espionage Acts and the magnanimous decision not to imprison Eugene V. Debs.

THE FREEDOM OF THE CITY

WHILE national and state governments have made more spectacular attempts to regulate discussion and imposed severer punishments, it is probable that cities and towns are in fact much more concerned with controlling the expression of opinion. To illustrate the many kinds of conflicts which may arise in a modern municipality, I have selected one important city, Boston, and shall present the material legal provisions in connection with some incidents which have occurred there in recent years.

At the outset attention may be called to the complexity of urban law. Where the authority of the nation or a state is involved, search may be quickly directed to accessible sources, the public statutes enacted by the legislature and the decisions of the courts interpreting them. On a question of municipal law one must of course consult these books, but he must also look much further. The powers of city officials and the police are often conferred by private statutes which are not contained in all libraries and are not so well indexed as ordinary legislation. In addition it is necessary to examine the ordinances of the city and perhaps also the regulations of a particular department. Under these circumstances the most careful writer is liable to overlook a material legal provision in considering a current clash between police and radicals, and a lawyer consulted on the eve of an unpopular meeting often could not complete the researches necessary to give a satisfactory opinion on the proper course to be pursued by his clients, who wish to keep within the law, until about two weeks after the date of the meeting has passed. With these obstacles clearly in mind, we may venturously consider affairs in Boston.

The wisest man who was ever born or lived in that Hub of the Universe, Benjamin Franklin, summed up the whole problem when he said, "Abuses of the freedom of speech ought to be repressed, but to whom dare we commit the care of doing it?" Numerous situations arise in which most people will agree that something which is said or written is objectionable in its nature, but in every case the suppression of such utterances requires that human beings, whether elected or appointed, be entrusted with the power to determine what is undesirable. Consequently the fitness of the particular officials involved to determine delicate questions of opinion becomes extremely important. The risks of unrestricted discussion are obvious, but we sometimes forget to balance against them the dangers of error on the part of censors.

BOOKS AND PERIODICALS

The Massachusetts statute against the sale of books and periodicals "containing obscene, indecent or impure language, or manifestly tending to corrupt the morals of youth,"[1] differs from similar laws in other states in testing a book by passages and not as a whole, but it has not been construed with especial severity by the Supreme

---

[1] Mass. Gen. Laws (1921), c. 272, § 28. For its construction, see Comm. v. McCance, 164 Mass. 162 (1895), *Decameron* conviction reversed; Comm. v. Buckley, 200 Mass. 346 (1909), *Three Weeks* conviction sustained.

Judicial Court. The interesting feature of the Boston book situation is that the determination of what books are indecent and the exclusion of such books from sale has not been made for the most part by the ordinary methods of the criminal law; that is, an arrest of a bookseller followed by a prosecution and a jury verdict. Private persons, not public agents and tribunals, have been the main factor in deciding what books should not be sold. Until 1926 this was done by the Watch and Ward Society,[2] a corporation for the suppression of vice, whose agents are not clothed with the powers of police, but are of course entitled like other private citizens to inform the police of suspected crimes. The Society, however, did more than complain to the law-enforcing authorities. Whenever its representatives formed the opinion that a certain book was indecent, the Society gave notice of this fact to a committee appointed by the Boston booksellers' association. If any shop afterward sold a copy, the Society informed the police, and arrest and prosecution followed. Naturally few dealers cared to run this risk, so that the mere disapproval of a book by the Society was sufficient to cause its immediate and quiet withdrawal from sale by the members of the booksellers' association. Indeed the scheme possessed distinct advantages for a bookseller, since it freed him from the necessity of deciding on the legality of a book at his own peril, and from the danger of unexpected prosecutions for offering books which were in his opinion proper, but which a jury might afterward find indecent. The general public was, as usual, inarticu-

[2] See the address by its agent, Rev. Frank J. Chase, "The New Puritanism," *Harvard Advocate,* May, 1926; A. L. S. Woods, "Keeping the Puritan Pure," *Am. Mercury,* September, 1925; H. L. Mencken, *To the Friends of the American Mercury,* 1926.

late under the control of its reading by a group of private citizens whose standards of decency were more strict than those of legal tribunals in other parts of the country.[3]

Publishers and authors outside Boston, who found a good market cut off without a chance to defend their wares in court, were more outspoken, and the scheme eventually received a deadly blow from the hands of H. L. Mencken. The *American Mercury*, edited by him, had described the situation with disapproval, and when its April, 1926, issue was withdrawn from sale in Boston under the ban of the Watch and Ward Society because of a short story, Mr. Mencken journeyed from Baltimore to Boston with a corps of lawyers and journalists, and on April 5 sold one copy of the proscribed issue to Mr. Chase, the Society's agent, in the presence of an immense crowd who had gathered in response to press announcements. The transaction was planned to be on "Brimstone Corner" by the Park Street Church, but the police, to avoid obstruction of traffic, ordered everybody across the street to the Common, where the sale and Mr. Mencken's arrest took place. Next day he was acquitted in the Boston Municipal Court by Judge Parmenter, who decided that the magazine did not violate the indecency statute.[4] A Cambridge bookseller who had previously been arrested for selling a copy was less fortunate, since he was found guilty by a different judge and paid a heavy fine.

[3] In his address, cited in note 2, Mr. Chase complains that the postal authorities, relying on the decisions of New York judges, had refused his request to declare unmailable a popular novel, for sales of which he had secured four convictions in Boston. A list of suppressed books is given by Mr. Woods' article cited in note 2.

[4] Comm. *v.* Mencken (unreported), opinion reprinted in *To the Friends of the American Mercury,* cited in note 2.

The *American Mercury* then began suit against Mr. Chase and his associates in the United States District Court in Boston, and on April 14 obtained from Judge Morton a preliminary injunction against future boycottings of the magazine.[5] The judge said:

May an unofficial organization, actuated by a sincere desire to benefit the public and to strengthen the administration of the law, carry out its purpose by threatening with criminal prosecution those who deal in magazines which it regards as illegal; the effect being, as a practical matter, to exclude such magazines from sale through ordinary channels, and thereby to inflict loss upon their proprietors?

The injury to the persons affected does not flow from any judgment of a court or public body; it is caused by the defendants' notice, which rests on the defendants' judgment. . . . In my judgment, this is clearly illegal. The defendants have the right of every citizen to come to the courts with complaints of crime; but they have no right to impose their opinions on the book and magazine trade by threats of prosecution if their views are not accepted. . . . Of course the distributors have the right to take advice as to whether publications which they sell violate the law, and to act on such advice if they believe it to be sound. The defendants have the right to express their views as to the propriety or legality of a publication. But the defendants have not the right to enforce their views by organ-

[5] *American Mercury v.* Chase, 13 F. (2d) 224 (1926), adversely criticized in 25 *Mich. L. Rev.* 74. After the April, 1926, issue of the *Mercury* had been mailed to subscribers and distributors, the Postmaster General on April 8 declared it unmailable because of the same story and other material. A preliminary injunction was granted against the enforcement of this order by the United States Court in the Southern District of New York, but reversed by the Circuit Court of Appeals because the question of mailability had become purely academic. *American Mercury v.* Kiely, 19 F. (2d) 295 (1927). For later events and proposed legislation, see the Boston *Herald*, Aug. 17, 1927, January 14, 1928; Elmer Davis, "Boston," *Harper's Magazine*, January, 1928.

ized threats, either open or covert, to the distributing trade to prosecute persons who disagree with them.

If other prominent persons took as much trouble as Mr. Mencken to establish the right to freedom of speech, we should have much more liberty in this country.

The final result of the *Mercury* case is hard to ascertain. It was followed by an abandonment of the coöperation between the booksellers and the Watch and Ward Society, whose agent, Mr. Chase, died soon afterwards. According to one account another group of private citizens, the Boston booksellers' association, thereupon undertook to determine for its members what was suitable to be sold or not, and submitted doubtful books to Superintendent Crowley of the police with the hope of obtaining a ruling from him before any sales were made. The ultimate decision on the morality of contemporary fiction seems to rest in his hands and he is reported to have become a diligent reader of novels in his spare hours, but he grew increasingly reluctant to draw up blacklists. District Attorney Foley also refused to proscribe books before arresting men for selling them, stating that he was not a public censor. Mr. Foley assured the Catholic Total Abstinence Union on August 16, 1927, that he would insist on jail rather than fines for offending booksellers, and intended to maintain "the standards of decency, purity, and morality that have been set up by past generations." There must be something in the Boston climate that has made the Roman Catholics as Puritanical as the Puritans. The booksellers, terrorized by such threats, and not knowing where they stood, played safe by withdrawing over sixty books from their shelves. Even Upton

Sinclair's public sale of *Oil,* which had been suppressed, did not relieve the situation. The booksellers on January 13, 1928, had a bill introduced in the legislature, of which one section requires knowledge by the seller [6] that a book is objectionable before its sale becomes a crime, and another makes possible the control of indecent books through a proceeding in equity brought by the state against the book in the Superior Court, a decided improvement on the present method of criminal prosecutions of the booksellers before police judges, who sometimes reach different conclusions about the obscenity of the same publication. Meanwhile it is impossible to buy in Boston many novels which are bestsellers in other parts of the country. Possibly this greater strictness is due to the conviction that other regions are unduly lax, or it may be the fact that Bostonians are peculiarly susceptible to immoral influences and so need a greater measure of protection than the inhabitants of other cities, who possess a superior ability to abstain from vice.

THEATERS

The Mayor of Boston grants licenses to theaters for the theatrical season; but a board consisting of the

[6] Under the existing law a bookseller may be punished for selling a book with indecent passages although he does not know of them. Under the proposed law (House No. 577) his knowledge would presumably be acquired from a warning by the police. Also if a book be enjoined in equity, this will be equivalent to knowledge of its indecency on the part of any dealer who subsequently sells it, and he will be criminally liable. A different bill (House No. 680), supported by Mr. Ellery Sedgwick, editor of the *Atlantic Monthly,* prevents convictions for isolated indecent passages by requiring that they must be considered in connection with the entire context and theme of the book. Mr. Roland D. Sawyer has asked for a commission appointed by the governor to investigate the whole question of proper regulation of obscene publications (House No. 59).

Mayor, the Police Commissioner, and the Chief Justice of the Municipal Court may by a majority vote revoke or suspend any such license "at their pleasure." [7] Thus they can close a theater if a play which they think indecent is performed notwithstanding an intimation of their view to the manager. It used to be said of a former mayor that he journeyed to New York to see dramas that were exciting comment, and then as a result of his observations banned them in Boston. This statutory provision extends to motion-picture theaters over which there is no state censorship, a bill for this having been rejected by a popular referendum a few years ago after passing the legislature. A systematic state censorship would be far more vigorous than the informal municipal control now existing. How far this possible supervision over films is actually exercised is uncertain, and at least no prohibition of a motion picture play has been sufficiently important to attract public attention.

The Boston scheme for theatrical regulation has some advantages for the managers over the common law method, which would render them liable to prosecution without warning after they had gone to great expense in the production of a play. If some kind of dramatic censorship is desirable, this scheme of board control is better than the English censor, whose absurdities have long been a target for George Bernard Shaw. A single censor is liable to become unduly preoccupied with questions of morality, while the three Boston officials have other things to think about. Nevertheless, the Boston scheme has dangers which deserve consideration. The difficulty is not merely that the Mayor, the Police Commissioner, and the

[7] Mass. Special Acts, 1915, c. 348.

Chief Justice of the Municipal Court are not put into office because of their qualifications for dealing with the rightness and wrongness of abstract ideas. Objections would still exist if this power to censor the drama were entrusted to a board consisting of the Presidents of Boston University, Boston College, Harvard, and Tufts, the Episcopal Bishop, the Roman Catholic Cardinal, a Jewish rabbi, and the editors of the *Transcript* and the *American*. The question is, whether even these persons could safely be entrusted with the arbitrary power to control the drama, or whether it would be better to allow the producers to make their own decisions on their plays, at the risk of being punished after conviction before a jury. In the latter way, if a crime is committed, it can be severely dealt with. The present method is more than a power to punish crime. It is a power by which, it is true, crime may be headed off, but on the other hand the threat of revocation of a theater license may deprive the public of a play which would be approved by a jury, merely because this board of officials—or the most influential member thereof—happens to be opposed to its subject matter. The problem still remains, whether any human being is good enough to be a censor.

It may be asked in what respect control of plays by jury verdicts is better than control by censors, since in either case the decision is made by human beings. Unless we are to have absolutely unrestricted drama, we can not eliminate the risk of human caprice either before or after production. The answer is, that the censor is in danger of becoming professionalized and out of touch with public standards of tolerance, while the jury comes to the issue of decency fresh from ordinary occupations, represents the views of twelve persons instead of one or three, and on the whole brings in the opinion of the mass of playgoers upon the question of what they want to see and hear. The difficulty that the jury ordinarily sits after the harm is done and punishes the producer without warning, might be met, if really important, by the New York device of calling a jury when the play is first put on.

No solution of the problems of indecent dramas, books, and periodicals is entirely satisfactory. Still, the most outrageous can easily be stamped out by prosecution, and I sometimes wonder if we are not overanxious to get rid of the others by operation of the law. It is true that many of our current writers seem like the young woman who said she could talk about anything, but the trouble was that she couldn't talk about anything else. However, the situation may prove its own best corrective. Nothing nauseates so quickly as a surfeit of licentiousness. Audacious ballets once shocked some and allured others, but of late years they have reduced the public to the state of mind of the London bus driver who ejaculated to the coyly descending damsel, "Step lively, Madam, legs ain't no treat to me."

PUBLIC HALLS

No statute declares that the Mayor of Boston shall have power to forbid public meetings in advance because of their purpose, or to punish the owner of a hall for permitting a meeting against the Mayor's will. Yet in actual practice, as stated in my discussion of the Bimba case, the Mayor has often exercised such a power by threatening halls where forbidden meetings are held with proceedings for structural defects. A statute [8] allows the

[8] Statutes relating to the City of Boston (1908), p. 190, c. 47, § 18.

license of a public hall in Boston to be revoked by the
Mayor because of unsatisfactory structural conditions,
and his decision is subject to confirmation by a board of
real estate men and architects and master builders and
members of the building trades. Mayor Curley made use
of this statute to prohibit meetings to promote the Ku
Klux Klan or to advocate the repeal of the Massachusetts
law against birth control, and no owners of halls dared
disobey him, since no matter how much care was taken in
the construction and repairs of a hall, some violation of
the complicated building regulations probably existed for
which the Mayor could, if defied, revoke the owner's
license and deprive him of all profits from his investment
for some time to come. The present Mayor Nichols, although of a different faith, has continued the same attitude toward meetings on proscribed topics.

Democratic Boston did not originate this shrewd device
for establishing censorship without legal authorization,
but is merely following the example of despotic Vienna
before 1914: [9]

Under the "architectural police regulations" in Vienna it is
technically impossible to build a theater so as to make it a
profitable undertaking. Yet new theaters are built and flourish,
while old theaters that violate the main principles of the regulations are maintained. The good-natured authorities are willing to close one eye to illegalities, on the tacit understanding
that he who profits by such indulgence will not be recalcitrant
should the convenience of the state require pliancy on his part.
The manager of a theater who should refuse to remove from
the playbill a play displeasing to the authorities, or should

[9] Wickham Steed, *The Hapsburg Monarchy* (1914), p. 76.

insist upon the circumstance that the play had been authorized
by the censor, might find the sanitary arrangements of his
theater declared to be insufficient by a special commission, or
the condition of the ceiling perilous, or the fire exits much
too narrow.

If a speaker in a Boston public hall utters indecencies,
or advocates crimes such as the overthrow of the government by violence,[10] he can be punished after conviction by
a jury. If the speeches break no law, nobody should be
punished. Each man should be responsible to the limit
of the law for his own crimes. The prohibition of meetings
in advance is not a power to punish crime. It is a power
which, under the guise of heading off crime, may suppress
any discussion to which the Mayor happens to be opposed,
even though no jury would ever convict for it. It is just
as much a censorship of oral discussion as his power to
suppress a newspaper for distasteful editorials would
create a censorship of written discussion. And the basis
of the objection is not merely the lack of legal authority,
but the doubt whether any human being is wise enough to
be a censor.

Upon some matters, administrative boards are undoubtedly well qualified to pass. The Mayor and the real estate
men, architects, and builders empowered by the legislature to revoke the licenses of halls are thoroughly trained
to judge whether stairs are strong enough to hold a crowd,
whether there are large enough exits, or too few fire-
escapes. Those are things that can be weighed and
measured and figured, and they know how to do it. But
who can be trusted to weigh the wisdom of an idea?

[10] The Massachusetts Anti-Anarchy Act is G. L. (1921), c. 264, § 11.

Who has the experience that qualifies him to say that a statute is so essential to the welfare of the community that any advocate of its repeal must be forbidden to speak? Men measure and weigh with foot-rules and scales whose accuracy is determined beforehand by scientific tests and impartial persons. There is no foot-rule to measure the hurtfulness of an argument on whether a group is antagonistic to our system, no scale to weigh the permanent value of a statute whose repeal is sought. The censor will have to measure and weigh with his own mind. His prejudices, his bias, his personal views, however well considered, must be the standard of decision, for he has no other.

The danger is not in the suppression of any particular doctrine or group, but in the very existence of suppression. Let no one remain content with the thought that the particular victims of recent decisions of the Mayor were distasteful to him. Intolerance is the most contagious of all diseases, and no party or creed is immune. The suppression of opponents has the same delightful fascination in our day that cutting off their heads had in the French Revolution. But the moderate republicans who first rejoiced in that method soon found it employed by *their* opponents, and the control of the guillotine shifted from group to group, of increasingly extreme views, until finally the conservatives seized it and beheaded Robespierre. So with the weapon of intolerance. Substantial citizens of St. Paul who urged the banishment of radical professors from the University of Minnesota were outraged when the Non-Partisan League in North Dakota purged the critics of public ownership from their State

University Faculty. Roman Catholics who acquiesce in the suppression of birth-control or Ku Klux meetings in Boston should watch the same spirit of intolerance infecting Protestants and leading to laws against the teaching of evolution in Tennessee and Mississippi, against the existence of parochial schools in Oregon. Nor is it just a matter of legislation. Intolerance can work by more subtle and sinister but equally effective methods. Probably no true construction of any statute or ordinance enables the Mayor of Boston to prevent public discussions of what he objects to, but he does it. No statute in Ohio authorizes the exclusion of Roman Catholic school teachers from the public schools, but a letter in the *New Republic* states that an inquisition into the religious views of teachers is conducted in violation of law, and only Protestants get positions. Intolerance can always find some crevice in the administration of the law through which to creep and accomplish its purpose. The only remedy is to build up every day and every hour the opposite spirit, a firm faith that all varieties and shades of opinion must be given a chance to be heard, that the decision between truth and error cannot be made by human beings, but only by time and the test of open argument and counter-argument, so that each citizen may judge for himself.

Of late years, whenever any controversy has arisen over discussion, constitutional free speech seems to be always just around the corner. People praise this magnificent fundamental right and then deny that it is applicable to this particular agitator or minority group. We are like Oliver Cromwell when he was besieging a Roman Catholic town in Ireland, which offered to surrender on the one condition of freedom of conscience. Cromwell replied: [11]

> As to freedom of conscience, I meddle with no man's conscience; but if you mean by that, liberty to celebrate the mass, I would have you understand that in no place where the power of the Parliament of England prevails shall that be permitted.

We should do much better to imitate a contemporary Englishman, Lord Justice Scrutton, who freed an Irishman from illegal arrest with these words: [12]

> The law of this country has been very jealous of any infringement of personal liberty. This care is not to be exercised less vigilantly, because the subject whose liberty is in question may not be particularly meritorious. It is indeed one test of belief in principles if you apply them to cases with which you have no sympathy at all. You really believe in freedom of speech, if you are willing to allow it to men whose opinions seem to you wrong and even dangerous.

While there has been little tendency in Boston, even during the war, to prosecute and imprison persons for heterodox opinions,[13] it is of small avail to refrain from putting a speaker in jail if he can find no place to speak. I have seen times in Providence when the Democrats

[11] Quoted by W. M. Evarts, *Arguments and Speeches,* I 464.
[12] Rex *v.* Secretary of State, *Ex parte* O'Brien, [1923] 2 K.B. 382.
[13] The three hundred reported cases under the Espionage Act (*Freedom of Speech,* Appendix II), do not contain any prosecution in Massachusetts. Despite the opportunities for harm from discussion in the neighborhood of Camp Devens, munitions factories, Charlestown Navy Yard, and Boston Harbor, no explosions or desertions or evasions of the draft were traced to speeches and books. The deportation raids of 1920 were entirely actuated from Washington. Except for Bimba, the Anti-Anarchy Act has lain inactive till 1927, though occasionally used to arrest aliens and hold them for federal deportation proceedings.

could not find any owner of a hall who was willing to rent it to them for a rally. The party was as effectively silenced as if a Republican legislature had made the promulgation of Democratic arguments a crime. No such obstacle to open discussion of ordinary political issues is likely to arise in Boston with its multitude of halls, and fortunately Faneuil Hall, Ford Hall, and the Old South Church are usually open for the expression of unpopular views. Despite energetic protests on both occasions, Faneuil Hall has been used within the last few years for meetings to advocate the recognition of the Soviet Republic and to celebrate the anniversary of the Fascist march on Rome. This is as it should be, but the arbitrary municipal power to ban meetings still remains.

The only time when considerable difficulty was found in getting a hall for a minority meeting was in August, 1927, just before the execution of Sacco and Vanzetti for the murder of a paymaster. Even then those who believed the two Italians were innocent were able, after prolonged search, to secure the Scenic Theater. The city authorities sensibly refrained from interfering, merely placing policemen in the hall. The outlet thus afforded for their views probably prevented some extremists from resorting to illegal action.

In a city where heterodox gatherings prove impossible for lack of rentable halls, the municipality itself would be wise in building an auditorium available for them, believing that revolution is made improbable when its advocates have an opportunity to bring their case into the open. Grievances may then be known and redressed, extremist arguments may be answered from the floor or later in the press and other meetings, the discontented are deprived of the dangerous incentive to violence which comes from suppression, and actually criminal talk on such occasions can be dealt with directly through arrests by the police present in the hall and prosecutions. This method is far better than compulsory silence, whether caused by censorship or inability to obtain a hall, since this drives discontent underground to fester out of sight and suppresses indiscriminately all arguments and presentations of fact, whether good or bad, on behalf of a distasteful cause.

THE COMMON

Even if the Mayor and his associates abandoned their assertion of power over public halls, there are many speakers who have not the funds to hire a building, and yet have views which they ardently desire to express, and which perhaps it is for the advantage of citizens to be able to hear. For such men there exists in the center of Boston an open forum, an open-air forum, the Common. But here again municipal censorship exists, this time with the express sanction of the law. An ordinance provides: [14] "No person shall, in any of the public grounds, make a public address . . . except in accordance with a permit from the mayor." The validity of this ordinance, under the free speech and personal liberty clauses in the state and federal Constitutions, has been sustained by the supreme courts of the Commonwealth and the United States.[15] Without such a permit the speaker can be arrested for a crime, and the permit can be refused in the

[14] Boston Ordinances (1914), c. 40, § 81.
[15] C. v. Davis, 140 Mass. 485 (1886), 162 Mass. 510 (1895); C. v. Abrahams, 156 Mass. 57 (1892); Davis v. Massachusetts, 167 U.S. 43 (1897).

uncontrolled discretion of the Mayor; or he may issue a conditional permit which is revocable if the condition be violated.[16]

This power has existed for many years, and I assume that for the most part permits have been issued as a matter of course. Before the war the police were very tolerant. For instance, when a woman urged a social revolution in which the rich should lose their money-bags and their heads, and the blood of the oppressors should flow from the State House down the gutters of Park Street, the officer leaning nonchalantly against a near-by tree merely murmured to a bystander, "The lady is getting a trifle hot." The Boston authorities pursued the same wise policy of avoiding violence by letting the agitators blow off steam in the open air that was followed by Arthur Woods[17] when he became Police Commissioner of New York City in the unemployment of 1914, after a series of suppressed outdoor anarchistic meetings had produced a very dangerous tension. Instead, he ordered that meetings in Union Square and other parks should be left alone unless an actual disturbance took place, but that plenty of police should be kept in readiness to suppress a disturbance if it occurred. Consequently, the atmosphere immediately cleared up. The success of his method is illustrated by an incident in Bowling Green Park. An earnest young woman was urging revolution to a noonday crowd calmly puffing their cigars in the spring sunshine, when one listener began to object to her continuing. The crowd at once closed in, and trouble seemed imminent. The policeman on duty walked up to the listener, who said, "Do

16 Boston Ordinances (1914), c. 3, § 21.
17 A. Woods, *Policeman and Public* (1919), pp. 73-78.

you hear what she's saying, officer? Why don't you stop her? If you don't, I will." "Now see here," the policeman replied, "she isn't violating any law, and as long as she doesn't, I'm going to protect her in her meeting. If you want to hold a meeting, go over to the other side of the street, and I'll protect you too."

An entirely different policy was adopted in August, 1927, when Boston Common was made unavailable to speakers who wished to protest against the execution of Sacco and Vanzetti.[18] On the first Sunday after the Governor had refused to alter the death sentences (August 7), when speakers with permits assailed the courts and the state's witnesses, the Superintendent of Police ordered the meeting to disperse. There was no general disorder, but the crowd fell back slowly; altercations followed, and several arrests were made. Permits to Socialists and Communists were thereupon revoked on the ground that the courts had been criticized and the Governor abusively denounced. The following Sunday (August 14), the announcement of an effort to meet without a permit attracted a crowd of two or three thousand. A score of uniformed police and as many plain-clothesmen were on hand, and after the arrest of the unlicensed speaker, Powers Hapgood, a hundred patrolmen and several mounted police were on the Common. The last Sunday before the executions (August 21), the Common was closed to all meetings. The police said they feared addresses might lead to arguments and thus to rioting. The *New York Times* remarked, "As a result of the occurrences on the Common, public tension was heightened."

It seems probable that the crowd came to see the ar-

[18] The facts are taken from the *New York Times*, Aug. 8, 14, 15, 22.

rests rather than to listen to the speakers, and that if the
usual permits had been issued and no interruptions made
by the police, the situation could have been easily handled.
It is significant that on each Sunday, the disturbances
appear to have followed and not preceded police interference. Of course, the authorities of Boston had a duty
to prevent a riot, and it may be that the state of feeling
was such that their action in closing the Common was a
justifiable precaution. However, one ground of objection
to the speakers deserves attention, that the courts should
not be unfavorably discussed. In a democracy no elective
and no appointive official should be kept beyond the reach
of public opinion. The very judge whose regard for the
courts was conclusively shown when he sustained the
Debs injunction [19] afterward said: [20]

It is a mistake to suppose that the Supreme Court is either
honored or helped by being spoken of as beyond criticism. On
the contrary, the life and character of its justices should be
the objects of constant watchfulness by all, and its judgments
subject to the freest criticism. The time is past in the history
of the world when any living man or body of men can be set on
a pedestal and decorated with a halo. True, many criticisms
may be, like their authors, devoid of good taste, but better all
sorts of criticism than no criticism at all. The moving waters
are full of life and health; only in the still waters is stagnation
and death.

It may be argued that, after Governor Fuller had made
his final decision, there was no further value in public
discussion of the Sacco-Vanzetti case, so that nothing was

[19] *Infra*, p. 200.
[20] Justice Brewer's address on Lincoln Day, 1898, quoted in 41 *Harv.
L. Rev.*, 164 note.

lost when speaking on the Common was forbidden. On the contrary, if the case were shown to reveal defects in the judicial system of Massachusetts, steps to remedy these ought to be taken for the common good. The formation of public opinion on changes in criminal procedure could best have been accomplished while all men's minds were focused on the matter, for in ordinary circumstances few people are interested in law reform. *Les morts vont vite.* After the executions came the World Series and other distractions to drive the intricacies of this case out of popular consideration, and the subsequent recommendation of the judges who form the Massachusetts Judicial Council,[21] for the removal of the procedural defects denounced on Boston Common till the police stepped in, is not likely to receive much attention from the mass of citizens. In questions of law reform we need every effort that can be made to arouse the public from its customary indifference to legal shortcomings.

In contrast to the requirement of permits from the Mayor for speakers on Boston Common is the system adopted in a much greater park and a much larger city, Hyde Park in London. There, a man may get up and address a meeting or gather a crowd of listeners as he talks, without any previous formalities. That is the point— without any previous formalities. No permit whatever is necessary. He is absolutely free to talk, subject of course to being arrested if he says anything in violation of law. The police may, if they choose, close the gates of Hyde Park and exclude all persons, soap-box orators and the wealthy paraders in Rolls-Royces alike; but so long as

---

[21] See the extract from their report in the *New Republic*, Dec. 21, 1927.

the gates remain open, any one can speak without any official's license.[22] For many years this plan has been in operation, and only once has there been disorder; that was the day in 1866 when the police closed the gates and the crowd leaned against the fence till it fell down. As for its value, hear Charles E. Hughes: [23] "Hyde Park meetings and soap-box oratory constitute the most efficient safety-valve against resort by the discontented to physical force."

I believe that the time is ripe to endeavor to make Boston Common like Hyde Park. It is not any abuse of the Mayor's present power as to the Common that calls for change, but the existence of the power, which may some day make abuse possible. There are abundant instances of cities where the requirement of a permit existed, where during a strike the Mayor refused permits to any person presenting the strikers' cause to the public, so that their side of the controversy had no chance to be heard. All sorts of controversies might arise where the Mayor at that time might be prejudiced and deny a hearing for a legitimate cause, and from his decision, be it remembered, there is absolutely no appeal.

My contention is that speakers should be free to talk without any previous permission from anybody, but that they should be fully responsible for what they say. In Hyde Park the police are near enough to arrest an advocate of assassination or an indecent person, or to keep an enthusiast within bounds by a word of caution. If it be

[22] Timbs, *Curiosities of London,* 649; Spencer Walpole, *History of Twenty-five Years,* II 172; A. G. Gardiner, *Sir William Harcourt,* I 236.
[23] Brief of Bar Assn. of City of N. Y. for the Socialist Assemblymen (1920), p. 41.

thought there is danger in Boston that without the permit the police would not know of the speech so as to be on hand in case of trouble, it would be practicable to adopt a plan which works well in France. The prospective speaker does not apply for a permit; he merely notifies the city authorities that he is going to speak. They then send him a receipt, which they can be legally compelled by him to do if they will not send it voluntarily. This receipt can be shown to any policeman as evidence that the meeting is legal. His notice serves as a warning to the city to have as many police on hand as seem desirable under the circumstances. Notice that under this system there is no censorship, no control by officials. Any man is free to speak. No permission in advance is necessary. And the public safety is amply protected.

THE STREETS

In August, 1927, the Sacco-Vanzetti sympathizers who were forbidden to speak on the Common took to the streets, and without attempting speeches, paraded in small groups, although all picketing and other demonstrations had been forbidden by the city authorities.[24] Incidents were most frequent on the last Sunday and on the day preceding the executions. Persons were arrested for carrying or following placards and for wearing raincoats painted with words commenting on the case. On August 22, the final day, thousands blackened the northwest corner of the Common while picketers were taken in

[24] The facts are taken from the *New York Times,* Aug. 11, 12, 13, 22.

custody. Here again it was a question whether disorders
caused the arrests or *vice versa.*

The material provisions of law were as follows: First, a
regulation forbids processions or parades of more than
two hundred persons on any public street of the city except in accordance with a permit from the street commissioners.[25] This does not appear to have been violated,
since the groups of picketers were fewer than two hundred in number. Secondly, an ordinance forbids any person on foot in any street to carry and display a placard
or sign without a permit from the Commissioner of Public
Works.[26] This was undoubtedly violated by the persons
who carried placards, and the printing on a raincoat would
probably be construed as a placard. However, the convictions of the picketers in the lower court were obtained
under another ordinance: "No person shall, in a street,
unreasonably obstruct the free passage of foot-travelers,
or willfully and unreasonably saunter or loiter for more
than seven minutes after being directed by a police officer
to move on." [27] The police appear to have relied on this
ordinance, since they gave the picketers seven minutes'
notice. A very wide discretion is entrusted by its terms to
the police. They may allow large crowds to watch baseball scores on a business street, or halt much smaller gatherings on behalf of unpopular causes. It was under this
same provision that woman suffragists were arrested for

[25] This regulation of the street commissioners, under Mass. Laws,
1854, c. 448, § 35, amended by Laws, 1908, c. 447, is quoted and upheld
in C. *v.* Frishman, 235 Mass. 449 (1920). On street meetings without
a permit, see P. *ex rel.* Doyle *v.* Atwell, 232 N.Y. 96 (1921).
[26] Boston Ordinances (1914), c. 40, § 37.
[27] *Ibid.*, § 36.

a demonstration when President Wilson landed in Boston
on his first return from Europe in February, 1919.[28]

Three legal questions are raised by this ordinance.

(1) Is it obstruction of traffic for several persons to
march in single file at an ordinary footpace? Is it enough
that the demonstration attracts spectators, although in
himself the picket does not obstruct any one?

(2) What is sauntering and loitering? The only construction of this phrase by an appellate court that I have
been able to find holds that an ordinance against loitering
on a street by vehicles for hire was not violated by a
driver who drove slowly up and down the same street,
turning and returning without obstructing traffic; and
the court defined loitering as being slow in moving, to
delay, to hinder, to be dilatory, to spend time idly, to
saunter, to lag behind.[29] The *New York Times* does not
make it apparent that the pickets were within this definition.

(3) The Boston ordinance was amended in 1916 by the
addition of these words: [30] "But nothing in this section
shall be construed to curtail, abridge, or limit the right or
opportunity of any person to exercise the right of peaceful persuasion guaranteed by" a statute of 1913. This
statute [31] declares that no person shall be punished criminally "for persuading or attempting to persuade by printing or otherwise any other person to do anything or to
pursue any line of conduct not unlawful or actionable or
in violation of any marital or other duty," unless such

---

[28] Leon Whipple, *The Story of Civil Liberty in the United States*
(1927), 316.
[29] Stephens *v.* District, 16 App. D.C. 279, 281 (1900).
[30] Boston Ordinances, Supplement (1915-22), p. 6.
[31] Mass. Laws, 1913, c. 690.

persuasion or attempt to persuade is accompanied by injury, threats of injury, disorder, or other unlawful conduct, or is part of an unlawful conspiracy. This legislation was evidently meant primarily to protect pickets in labor disputes, but in the absence of any definitive construction in the courts, it would seem to apply to other persons. Although the word "printing" does not perhaps include the carrying of placards, it would certainly allow leaflets to be distributed; and the whole statute may apply to a small group of persons who wish by marching in line to convince bystanders that proposed official action is unjust.

Consequently, it is doubtful whether the ordinance against obstruction of traffic and sauntering and loitering was violated by the demonstrations of August, 1927. Such at least was the opinion of the jury who in November acquitted all those tried for these offenses.[32] However, these legal considerations are practically irrelevant. Whenever city authorities make up their minds that public safety demands the suppression of certain gatherings, they are going to use the police to break them up on the spot. They trust that the courts will later sustain their action, but if not, it is no great matter, since illegally arrested agitators will have no criminal or civil remedy against the city or the police that is worth trying.[33] Although the jury acquitted the picketers, the picketing was

[32] *New Republic*, December 21, 1927. Powers Hapgood was convicted at the same time for speaking on the Common without a permit, but the jury disagreed on the charge of inciting a riot.

[33] A civil action for damages could be maintained against the policeman making the arrest, but his small means would make the suit unprofitable and oppressive. The officials higher up would ordinarily not be liable unless they instituted a prosecution which was both malicious and without probable cause. The city would not be liable at all.

stopped, so that the main object of the authorities was accomplished.

In short, there is no constitutional right of assembly of real value, first, because the right is subject to wide administrative powers for the regulation of public places, and secondly, because even when the right is violated, our law provides no effective means of redress for the injured persons.

One more question remains: Is street picketing by persons protesting against a governmental policy one of those situations where it is good policy to tolerate the minority, even though suppression is not unconstitutional or otherwise illegal? This policy is less strong for picketing than for speaking on the Common, since it is more remote from discussion of facts and principles and involves greater possibilities of interference with public convenience. Still, when the authorities are sufficiently strong to prevent violence and breaches of the peace, they may be wise in permitting persons who are driven by an overpowering sense of injustice to give vent to their emotions by a silent parade which enables them to show the public how they feel. Though not an effectual method for the discovery and dissemination of truth, which is the main purpose of freedom of thought, such a parade does serve as one more safety-valve for pent-up impulses. Of course, it must be small enough in numbers not to create the risk that the police will be overawed. The often-emphasized danger that the paraders will be attacked by hoodlums can usually be met by arresting the hoodlums when they do attack instead of by taking the paraders into custody in advance. It is possible that the picketers in August, 1927, were more anxious to be stopped than to go on, and that if they had been left alone the crowd would quickly have become bored and the demonstrations have faded away. On the other hand, it may be that the situation was so tense that any collection of protesters was dangerous. These are questions of fact on which it would be presumptuous for a writer to pass who has not heard the evidence and was not even an eyewitness. The authorities evidently feared that Charlestown Prison, despite the armed guards, machine-guns, and searchlights with which it was surrounded, might be attacked like a second Bastille, with a seventy-year-old Wellesley professor and a young woman in a red raincoat from Greenwich Village playing the part of the "knitting women." It was the duty of the city government to make the ultimate decision in the emergency, but it is to be hoped that it will not form a precedent for future occasions when the situation is less grave.

This discussion may be closed by a few concrete suggestions: (1) A departure from the present practice of excluding well-known books from sale in Boston. (2) A different system for the regulation of speaking on the Common. (3) Tolerance of picketing except in serious dangers. (4) Confidence that the existing criminal law, including the Anti-Anarchy Act, has been amply sufficient to deal with the few speakers and writers who have been recent objects of prosecution in Massachusetts, so that further legislation, such as the California Syndicalism Act, is proved to be entirely needless.

Though I am not a citizen of Boston legally, all of us her neighbors are intellectually her citizens; for from her come our newspapers and books, and to her we must go

for all political and social discussion of importance. We
are spiritually fellow citizens of no mean city—the home
of leaders of national independence, of religious liberty
once terrifying to many, the city where great writers inter-
changed their ideas and freely published them, where
books were much sold and much read, where William
Lloyd Garrison issued the *Liberator* and Wendell Phillips
agitated. Shall we sacrifice all this to a sterile safety and
become the laughing-stock of the nation, which buys the
books and permits the meetings of which we are afraid?
Have we no confidence in our churches and schools, to
say nothing of our police, that we think *Elmer Gantry*
will turn us into a sink of corruption? I believe in the
institution of private property enough to think that it
will not be swept away by hostile critics, only modified
and improved. I believe in our system of justice and want
it made as near perfection as possible, which means that
its possible shortcomings must be freely pointed out. I
believe in the Constitution—the whole Constitution, not
just the war clauses and the Fourteenth Amendment protecting property, but also the First protecting free speech
and the Fifth Article allowing change. I believe in our
citizens, that they can be trusted to read and hear, to
choose good from bad, to consider carefully, and to alter
with deliberation. Let us have no cowardly distrust in
ourselves and our institutions which makes us erect
prison-walls against strange doctrines. Even if we no
longer want to be the land of the free in Massachusetts,
at least let us be the home of the brave!

THE INTERCHURCH STEEL REPORT [1]

THE Interchurch World Movement's *Report on the Steel Strike of 1919* was given to the press July 28, 1920, and subsequently issued in book form. Some of its conclusions were expressly based on the sub-reports of various investigators, and six of these were collected in the volume, *Public Opinion and the Steel Strike of 1919:* "Under-Cover Men," by Robert Littell; "Pittsburgh Newspapers and the Strike," and "The Pittsburgh Pulpit and the Strike," both by M. K. Wisehart; "Civil Rights in Western Pennsylvania," and "Welfare Work of the United States Steel Corporation," both by George Soule; "The Mind of Immigrant Communities," by David J. Saposs. In addition, the secretary to the Commission of Inquiry, Heber Blankenhorn, contributed a summary of the effect of the main report upon public opinion, and an addendum gave the details of the hitherto unreported interview of the commission with Judge Gary in their unsuccessful effort at mediation. The new book had a double importance—first, for its bearing upon the steel strike of 1919, and secondly, for the light thrown on the factors which shape public opinion about all strikes, and indeed about any significant event.

On the steel strike itself three conclusions may be stated in view of the two Interchurch publications and

[1] A review first printed in the New York *Evening Post,* March 18, 1922, of *Public Opinion and the Steel Strike of 1919: Supplementary Reports to the Commission of Inquiry, Interchurch World Movement.* New York: Harcourt, Brace and Company, 1921.

other events since the termination of the strike. First, the charge of Bolshevism which was made by the press, the steel officials, and Attorney General Palmer during the progress of the strike has been wholly disproved. It is now seen to be only a phase of the red hysteria which swept over the country in the last months of 1919 and closed with the expulsion of five Socialists from the New York Assembly. The charge possessed some plausibility because W. Z. Foster, the organizer of the strike, had once written a book on Syndicalism, but he had definitely abandoned that doctrine and become an enthusiastic member of the American Federation of Labor.[2]

Secondly, the Interchurch findings with respect to the twelve-hour shift and the seven-day week have been widely accepted. On December 3, 1920, at a joint meeting of the Taylor Society and sections of the American Society of Mechanical Engineers and of the American Institute of Electrical Engineers, Horace B. Drury, economist, presented to an approving audience a report showing the successful operation of three eight-hour shifts in the twenty steel plants which have adopted the eight-hour day. The United States Steel Corporation itself twice in 1921 announced its intention of abolishing the twelve-hour day.[3]

Thirdly, with respect to the absence of any share by the workers in the control of the steel industry (apart from the comparatively small ownership of stock), the case seems somewhat less clear than the Interchurch

---

[2] However, Foster in 1924 was the presidential nominee of the Workers' Party, which is avowedly revolutionary.
[3] The twelve-hour day was eventually abolished in 1923.

Commission would have had us believe. The lack of any
systematic method for the communication of grievances
and for their adjustment is an undoubted evil. On the
other hand, the strike was not merely an effort by the
steel workers to remove their grievances and procure
some reasonable method of conference. It was a campaign by the American Federation of Labor to obtain a
permanent position in the steel industry, and the Interchurch Commission did not sufficiently recognize that
this also might be an evil. It is true that the commission
recommended certain definite steps toward the democrati-
zation of the various unions involved, but there is no
evidence that such steps are likely to be taken. The
strike of 1919 presented just one alternative to the enlightened despotism of Mr. Gary, and that was the supervision of working conditions by twenty-four international unions, many of them committed to the policy of
restricted membership and high initiation fees, many of
them quarreling with one another over questions of jurisdiction. It is significant that the strike committee was
hampered by the reluctance of these unions to receive the
steel workers for a three-dollar fee, and by disputes
whether cranemen should belong to the Shovelmen's
Union or the Stationary Engineers. There must be some
other way than this out of the present no-conference
situation. The Steel Strike Committee of 1919 offered
nothing to compare with the Industrial Court which for
many years has settled labor questions in the great factories of Hart, Schaffner and Marx. Or it is possible that
the existing autocracy in the steel industry may give way
to a system of State adjudication like the Industrial

Relations Court in Kansas or the Australian Court of
Conciliation, which Chief Justice Higgins has described
under the title "A New Province for Law and Order." [4]
In other words, much time and thought are necessary
for a satisfactory solution of the relations of hundreds
of thousands of steel workers with their employers.[5]

The student of public opinion will obtain much aid
from this book in his struggle to answer two questions,
which must be answered in a democratic country if its
course is to be kept free from confusion and disaster:
To what extent does the mirror of public opinion present
a distorted picture of the real facts of a critical event,
and are the causes of this distortion remediable?

Satisfactory public opinion in a crisis is impossible
unless both sides can present their contentions in meetings and through the press. The right of assembly was
virtually denied to the unionists in western Pennsylvania
before and during the strike. In some cities meetings were
unlawful unless a permit was given, and it was often
arbitrarily refused by the authorities. In Duquesne the
Mayor did not even answer repeated requests for a permit, and when the strikers thereupon went ahead and met

[4] 29 *Harv. L. Rev.* 13 (1915); *32 ibid.* 189 (1919); 34 *ibid.* 105
(1920). The United States Supreme Court has unfortunately rendered
this solution of industrial disputes in the United States virtually impossible by the decisions holding the Kansas Industrial Relations
Court Act unconstitutional in certain essential provisions. Wolff Pack-
ing Company *v.* Court of Industrial Relations, 262 United States Reports 522 (1923), 267 *ibid.* 552 (1925); Dorchy *v.* Kansas, 264 *ibid.*
286 (1924). See *infra,* p. 216, note 28.

[5] The position taken by the author in this paragraph is vigorously
assailed by W. E. Walling, "Anti-Labor 'Liberals,'" *American Fed-
erationist,* May, 1922, in which this paragraph is said to be written
"in the typical pseudo-liberal manner," and the whole review to furnish "a complete epitome of the pseudo-liberal attitude both to free
speech and to the labor unions."

without one, he had their leader arrested.[6] In other cities, where the meetings were legal, the owners of halls refused to rent them to strikers, or after consenting to do so would break the contract on the night of the meeting. This is a splendid illustration of the truth that freedom of opinion is not safe merely through the absence of legal interference; there must exist affirmative channels of expression. The prohibition of meetings was defended on the ground that violence might occur. Yet thousands of strikers went over into Ohio and West Virginia, where they were free to assemble, without any disturbance; there is almost no proof of trouble when meetings did take place in Pennsylvania—for example, in Johnstown, where the strikers met daily. The true reason was that the strike was likely to fail if meetings were forbidden. The relationship of numerous city officials to steel officials may not have caused their action, but it is unfortunate in view of that relationship that they showed such partiality against the rights of the strikers.

A still worse interference with civil rights was the number of arbitrary arrests. In New Castle forty strikers were held without bail "as suspicious persons," but the sheriff offered to release those who would return to work. In McKeesport, where an attorney was taking affidavits of strikers who had been clubbed and arrested for meeting, the police broke in and arrested everybody. In Duquesne and Monessen men were fined without any charges. Some of the worst acts were by the State Constabulary, who came into Braddock and Johnstown without the consent of the local authorities. The victims of

[6] Duquesne v. Fincke, 269 Pa. 112 (1920), not mentioned by Mr. Soule.

these illegalities were remediless. It has long been obvious that the old actions of trespass and false imprisonment which were an effective check on the arbitrary proceedings of the officials of George III are worthless today because no jury will give a just verdict to a member of a minority group. Senator Borah introduced a bill in Congress [7] to make illegal arrests and searches by federal officials a crime, and similar state laws might have some effect; but prosecutions by the governments which tolerate such police are not likely to be vigorous. The only effective remedy for these abuses is for respectable citizens to protest vehemently against all violations of law and order, even when committed against persons with whom they bitterly disagree.

The strikers were equally voiceless in the Pittsburgh press. The newspapers there may have been right in concluding that the strike was unjustified and injurious to the nation, but they did not merely embody those conclusions in editorials. They neglected to state in their news columns the facts of the strike, so that their readers might reach their own decisions with as much evidence as possible. It is this want of facts that Mr. Wisehart condemned. The New York and Boston press gave much fuller accounts. In view of established newspaper traditions, the Pittsburgh journals should have started to cover the event as one vital to the community and not ignored it because it was inimical to owners' interests or to local pride. They should have investigated the conflicting statements of both sides of the strike and given an accurate record of actual events. They should have

[7] About 1921. The same or a similar measure in the House was H.R. 12816, 66th Congress, 2d Session. No legislation was enacted.

presented at the start an account of the background and
causes of the strike, hours, wages, the organizing campaign, a list of strikers' demands, just as they precede
an election with figures and predictions, or a World's
Series with batting averages. They should have reached
an editorial policy on the basis of their own inquiries, and
openly promulgated it. Instead, they all took one position
from the start and stuck to it. There was silence on
grievances. In four hundred issues there was only one
first-hand independent investigation, a report by an eyewitness of a brush between foreign workers and the constabulary. The editorial columns were reticent. The news
columns continually said that the strike was practically
over, and exaggerated the number of men returned to
work. Some one added the figures to show that two and
a half million men had been reported back in an industry
employing only one-half million. The newspapers were
not impartial as to violence on both sides, gave ready
credit to rumors of I.W.W. and German influence, printed
sermons only by clergymen opposed to the strike, and in
their headlines featured only the anti-strike evidence before the Senate investigation. The strike was the enemy,
and the press mobilized its forces to defeat it.

What is the cure for this partiality in reports of labor
disputes? Clearly, not public ownership. Apart from all
the evils of a censorship, there is no probability that a
journal controlled by Governor Sproul or the Mayor of
Duquesne would have chronicled illegal arrests and the
extent of the twelve-hour day. Again, the suggested remedy of a labor-owned journal merely gives us another
one-sided account without impartiality and without the
news-gathering facilities of the established press. The

best way out is that just as newspapers have financial
and sporting experts, they should have trained industrial
reporters, whose instinct of workmanship would force
them to tell the whole story regardless of their own pref-
erences. A sporting editor would never think of conceal-
ing the errors and blunders of the home team. This solution is advised by Mr. Richard Hooker, the editor of the
Springfield Republican, in his Bromley Lectures at Yale,
1921:

I doubt if in the coming years many larger services will be
performed than those of the industrial reporter who fits himself to write understandingly and with a clear comprehension
of any labor controversy with which he may deal. Such work
should be welcomed by both sides, for it should be sound and
constructive in its influences and free from sensation save
when the facts disclosed are themselves sensational. Such a
reporter should be a student both of human relations and of
statistics. . . . He should, for example, be alert to detect the
significance of intermittent employment in conflicting claims
as to hours and wages; no less alert on the other side to the
significance of uneconomic restrictions and arbitrary limitations
upon production.

In short, a newspaper is an expensive enterprise with
risks for which private capital is required. Mere mechanical alterations of control will not give us adequate news
of industrial controversies. The cure, as for so much
else, lies in the development of the individual knowledge,
intelligence, and conscience.

All told, this is a gloomy book. There are those who,
admitting all its statements of fact to be true, will say,
"Why waste time regretting its gloom? These things are
necessary. You cannot run one of our existing great busi-

nesses without espionage, without the suppression of meetings which attack the true welfare of the employees as well as that of the business, without the hearty support of the press and the pulpit in critical times." It is the argument for the Amritsar massacre; "British rule cannot be preserved without a whiff of grapeshot now and then." The reply is inevitable. Is the present system of control worth preserving if this is the price? Therefore it behooves us who believe that on the whole private enterprise gives the best opportunity for the progress of all to bestir ourselves and prove that these fetters on public opinion are not a necessary accompaniment of such enterprise. If the Interchurch reports lead to the abolition of espionage, shackled assemblage, illegal arrests, police clubbing, a partial press, an uninformed pulpit, no one will have sounder cause to rejoice than the supporters of our present industrial system.

COMPANY TOWNS IN THE SOFT-COAL FIELDS [1]

THE United States Coal Commission was established by Congress in 1922 to report on the various phases of the coal industry. Its chairman was John Hays Hammond, the distinguished engineer, and the other members were former Vice-President Marshall, Clark Howell, the editor of a leading Georgia newspaper; George Otis Smith, a prominent geologist and member of the Coal Mining Institute of America; Edward T. Devine, the well-known sociologist, and Charles P. Neill, who has had extensive experience as an arbitrator in industrial disputes. The secretary was Edward E. Hunt. The Commission issued its report on anthracite early in July, and its subsequent

[1] First printed in *The Independent,* Sept. 15, 1923.

On Feb. 14, 1923, the United States Coal Commission, which had been created by Congress in September, 1922, issued an invitation to "the United Mine Workers of America, the owners and operators of the mines and the public generally," to submit to the Commission in concrete form specific charges of the denial to any American citizen of any right guaranteed to him by the Constitution and laws of the United States and the decisions of the courts thereunder, and also specific instances of the breach of the civil or criminal law of the United States or any of the states. In response to this invitation a group of persons having at heart the preservation of constitutional liberties and civil rights formed a committee known as the Committee of Inquiry on Coal and Civil Liberties. Its members were Prof. Herbert A. Miller, Oberlin College; Father John A. Ryan, Director of the National Catholic Welfare Council; Kate Holladay Claghorn, head of the Department of Social Research of the New York School of Social Work; Rev. Arthur E. Holt, Social Service Secretary of the Congregational Church; and the author as chairman. The committee conducted an investigation of the violations of civil, constitutional, and legal rights in sections of the American coal fields, the field work being in charge of Winthrop D. Lane, for many years associate editor

endeavors to adjust the differences between the hard-coal operators and the United Mine Workers of America concentrated the attention of the public upon the problems of anthracite. Nevertheless, the report of the Commission on bituminous coal production was still more important. Necessary as anthracite is to the householder of the Atlantic seaboard, the output of soft coal is very much greater. It is soft coal which warms most of our homes, creates most of our electricity, moves our trains and steamers and machinery, supplies the fuel for the production of steel. With iron it constitutes the basis of modern industrial civilization. Therefore the conditions under which bituminous coal is mined are the concern of every thoughtful citizen.

The most important aspect of civil liberty in soft-coal fields does not lie in specific instances of the violation of the civil rights of individuals, but in those general conditions of the coal-mining communities which inevitably

of *The Survey* and an investigator of long experience in labor problems, especially in the coal industry, and Prof. Jerome Davis, now professor of sociology at Yale University and then assistant professor at Dartmouth College.

The report of the committee, submitted to the United States Coal Commission, consisted largely of documents on which a brief comment was made. The article here reprinted was written to summarize the results of the committee's investigations and appeared before the Report of the Coal Commission was published. The portion of its Report bearing on the topics discussed in this article will be found at pages 161-182 of Part One of the Report, Washington, Government Printing Office, 1925. Brief extracts from the Report are reprinted in subsequent footnotes. The position of the operators was presented in *The Independent* of Oct. 13, 1923, by Mr. William C. Chanler, a member of a prominent New York law office which represented the bituminous operators before the Commission. A brief reply by the writer will be found in *The Independent*, Oct. 27, 1923.

The investigations of the Committee have been more fully set forth in a pamphlet by Winthrop D. Lane, *The Denial of Civil Liberties in the Coal Fields*, published by the American Civil Liberties Union, New York, 1924.

tend to deprive the miners of ordinary incidents of citizenship. While there is bitter controversy on many questions of fact connected with the contests between unions and operators, there is absolutely no disagreement by any of the persons concerned about the widespread existence of the company town in the bituminous fields.

In such a community all of the land on which the town is built is owned or leased by the company employing the miners. All of the houses are owned by the company and rented to the employees. The store from which the employees buy their food, clothing, and other necessaries is commonly owned and conducted by the coal company. The movie theater, the recreation house, the playground, and whatever other facilities of amusement exist, have been built by the company on its land. Often the schoolhouse is upon this land, and the company assists in the selection of a teacher and sometimes pays part of his salary. The church or churches are often similarly situated on company property, and the minister looks to the company for part of his maintenance. The roadways over the land are private, owned by the company. The postoffice is usually located in the company store, and an employee of the company is postmaster. The communities are not incorporated as cities or towns, but activities that are normally run by municipalities or by public utility corporations—such as lighting, water supply, sanitary inspection, garbage removal, etc.—are private operations of the coal companies. In other words, the town itself is a privately conducted enterprise as much as the mine. These towns are the continuous residence places of scores of thousands of people. They stand to them for homes and for whatever degree of community life and social existence these people possess.

The situation is quite different in the anthracite regions. Hard coal is mined in eastern Pennsylvania, in well-settled districts. For example, it lies under such a populous city as Scranton, where serious difficulties have arisen from the subsidence of streets and public buildings because of the mining underneath. In such communities, the anthracite miner may, if he wishes, turn from the company house or the company store to those privately owned, and engage freely in the life of a normal American community. The bituminous miner is dependent on his employer for almost all the incidents of life.

An especially significant feature of this dependence of the soft-coal miner and his family is brought out by the leases under which the homes are rented from the companies. The employer in typical leases in Somerset County, Pennsylvania, reserves the right to keep out of the rented premises any person whom it considers objectionable, or limits the use of the house and the road or way thereto exclusively to the employee and his immediate family. The lessee covenants not to permit the use of the land or ways by any other persons. A lease issued by W. J. Rainey, Inc., in Fayette County, Pennsylvania, is even more explicit. The tenant agrees that no persons outside his family shall enter on the premises or ways thereto, "except physicians attending the lessee and his family; teamsters or draymen moving lessee and his family belongings into said premises or away from the same; and undertakers with hearse, carriages and drivers, and friends, in case of death of the lessee or any member of his family."

Very likely such drastic provisions in miners' leases are intended for the exclusion of union organizers and strikers who have left their own houses. It may be surmised that a lease is not ordinarily forfeited because the tenant has asked his fellow workman who lives down the hill to come up for a game of cards. Nevertheless any such friendly visit is a ground for forfeiture, which might be utilized by a tyrannical superintendent who was suspicious of this particular tenant. Certainly in a mine where working conditions were unsatisfactory, workmen would not be free to discuss their grievances in each other's houses, for fear of eviction. Nothing could be more alien than these leases from the Anglo-Saxon tradition that a man's house is his castle. And whether or not the Poles and Italians of the Pennsylvania mines may rightfully be denied the benefit of that tradition, in West Virginia and Alabama the miners who have to sign these leases are American mountaineers.[2]

A second kind of control by the operator over his employees is secured by clauses in the leases waiving rights usually retained by tenants. In Pennsylvania a tenant is entitled by statute to thirty days' written notice to quit before eviction proceedings begin, so that he has time to

[2] On these leases, see the Report of the United States Coal Commission, I, p. 169 ff., which says in part: "Thus the position of the miners in company-owned houses is anomalous. They are not tenants and have no more rights than a domestic servant who occupies a room in the household of the owner. The documents which pass for leases often give the company complete control over the social life of the families who live in the houses owned by the company."

After quoting from the Rainey lease above, the report continues: "Under existing laws the miners have a legal right to sign and the companies have a right to require them to sign such leases as a condition of obtaining employment. That they are ill-advised, obnoxious, and inconsistent with the spirit of free local communities hardly requires argument. Self-respecting American citizens will find a way to

find other premises and move his belongings. Yet every Pennsylvania miner's lease that has come to the writer's attention, twenty of them in all, obliges the tenant to surrender the benefit of this statutory protection and agree to leave his home in a much shorter time. The longest time allowed is ten days, and most leases allow only five days. One company allows its miners one day to vacate, while the Consolidation Coal Company requires that on the termination of his employment he "shall forthwith, without notice from or demand of the company, abandon said premises."

Not only is the miner obliged to waive his statutory thirty-day privilege, but in most Pennsylvania leases he must abandon the right to have any trial if ejectment proceedings are brought against him. Once the company starts suit, judgment is entered automatically, and execution may issue virtually at once. The miner never gets a day in court to present his case. The tenant gives up his right of appeal and any exemptions of his furniture from seizure for rent. In short, the Pennsylvania courts are for all practical purposes ousted of jurisdiction.

These provisions for summary ejectment of miners apply not only to those who abandon their jobs volun-

put an end to them. In the case of a helpless, submerged working population, the legislatures of the several states might well consider making such 'leases' illegal, like any other contract which is contrary to the public interest. Self-respecting American miners, who have on other occasions shown themselves by no means contemptible defenders of their own interests, may prefer to take the remedy into their own hands, and by insisting on reasonable leases, on the incorporation of their villages, and otherwise, win for themselves those elementary civil liberties which must always be won and held by free peoples for themselves rather than thrust upon them by external benevolence."

For an instance of rapid dispossession of a miner under a Virginia lease, see Virginia Iron, etc., Co. *v.* Dickenson, 143 Virginia Reports 250 (1925), noted in 99 Central Law Journal 112.

tarily, but also to those who are discharged for any reason or even, as some leases read, "without cause." In ordinary communities a workman keeps his home so long as he pays his rent and does not ill-treat the premises. The fact that he has struck or been laid off is immaterial. In the soft-coal fields he loses his home practically as soon as he loses his job. And this means that he must leave the neighborhood. There are no other houses open to him. Sometimes during a strike the men are anxious not to go elsewhere so long as there is a possibility of victory, and live in tents near the mine but on land not owned by the operators. Even the maintenance of such tent colonies may be impossible, for they have been enjoined by the courts because of the danger that such a large group of strikers in the vicinity may intimidate the men who still work in the mine. Thus the existing housing conditions of the bituminous miner are in marked contrast to those of the normal American citizen, whose home is not irrevocably bound up with his job.

The coal companies, besides owning the houses, stores, and streets in the mining towns, often substantially control the most important function of government, maintenance of order. The miners have no direct political control of their community through any city or town elections. The county is the unit, and the police are the deputy sheriffs, who in many states are selected and paid by the coal companies. As many deputies as one for every fifteen miners have been serving in some counties. It is these company-paid officials who are empowered to arrest miners on charges of disorder and evict them from their houses. The existence of such forces of policemen drawing all their compensation from private sources is bound to cause a bad administration of law. It is especially serious when a bitter controversy is waging between the unions and the operators who pay the deputies. The latter's function of keeping the peace rapidly turns into a duty to maintain the non-unionization of the particular field. According to the president of a coal company in Logan County, West Virginia, testifying before the Kenyon Committee of the Senate, these deputies ought to keep out of Logan County "the organizers of the United Mine Workers of America for exactly the same reason that those whose pictures are in the Rogues' Gallery are kept out of lower New York." The evidence indicates that the deputies performed their duty with satisfactory thoroughness. A region like this is an *imperium in imperio,* cut off from the normal political, economic, and social life of the United States.[3]

Such is the situation in company towns. Is it here to stay? On that question the statements of the operators to the Coal Commission threw important light. First, they regard the payment of deputy sheriffs as an evil, due to the necessity of having a large police force to suppress the disorders which they charge against the United Mine Workers, and the inability of the county to bear the expense out of public funds. (The extent to which the mines are taxed would seem to bear on this inability, but this

[3] On these deputies paid by the operators, see the Report of the Coal Commission, I, pp. 171-174, 180, which says in part: "That, however, a public police official should be privately paid is indefensible. It is so admitted to be by the Governor of West Virginia." The Commission also states of Logan County, West Virginia, "The clamor raised against these deputies caused a change in the method of paying them. The operators now 'loan' the county an amount equal to the extra cost of maintaining these special deputies. There is no record that these 'loans' have been repaid, and the operators do not seem to be pressing for payment."

aspect of the problem has not yet been considered.) The operators blame the unions for the persistence of the deputy system in West Virginia, as the unions have opposed a State Constabulary. Wherever the blame lies, the system ought to end; progress has already been made, but fee-yielding offices are proverbially hard to abolish.

Secondly, the exclusion clauses in leases are defended because of the evils which union organizers are said to bring in their train. The summary ejectment provisions are declared to be necessary, since strikers lingering on in the neighborhood cause intimidation of other workers and, besides, the company needs all its available housing space in order to accommodate the men who are required to operate the mine. Effective concrete illustrations are given of the difficulties caused by a strike in mines where no such clauses prevailed. It may be true that these leases are the price which must be paid to avoid unionization of the mines. If so, the public is likely to feel that the price is too high. Even if the drastic clauses are a necessary incident of the system of company-owned houses, need that system persist?

That brings us to the root of the whole matter, the permanence of the company town. In the past, such communities were probably desirable. Indeed, it is hard to conceive how the mining-towns could have grown up in the wilderness under haphazard development. The companies deserve great credit for the way they have brought in civilization and avoided many of the usual lawless and vicious features of frontier settlements. Much that the operators say about the excellence of the housing, the cheapness of rent and company-store prices, the electric cooking-utensils furnished free, the salaries paid to teach-

ers in excess of the public-school rates, is doubtless
widely true, and merits much praise. Yet, when all is
said and done, it is paternalism. It is done for the miners,
not by them, given in return for an abnegation of the
ordinary privileges of workmen. Surely those who pro-
foundly distrust state paternalism cannot view the continuance of private despotism, however benevolent, with
equanimity.

Children have to become men, and Territories cast off
the supervision of Washington and assume the responsibilities of Statehood, and the risks which always accompany responsibility. Is not a similar emancipation possible for these company towns, so that they may turn into
ordinary American communities, with competing land-
lords and stores, town governments, and streets administered by representatives of the voters, not as private
ways? The problem of transfer seems difficult, but not
insoluble. And those who oppose control of the laborers
by an absentee union, with headquarters in Indianapolis,
may equally wish to avoid the control of their housing
and shopping by absentee corporations. The president of
the Logan County Coal Company who spoke of the
Rogues' Gallery is a Boston lawyer. In short, it is the
old problem, who knows best what is good for a man,
the man himself or some wealthier and better-educated
person?

Much that is bad in the existing situation is due to the
trend of circumstances rather than to deliberate design.
Indeed, in this as in so many other matters, it is the
writer's belief that we should not waste time in appor-
tioning moral blame, but set our minds at work to produce a better state of affairs. Human beings were directed

to bring about the Kingdom of Heaven on earth and not
to take over the job of the Recording Angel. The future
above is all very well, but the present here below is certainly part and parcel of it.[4]

[4] A concluding paragraph of the original article, omitted here, urged
that action be taken to prolong the life of the Coal Commission, which
expired Sept. 30, 1923, and to carry into effect as many as possible of
its recommendations. It does not appear that such action was taken
either by the President or by Congress.

The following extract from the conclusion of the report of the
Committee of Inquiry on Coal and Civil Liberties embodies the author's position on the activities of the United Mine Workers in the
region described in this article:

"While we have not included in our investigations the charges of
violations of civil liberty which have been made against the United
Mine Workers, this omission arises from no desire to overlook or con-
done any illegal acts committed by that organization. Our only interest
in this investigation is as members of the public. With the limited
time and funds at our disposal, we have not felt it to be our task to
go over a second time ground already covered by another group, the
Bituminous Operators' Special Committee, but rather to lay before
you documents and classes of facts, especially documents, which would
naturally not be included in their investigations. The public, of whom
we form a part, will most benefit insofar as your invitation for facts
on civil liberty is met by information which taken together will present a well-rounded picture of the situation in the coal-fields.

"The reports submitted to you by others which have come to our
notice, and our own documents, point to the existence of what is practically a state of war in important areas of our country and in the
production of the mineral which with iron constitutes the basis of the
American industrial structure. If your Commission finds that in that
war individual rights and the laws of the land have been frequently
disregarded by either side or both sides, we earnestly hope that you
may be able to recommend plans of industrial adjustment which will
achieve a durable peace. We hope that an end may be put not only to
the outrages charged against the United Mine Workers of America,
but also to the far-reaching control of the operators over the homes
of their employees, to the abuses of liberty by public officials paid by
the operators, to the suppression of peaceful activities through injunctions and military force."

THE LABOR INJUNCTION [1]

THE case against the labor injunction has been presented in a book by a layman, the editor of the *International Molders' Journal,* with an introduction by Samuel Gompers.[2] Somewhat less than half the book is occupied by discussion, and the last hundred pages contain an abstract of the declaration of annual conventions of the American Federation of Labor about injunctions, the model anti-injunction bill drafted and approved by the Federation, and typical injunctions and leading judicial decisions.

Although a lawyer can find many defects in the book, he may at least learn from it the fact that lawyers have made the law much more difficult for laymen to understand than it ought to be. Here is a field of the law which intimately affects the lives and happiness of two or three million workingmen and women. Yet there is no book from which they can learn its principles. It has never been codified, and any trade-unionist who wishes to study it must either rely on the unofficial statements of long treatises, or else examine hundreds of judicial decisions, each in a different volume, and many of them wholly inconsistent with each other. Furthermore, the labor injunction cannot be correctly understood from the cases

---

[1] First printed in the *Harvard Law Review,* February, 1923.
[2] *The Labor Injunction: An Exposition of Government by Judicial Conscience and Its Menace.* By John P. Frey. Cincinnati: Equity Publishing Co., 1922.

on that topic alone. It demands an accurate knowledge of two much wider subjects, torts and equity jurisdiction, each of which in its turn must be studied in a mass of decisions. And not only the layman is baffled. Few leaders of the bar could advise a labor union how to conduct an effective strike with any assurance of avoiding an injunction and imprisonment for contempt. The essential quality of predicability is virtually absent from this portion of the law. Surely the time has come for the state to stop governing workingmen by uncertain rules, resembling the ingenuity of the Emperor Caligula in hanging drastic statutes so high in the air that nobody who might possibly violate them could understand what they said.

Such being the difficulties of the labor injunction, it is not surprising that Mr. Frey has failed to comprehend several important points. Thus, he begins by contrasting the modern equity judge, who protects the rich, with the medieval chancellor who devoted all his attention to the safety of the poor.[3] A layman might derive this impression from stray statements in text writers, but a lawyer would know, first, that the modern equity court frequently relieves the poor against fraud, and secondly, that the fifteenth-century chancellor spent a large portion of his time enforcing trusts for the benefit of large monasteries and wealthy landowners. Again, the author quotes [4] Selden's famous gibe at the arbitrary nature of the chancellor's conscience, apparently supposing that it represents the situation today, and that the definitions of coercive picketing or the secondary boycott depend on the uncontrolled conscience of the particular equity judge.

[3] Page 4.
[4] Page 8.

Since Lord Eldon's time, a century ago, the rules of equity have become almost as rigid as those of the common law, especially in the field of civil injuries, where equity necessarily follows the law. The question whether the trade unionist has wronged the employer is not a matter for the equity judge's discretion at all, but is determined by rules in the same way as the question whether a street railway has negligently injured a passenger.

The true reasons which make the labor injunction much more questionable than the negligence suit are not any refusal of courts of equity to attempt to lay down rules; they are, first, the greater difficulty in stating the rules, and the conflicting decisions in different states or even the same state; secondly, the possibility that in so far as these rules are settled, they give the laborer an unjustly narrow scope in his competitive struggle with the employer, both in defining what constitutes a tort and in regulating the grounds and scope of injunctions; thirdly, the grave doubts whether the injunction is the most suitable method to accomplish the legitimate purposes of safeguarding business and public order against the coercion and violence which so frequently accompany strikes. It may be that the criminal law ought to deal more with the actual manifestations of disorder, while the adjustment of the disputes which underlie the strike must be placed in the hands of conciliation courts or administrative tribunals. Certainly, even though Mr. Frey's wish for the abolition of the labor injunction were granted, the public would still demand a vigorous weapon against the excesses of strikers.

It is to be hoped that Mr. Frey will consider such

questions as these in his next book, and that he will have the opportunity to make a broader study of equity jurisdiction in its preparation. This might lead him to modify several of his positions. For instance, he asserts that "American courts of equity had no English precedents to justify them in the issue of labor injunctions," [5] and ridicules the American judicial theory that business is property,[6] as if it were an outrageous legal innovation invented to justify labor injunctions. The fact is that during the last half of the nineteenth century, business has been protected in equity, both in England and this country, against numerous wrongs which have nothing to do with industrial disputes. Thus, equity has enjoined the action of a competitor in putting up his wares so as to pass them off on the public as the plaintiff's, and has required compensation for the good will of a dissolved partnership. On the same principle, equity under statutes safeguards the union label. When equity had taken

[5] Page 27. The author states that there are only two instances of labor injunctions in England, Springhead Spinning Co. v. Riley, L.R. 6 Eq. 551 (1868), and Taff Vale Railway Co. v. Amalgamated Society of Railway Servants, [1901] A.C. 426. These he declares to have no authority, because the first was repudiated by the Court of Appeal in Prudential Assurance Co. v. Knott, 10 Ch. App. 142 (1875), and the second was immediately superseded by the Trade Disputes Act of 1906, 6 Edw. 7, c. 47. This does not quite state the true situation. The Springhead case was attacked, not because it was a labor injunction but because it enjoined a libel, and its authority has been virtually restored by later English cases enjoining libels. See Roscoe Pound, "Equitable Relief Against Defamation and Injuries to Personality," 29 *Harv. L. Rev.* 640, 657-666 (1916). The Taff Vale case was attacked, not because of the labor injunction, but because it treated the union as an entity, thus making its funds liable to seizure to pay damages, like United Mine Workers v. Coronado Coal Co., 258 U.S. 344 (1922). The statute of 1906 did not prohibit labor injunctions, but affected law and equity together by narrowing the tort liability of the unions. Labor injunctions have been very infrequent in England, but are not opposed to English authorities, and rest on general equitable principles which are well recognized in that country.

[6] Page 33 ff.

this entirely proper proposition in recognizing the business man's opportunity of access to the market as a right, just as valuable as the ownership of land or machinery, it was a natural though perhaps unwise step, to protect his access to an open labor market by injunction.

Again, it is stated that the principle that equity must not be used to punish crime has been violated by the issue of labor injunctions against criminal acts in strikes.[7] The author is probably not familiar with the numerous injunctions in matters wholly dissociated from labor against acts which were in fact criminal, but which were enjoined because they also threatened private rights. Thus a man may be enjoined from repeatedly breaking into the plaintiff's house, from pouring dense smoke over the plaintiff's land, from manufacturing TNT next his residence, though these acts are also punishable by the state through prosecution. Large corporations under the Sherman Act may be broken up in equity, although they may also be proceeded against criminally. The point is, that equity does not deal with criminal acts because they are crimes, but only if in addition they present grounds for equitable relief, to protect private rights, etc.

Yet, although no reliance can be placed on the theoretical discussion in Mr. Frey's book, the collection of labor cases has distinct value for lawyers. Still more important is the opportunity which this book gives for lawyers to see how law in action looks to laymen who are intimately affected by it, however untrained in law in books. Some houses have been described as combining a Queen Anne front with a Mary Ann back, and we members of the bar often rest satisfied with the symmetrical

[7] Page 72.

façades of the logical structures we have raised, without realizing the opinions of those who inhabit the working-quarters behind. Against the theoretical justifications of the labor injunction which I have just given must be weighed its mental and emotional effect upon trade-unionists. Imprisonment for contempt by a single judge is logically different from imprisonment for crime by a grand and a petty jury, but the prison walls and prison food are just the same. The lawyer who reads a judicial opinion in a labor case with care is not likely to consider the language of the injunction itself as it must sound to the men against whom it is directed. Here is Mr. Frey's impression: [8]

The strikers, unfamiliar with legal phraseology, knowing if they are cited for contempt, that no jury will be permitted to pass on the facts, are intimidated by the phraseology and deterred from doing anything to protect their interests because of the indefinite language used, which they realize the court can interpret in any manner satisfactory to itself, because the wording of the injunction has failed to convey the clear, direct implication and interpretation of the language used.

The lawyer who finds that an erroneously granted injunction against picketing has been reversed by the appellate court will probably feel that justice has been attained. The unionist only sees that the strike was effectively broken by the erroneous injunction; the reversal comes months too late to reinstate the contest.[9] The

---

[8] Page 74. Compare page 191, *infra.*
[9] In the Tri-City case, 257 U.S. 184 (1921), an injunction was held too sweeping seven and one-half years after it was granted. Prof. W. W. Cook of Yale and Johns Hopkins suggests in 32 *Yale L. J.* 170 that we should not permit a single judge to use the drastic remedy of an injunction in these labor cases involving burning economic issues and fundamental human rights, unless we make adequate pro-

lawyer is too familiar with conflicting and inconsistent decisions to view them with surprise or indignation. Mr. Frey is immediately struck by the contrast between frequent injunctions against boycotts by strikers and frequent refusals to enjoin boycotts by associations of business men against firms who violate the association's rules.[10] It may be that Mr. Frey overlooks cases that do enjoin the employers, and that on the whole there has not been discrimination. The point is, that as a union member reads the cases collected here, he thinks they do discriminate against him, and feels aggrieved. What are we going to do to remove that impression of injustice? It is not enough that the people get justice; they must feel that they are getting justice.

vision for immediate review by the proper appellate courts. Otherwise in granting an injunction to prevent irreparable damage to the plaintiff the judge may through an error cause irreparable damage to the defendants, which could be avoided by the immediate review suggested. He remarks the possibility that labor may turn the tables by invoking the injunction against the employer as was once done in New York, and that a single judge inclined to favor the unions might do serious damage to the employer by a sweeping injunction with the delayed review which we now have. Besides the immediate review recommended by Professor Cook, an additional safeguard against error might be found in an injunction bond. A patentee who seeks a temporary injunction against an infringer is forced to file a bond to pay damages caused by the injunction if it is later dissolved. A similar bond might be required from the plaintiff in labor injunctions, the damages being fixed at so much for each week the injunction is in force and bearing a rough relation to the expenses caused to the union by the strike which has been erroneously ended by the injunction.

[10] Page 63. Mr. Frey cites the following cases: Montgomery Ward & Co. v. South Dakota Retail Merchants' and Hardware Dealers' Ass'n., 150 Fed. 413 (1907); Delaney Bros. v. Master Plumbers' Association of St. Paul (Minn. Dist. Ct. 2nd Dist., 1920); Cote v. Murphy, 159 Pa. St. 420 (1894); Master Builders' Association v. Domascio, 16 Colo. App. 25 (1901); National Fireproofing Co. v. Mason Builders' Association, 169 Fed. 259 (1909).

STRIKE INJUNCTIONS OBTAINED BY COAL OPERATORS [1]

THE use of injunctions in coal strikes is important for civil liberties only as they operate to restrict the ordinary activities of citizens, such as the holding of meetings, the expression of opinion, and peaceful persuasion of others to adopt their views. We are not here concerned with the employment of the injunction against violence, coercion, intimidation by picketing, and similar illegal or abnormal conduct of strikers. Although some of the injunctions subsequently discussed are partly directed against such illegal or abnormal conduct, they also contain clauses of such sweeping or vague language as to place those enjoined in peril of imprisonment for contempt if they carry on activities ordinarily regarded as lawful. It should also be observed that the present paper deals only with coal-strike injunctions which were obtained by the operators, for suits by the United States against strikers raise special problems, which may better be dealt with elsewhere.[2]

[1] This paper is based on the author's examination of twelve coal-strike injunctions and his commentary thereon in the report to the United States Coal Commission (p. 172 *supra,* note 1), with which were filed (in Envelope E) the twelve injunctions. Seven were from West Virginia (three in the state courts and four in the United States Courts), four from Pennsylvania county courts, and one from a United States court in Alabama. Many other injunctions in similar terms have been issued in the bituminous fields since 1919. Thus, at least eleven companies in Somerset County, Pennsylvania, filed bills in equity in April, 1922, asking for broad injunctions, which were accordingly issued, but only one of these was procured for examination.

[2] See "Strike Injunctions Obtained by the United States," *infra.*

Discussion of labor injunctions usually turns upon questions of substantive law, that is, upon the circumstances under which such relief is given and the theoretical bases of the employers' right of action. It is, however, worth while to approach the question from a different angle and to consider what the courts actually do in such cases, as shown in the wording of their decrees. Since the materials for such study are often not readily accessible,[3] the examination of an important group of unpublished injunctions may not be without value.

The selection of clauses from coal-strike injunctions for comment has been guided by two propositions as to the proper scope of an injunction which have been laid down by courts of high authority.

First, an injunction should not be issued in such general terms that the person enjoined cannot ascertain what specific acts he is forbidden to commit.

Justice Holmes, speaking for the Supreme Court of the United States in Swift *v.* United States,[4] said:

The defendants ought to be informed as accurately as the case permits what they are forbidden to do. . . . The words quoted are a sweeping injunction to obey the law, and are open to the objection which we stated at the beginning that it was our duty to avoid.

The same principle was enunciated in a leading case by an eminent New York judge, Chancellor Walworth:[5]

[3] Some injunctions are reprinted in the official law reports, but many such orders never come before appellate tribunals. Their text is printed, if at all, only in such useful unofficial publications as *Law and Labor,* or in the daily press.

[4] 196 U.S. 375, 401 (1905).

[5] Laurie *v.* Laurie, 9 Paige 234 (1841).

As the defendant is bound to obey the process of the court at his peril, the language of the injunction should in all cases be so clear and explicit that an unlearned man can understand its meaning, without the necessity of employing counsel to advise him what he has a right to do to save him from subjecting himself to punishment for a breach of the injunction.

And Judge Amidon of the Eighth United States Circuit has said: [6]

Injunctions are addressed to laymen. They ought to be so brief and plain that laymen can understand them. They ought to be framed in the fewest possible words. The order should not express the bias or violence of a party to such a controversy or his attorney. . . . The purpose ought to be to state the specific acts that are forbidden. So I attempted to do that in the orders that were issued. . . . The result has been that the strikers have been able to understand the orders, and have shown a keen desire to do so and obey them.

Several of the coal-strike injunctions examined were issued by inferior courts in Pennsylvania. Certain of their vague and general terms should be compared with the requirements for an injunction laid down by Chief Justice Moschiszker of the Supreme Court of that state: [7]

The entry of an injunction is, in some respects, analogous to the publication of a penal statute; it is a notice that certain things must be done or not done, under a penalty to be fixed by the court. Such a decree should be as definite, clear and precise in its terms as possible, so that there may be no reason or excuse for misunderstanding or disobeying it; and when

[6] Gt. Nor. Ry. v. Brosseau, 286 Fed. 414, 415 (N.D., 1923).
[7] Collins v. Wayne Iron Works, 227 Pa. 326, 330, decided in 1910 while he was still Associate Justice.

practicable it should plainly indicate to the defendant all of the acts which he is restrained from doing, without calling upon him for inferences or conclusions about which persons may well differ.

Second, an injunction should be limited to unlawful acts and should not also forbid lawful acts. The Supreme Court has taken this position in a non-labor case. A manufacturer of a quinine preparation flavored with chocolate complained that a rival was putting just enough chocolate into a similar preparation so that its color would exactly resemble the plaintiff's and the public be deceived into supposing that they were getting the plaintiff's preparation in drug stores when they were really drinking the defendant's. The lower court said that the defendant, having shown himself unfit to be trusted, should be forbidden to use chocolate altogether in any preparation of quinine; but this decision was modified by the Supreme Court of the United States, which held that the defendant was entitled to put chocolate in his beverage so long as it was clearly distinguishable from the plaintiff's.[8] The application of this principle to strike injunctions has been clearly stated by Judge Baker in the United States Circuit Court of Appeals for the Seventh Circuit:[9]

Surely men are not to be denied the right to pursue a legitimate end in a legitimate way, simply because they may have overstepped the mark and trespassed upon the rights of their

[8] Warner *v.* Lilly, 265 U.S. 526 (1924), modifying 275 Fed. 752 (1921).
[9] Iron Molders' Union *v.* Allis-Chalmers Co., 166 Fed. 45, 49 (C.C.A. 1908). Numerous other cases are collected in Sayre, *Cases on Labor Law,* 199 n.; Chafee, *Cases on Equitable Relief Against Torts,* 242 n.

adversary. A barrier at the line, with punishment and damages for having crossed, is all that the adversary is entitled to ask.

The same judge said in Borderland Coal Company *v.* Gasaway,[10] when modifying a sweeping injunction granted by Judge Albert B. Anderson:

No injunction, preliminary or final, should forbid more than the particular unlawful invasions which the court finds would be committed except for the restraint imposed. . . .

In the present state of the law, and without a constitutional exercise of the legislative power of regulation, appellee had no greater right to a decree suppressing lawful action (such as the publications, speeches and personal persuasions heretofore mentioned in this paragraph) in support of the closed union shop program than appellants had to a similar decree suppressing similar lawful action in support of the closed non-union shop program. Neither side had any such right.

While it is true that there are decisions to the contrary [11] in which the judges contend that a defendant who has once crossed the line which separates legal from illegal action shows as a matter of common sense that he must not be allowed in the future to come anywhere near the line upon the legal side thereof, nevertheless Judge Baker's position, supported as it is in principle by a decision of our highest court, is much more likely to preserve the liberty of citizens. If we permit a judge to for-

[10] 278 Fed. 56, 63, 65 (1921). The modification of the injunction is approved in 4 *Law and Labor* 15.
[11] Holyoke *v.* Palmer, 3 *Law and Labor* 65 (Mass. Supreme Ct., 1921); Pacific *v.* United Mine Workers, 4 *ibid.* 42 (Wash. Superior Ct., 1921); Jenckes Spinning *v.* McMahon, 4 *ibid.* 251 (R.I. Superior Ct., 1922); and a case of unfair competition, Cheney *v.* Gimbel, 280 Fed. 746 (S.D.N.Y., 1922).

bid lawful acts as a punishment for previous unlawful action, we are transferring the notion of punishment from the criminal law, where it belongs, into equity, where it has no place. We are allowing men to be imprisoned for doing what the law permits. We are clothing the equity judge with powers of an immense and vague range, since no standard exists to separate the lawful acts which he may enjoin from those which cannot by any possibility be brought within his control.

If either of the two propositions already submitted be disregarded by an injunction, it operates to deprive citizens of their liberty in violations of law.

The first proposition that a defendant in equity should not be subjected to what Justice Holmes calls "a sweeping injunction to obey the law" seems to be disregarded by clauses in the coal-strike injunctions under consideration which prohibit the defendant from doing "any act or thing that will suppress or unduly limit the rights of the plaintiff to employ non-union labor"; from "doing any act or thing that will in any way interfere with or restrain free competition among those seeking employment of the plaintiffs"; "from in any manner interfering with the lawful right of the plaintiffs to employ such laborers as they may choose"; from "interfering in any unlawful manner" with the plaintiffs, etc. One injunction goes so far as to forbid the defendants "from in any way interfering with the plaintiff, its agents or employees, in the conduct or operation of its mines." Such clauses oblige the defendants to ascertain at their peril what acts are unlawful. The penalty for a mistake is imprisonment for contempt at the will of the judge who issued the injunction.

The second principle, that the injunction should limit itself to the prohibition of unlawful acts and not extend to the ordinary lawful activities of the defendants, may well be considered in connection with the clauses which forbid all mass meetings; which forbid all use of money to assist "in unionizing the mines of these plaintiffs";[12] which prohibit the defendants from representing to any person that he is likely to suffer some loss or trouble in continuing in or in entering the employment of the plaintiff, and forbid the use of persuasion to induce any persons not to enter the plaintiff's employment. Two of the injunctions contain clauses applying to tent colonies. The ownership of the houses near the mines by the operators, which has been discussed in a previous paper,[13] necessarily means that the miners who go on strike must leave their houses. If they are not to leave the region altogether, the only place where it is possible for them to live is in tents, which are frequently maintained by the unions on land not belonging to the operators. An injunction granted to the Borderland Coal Corporation and numerous other operators by the United States District Court for the Southern District of West Virginia in 1922 forbids the United Mine Workers of America to maintain tent colonies in Mingo County, or to furnish to the inhabitants of

[12] Such an injunction was declared improper in Borderland Coal Co. *v.* Gasaway, supra, note 10.

An editorial in the Boston *Herald,* Jan. 14, 1928, reports an injunction issued on Nov. 8, 1927, at the suit of the Clearfield Bituminous Coal Corporation, by the Court of Common Pleas of Indiana County, Pennsylvania, which includes among the acts forbidden to the strikers, "distributing pecuniary contributions in furtherance of the conspiracy to keep men from employment or seeking employment" with the company. Since the strike benefits thus prohibited constitute the only support of the strikers and their families, this forces them to return to work or starve.

[13] "Company Towns in the Soft-Coal Fields," *supra,* p. 172.

such colonies any money or merchandise, etc., so as to make possible the continuance of such colonies, on the ground that they are a source of menace and intimidation to the employees of the plaintiffs. A similar provision appears in an injunction obtained by the Quemahoning Creek Coal Company in Somerset County, Pennsylvania, in 1923. The most far-reaching provision is contained in an injunction obtained by the Pond Creek Coal Company in 1920 from the United States District Court for the Southern District of West Virginia. This prohibits the defendants "from advertising, representing, stating by word, by posted notices, or by placards displayed at any point in the State of West Virginia or elsewhere, that a strike exists in the Pond Creek Field, or at plaintiff's mines, and from warning, or notifying persons to remain away from said Pond Creek Field or from plaintiff's mines."

STRIKE INJUNCTIONS OBTAINED BY THE UNITED STATES

SINCE the Armistice of 1918 two large strikes have been broken up by injunctions issued in United States District Courts at the suit of the government. These were directed not merely at violence and intimidation, but at the very existence of the strikes. Since the use of federal jurisdiction for this purpose and the broad terms of the decrees may have an important effect as precedents in future labor controversies, it is worth while to discuss some aspects of these two injunctions.

THE COAL STRIKE INJUNCTION OF 1919 [1]

In the middle of October, 1919, the United Mine Workers, from its headquarters in Indianapolis, issued a strike order to the union miners in all the bituminous coal fields, to take effect at midnight on October 31. Attorney General Palmer on October 31 started a suit in equity in the United States District Court of Indiana, *United States v. Frank J. Hayes* [2] and others, and on the

---

[1] First printed in the *Harvard Law Review,* February, 1921; some additions have been made.

[2] U. S. D. C. Ind., Nov. Term, 1919, In Equity, No. 312; Oct. 31, 1919; Nov. 8, 1919. The bill and temporary restraining order have been printed (Wash. 1919); and all the pleadings and decrees up to Dec. 3, 1919, are included in the printed Information for Criminal Contempt (in Harvard Law School Library). No report of the decision has been published, and so far as can be ascertained, no opinion was filed by the court. The case is approved in 5 *Cornell L.Q.* 184. The temporary injunction is reprinted in Sayre, *Cases on Labor Law,* 757.

same day obtained from Judge Albert B. Anderson a temporary restraining order against specified officers of the union and their unnamed associates commanding them, among other requirements,

to desist and refrain from doing any further act whatsoever to bring about or continue in effect the . . . strike . . . ; from issuing any further strike orders . . . ; from issuing any messages of encouragement or exhortation to striking miners . . . to abstain from work and not to return to the mines . . . ; and from . . . taking any steps to procure the . . . distribution . . . of . . . strike benefits, and from conspiring . . . with each other or any other person to limit the facilities for the production of coal, or to restrict the supply or distribution of coal. . . .

There is no mention of violence, intimidation, boycotting, or other incidents of a strike. It is the strike itself which is forbidden. After a hearing on November 8, the order was continued as a temporary injunction *pendente lite,* with a mandatory provision for the recall of the strike before the end of the third day following. An order of the union officials for that object was subsequently approved by the court. No appeal was taken and no written opinion filed.

For the purpose of this article, it may be assumed that the wage agreement between the coal operators and the union members, which had been approved by the government, was still in force, that this was violated by the strike, and that the miners could therefore have been sued by the operators. The only question here is how a court of equity had power to grant relief at the suit of the United States.

The following grounds have been suggested:

1. *Public Nuisance.* This was the basis of the injunction issued by the California court against the I.W.W., discussed in a previous article.[3] Even if we concede the dubious proposition that a large strike is a nuisance in itself, without proof that any violence or intimidation is used, the United States courts have not the powers of state courts to enjoin public nuisances. Some language in the Debs case,[4] in which the injunction against the Pullman strikers in 1894 was sustained by the Supreme Court, has fostered the belief that the United States may obtain an injunction on this ground. Doubtless the federal interest in the mails, threatened by that strike, was analogous to the interests infringed by public nuisances, so that it was easy to exercise equitable jurisdiction once a federal right had been established. The right must, however, be based on something besides the nuisance. There is no clause in the Constitution which gives the United States power to abate public nuisances unless they also infringe some federal right created by the Constitution. The health, comfort, and general welfare of citizens are in charge of the state governments and not of the United States. Or, to put the matter in another way, the injunction of public nuisances is based on the police power, and the federal government has no police power independent of its express powers. The Constitution did not see fit to entrust to the general government the control of conduct on the sole ground that in the opinion of Congress, or United States judges, such conduct threatened widespread injury to the country at large.

[3] "The California I.W.W. Injunction," p. 74, *supra.*
[4] 158 U.S. 564 (1895).

2. *Protection of federal property rights,* in the mails
and the operation of the railroads, then under control of
the Director General. This is in my opinion the strongest
argument in favor of the coal-strike injunction, and finds
an analogy in the Debs injunction of 1894. Nevertheless,
the analogy is far from complete. It is one thing for the
government to restrain the direct interference with the
operation of mail trains through violence on the spot. But
it is a very much wider exercise of federal authority to
prevent indirect interference through the curtailment of
the production of coal. Where is the jurisdiction to stop?
Have the federal courts equitable jurisdiction over all the
employees of persons who make contracts with the United
States for the supply of essentials? Furthermore, if the
action of the strikers is not to be considered too remote to
be an injury to the property rights of the government, it
must also constitute a tort to private persons. A manufacturer who has a contract for the delivery of coal to
him would also have the right to obtain an injunction
against striking miners. It seems very probable that the
causation is here too remote to constitute a tort in the
absence of legislation. In a converse case, where a failure
of the railroad to furnish rolling-stock led to the shut-
down of a coal mine, the miners were held to have no
cause of action against the railroad.[5] The argument that
the strikers are causing the mines to break contracts with
the United States, and hence are liable to the United
States in a civil suit,[6] is open to similar difficulties, espe-

[5] Ill. Cent. R.R. *v.* Baker, 155 Ky. 512 (1913).
[6] See F. B. Sayre, "Inducing Breach of Contract," 36 *Harv. L. Rev.*
663 (1923). The strongest case for liability where the strike is not
directed against the contract is Niles-Bement-Pond Co. *v.* Iron Molders' Union, 246 Fed. 851 (1917), discussed in 31 *Harv. L. Rev.* 1017.

cially as the strike was not specifically directed against these contracts. Finally, if the injunction is based on a federal property right in the supply of coal, it should restrain the strike only to the extent that it prevents the delivery of coal to the railroads and should not also compel the production of coal for private consumption.

3. *Interference with interstate commerce.* This raises the same questions as the preceding ground, even if, as was stated by the Supreme Court in the Debs case, such commerce may be regulated by the courts as well as by Congress.

4. *Violation of the Sherman Act,*[7] by which Congress has declared every conspiracy in restraint of interstate commerce illegal and subject to injunction in the federal courts at the suit of the Attorney General. This ground is not alleged in the bill and involves serious difficulties, among which these may be mentioned: (a) The strike was a cessation from production of coal within separate states and not in businesses engaged in transporting coal, so that interstate commerce was not directly attacked. Whether it was sufficiently affected by the scope of the strike is a difficult question.[8] (b) The Supreme Court has ever since the Standard Oil case [9] interpreted "restraint" in the Sherman Act to mean only unreasonable restraints, and has never held that a widespread cessation of work is in itself unreasonable where no violence, intimidation, secondary boycott, etc., accompanies the strike. (c) The

[7] Act of July 2, 1890, c. 647; U.S. Code (1925), Title 15, c. 1. This ground is rejected by the note in 5 *Cornell L.Q.* 187.
[8] Compare United Mine Workers *v.* Coronado Coal Co., 259 U.S. 407 (1922) and 268 U.S. 310 (1925). See also United Leather Workers *v.* Herkert, 265 U.S. 457 (1924). The unconstitutionality of the first Child Labor Law raises a similar problem.
[9] 221 U.S. 1 (1911).

Clayton Act [10] forbids federal courts to enjoin any persons "from terminating any relation of employment . . . or from recommending, advising, or persuading others by peaceful means so to do. . . ." This section surely invalidates Judge Anderson's injunction, unless, as is possible, Congress was speaking only of suits brought by private persons and not by the government; [11] but this question has not been determined by the Supreme Court.

5. *Specific performance of the wage agreement.* Even if we overcome long-standing objections to the enforcement of compulsory personal service by injunction, the government has no interest which would enable it to enforce this contract. It is not a party thereto, and is a beneficiary only in a remote sense.

6. *Interference with the war.* If we assume that the war was raging in November, 1919,[12] then the coal strike was a sufficient hindrance thereto for Congress to legislate against it. Such legislation might have conferred equitable jurisdiction on the courts in furtherance of the war power, by analogy with the statutory extension of equitable jurisdiction in the Sherman Act. Since, however, Congress did nothing of the sort, the supporters of the injunction on war grounds must rest on either of two contentions: (a) It might be argued that a United States

[10] Act of Oct. 15, 1914, c. 323, § 20; U.S. Code (1925), Title 29, c. 5, § 52.

[11] Judge Wilkerson in the Railway Shop Workers case, *infra* note 21, held the Clayton Act inapplicable to government suits. For the opposite view see W. W. Cook, 32 *Yale L.J.* 168, note 10.

[12] It was not ended for purposes of law-suits until the joint resolution of Congress on July 2, 1921, although the armistice was concluded a year before the injunction. Manley O. Hudson, "The Duration of the War Between the United States and Germany," 39 *Harv. L. Rev.* 1020 (1926). The termination of hostilities was, however, a material fact to be weighed against the argument of the government that interference with the war was a reason for drastic judicial action.

court had power to enjoin any act which hindered the war, regardless of the absence of Congressional authorization. The sweeping character of this claim is its own refutation, and the Constitution vests the war power in Congress, not the courts. (b) It might be argued that if the defendant's conduct violated a war statute so as to cause widespread injury analogous to a public nuisance, then although this statute conferred no equitable jurisdiction, nevertheless the illegal conduct might be restrained. Some such view probably lay behind the reliance on the Lever Act, discussed below. If it was sound, then the silence of Congress about equitable jurisdiction need not have prevented mandatory injunctions to compel men to register under the Selective Service Act, and prohibitions against the distribution of books considered by the judges to violate the Espionage Act. The fact that Congress had provided very different methods for enforcing these war statutes is a very serious objection to the assumption that they were also within the jurisdiction of equity, which Congress had not mentioned.

7. *Violation of the Lever Act*,[13] which punished conspiracies to restrict the production or distribution of necessaries in war-time. This is the main ground put forward in the bill.[14] It seems to me very questionable, even if the statute were violated by the strike so that the miners could have been criminally prosecuted by the government. If there is one principle of equity which can be regarded as settled, it is that a crime will not be enjoined merely because it is a crime. Some other aspect

[13] U.S. Act of Aug. 10, 1917, c. 53, § 4, amended by Act of Oct. 22, 1919, c. 80, § 2. Another portion of this section was held unconstitutional in U.S. *v.* Cohen Grocery Co., 255 U.S. 81 (1921).
[14] It is accepted as sufficient in 5 *Cornell L.Q.* 184.

of the defendant's conduct must bring the case within the established jurisdiction of chancery. The Lever Act declared violations thereof to be crimes subject to criminal penalties. Not a clause made them a ground for equitable relief.

The coal-strike injunction could be supported only if it was based upon the infringement of a definite federal right. The existence of such a right must remain conjectural in the absence of any written opinion from the United States District Court of Indiana. Over a century has elapsed since the greatest of chancellors declared, "I have no jurisdiction to prevent the commission of crimes." [15] A conservative lawyer of today may be permitted to share Lord Eldon's doubts and express regret that Judge Albert B. Anderson felt unable to make public the reasons which led him to differ from the foremost English advocate of law and order, who even during the disturbance of the French Revolution refused in the absence of legislative authority to strengthen the power of the government by placing the Court of Chancery at the disposal of the criminal law.

Even though the court had jurisdiction to enjoin the coal strike, the question still remains whether that jurisdiction should have been exercised. Undoubtedly an emergency confronted the government, but if an injunction had been refused, there were alternative remedies through legislative or executive action. The question deserves serious consideration, whether such types of action are not more expedient than an injunction in the case of a

---

[15] Gee v. Pritchard, 2 Swans. 402 (1818). See Cope v. Dist. Fair Assn., 99 Ill. 489 (1881). An early case is Wakeman v. Smith, Toth. 12 (1585).

huge industrial dispute unaccompanied by violence. In favor of judicial proceedings is the fact that they guarantee a chance for both sides to be heard, whereas if Congress had handled the strike with legislation like the Adamson Law, or if the President had taken over the mines under his war powers, a hearing might have been denied. On the other hand, there is no obstacle to a hearing before Congress or the Executive which should be just as adequate and fair as that given by Judge Anderson, and such legislative or executive action has certain great advantages for the settlement of a huge industrial controversy which are not possessed by a court of equity. Such a court can stop the strike, but it cannot remove the causes of the strike. There is a familiar equitable principle that a bill will be dismissed if the absence of necessary parties makes it impossible for the court to give a decree which will wind up the whole controversy in a just manner. A similar consideration might well have led to the dismissal of the government's coal-strike bill on the ground that the main controversy between the operators and the miners ought not to be left hanging in the air after the incomplete remedy of an injunction, but could only be finally and justly settled by an investigation into the complex conditions at the mines and possibly a new wage agreement. Such an investigation could not be made by a court of equity. It could be made by the Executive. It was in fact eventually so made after the injunction. Consequently, since the court could not meet the real issue of the controversy, it might well have refused to have any halfway dealings with it in the absence of well-recognized grounds for judicial action, and might have left the government to make use at once of the executive powers which obviously must be employed sooner or later. Moreover, such action shifts a great and bitter dispute involving masses of people and wide economic ramifications from appointive judges who rarely have expert knowledge of such economic problems to the President, an elective official clothed with powers which enable him to treat this problem like other war problems, drawing on the extensive assistance of experts and enforcing his decision by methods which are not available to courts. This shift relieves the judiciary of a terrific strain which it is not well fitted to bear. Under our constitutional system, the highly important task of adjusting conflicts between different portions of the system belongs to the courts. This task requires that the firmest confidence of the people in the correctness and fairness of judicial decisions shall be maintained. There is a genuine danger that this confidence will be shaken if the Attorney General calls on judges who are not equipped by long experience to solve difficult economic problems and who lack the powers necessary to solve them finally and obtains from them summary remedies affecting the industrial life of thousands. Perhaps eventually we shall establish Conciliation Courts fitted by training and experience and the possession of powers not now conferred on a United States District Court to settle great strikes to the satisfaction of all concerned. Until then, may it not be wise to entrust such controversies to Congress or the President, who are at least as able to decide them as the courts, rather than cast a great burden on the judiciary, which may weaken its accomplishment of its customary and invaluable work?

THE RAILWAY SHOP STRIKE INJUNCTION OF 1922 [16]

Although a conciliation tribunal, as suggested in the preceding paragraph, does not yet exist for coal-mining, something of the sort has been provided by Congress for another great industry, the railroads. The Transportation Act of 1920 [17] established a national Railroad Labor Board, and also permits Railroad Boards of Labor Adjustment to be arranged by agreement between carriers and their employees. Disputes may go first to the local boards or directly to the national board, which has power to compel the appearance of witnesses and the production of documents. The decisions of all the boards are to establish rates of wages and salaries and standards of working conditions "which in the opinion of the board are just and reasonable," in view of certain specified classes of facts. The Labor Board may, after a hearing, determine that a ruling of its own or of a subordinate board has been violated and "make public its decision in such manner as it may determine," but the statute provides no other remedy, civil or criminal, for disregard of board rulings, and it does not say that such a violation is a crime or otherwise illegal. The Supreme Court, through Chief Justice Taft, declared in 1923: [18]

The decisions of the Labor Board are not to be enforced by process. The only sanction of its decision is to be the force of public opinion invoked by the fairness of a full hearing, the

[16] The latter portion is reprinted in part from *Weekly News*, League of Women Voters of New York, Feb. 9, 1923.
[17] Act of Feb. 28, 1920, c. 91, §§ 300-316; U.S. Code (1925), title 45, c. 7.
[18] Penn. R.R. Co. *v.* U.S.R.R. Labor Board, 261 U.S. 72 (Feb. 19, 1923).

intrinsic justice of the conclusion, strengthened by the official prestige of the Board, and the full publication of the violation of such decision by any party to the proceeding. . . . The function of the Labor Board is to direct . . . public criticism against the party who, it thinks, justly deserves it.

Unfortunately, respect for public opinion has not been sufficient to secure obedience to the Labor Board in all cases by either carriers or their employees. Thus, in 1921 the Pennsylvania System refused to abide by its decision that the railway shop employees in their conferences with the railroad on working conditions might be represented by an organization affiliated with the American Federation of Labor. After the Pennsylvania had failed in judicial proceedings [19] to stop the Board from publishing this violation, it continued to disobey even after publication.

In 1922 it was the turn of the railway shop employees to be recalcitrant. Being dissatisfied with another ruling of the Labor Board, fixing wages, several unions affiliated with the American Federation of Labor, and chiefly those known as the federated shop crafts, ordered a strike to secure wages above those fixed by the board. On July 1, 1922, about 90 per cent. of the members of the unions quit work in a body.

Disobedience of the Labor Board by a railroad did not inconvenience the public or move the government to action. A widespread cessation by employees from maintenance of rolling-stock and equipment produced a very different result. Attorney General Daugherty on behalf of the United States brought a suit in equity in the United

[19] See note 18.

States District Court for Northern Illinois to enjoin the unions under the general federal equity jurisdiction and the Sherman Act. The bill charged that the unions had a duty to observe the order of the Labor Board, but had entered into a conspiracy to disregard it, and, by striking, force the railways through public pressure to do so as well; and that this conspiracy constituted a violation of the Sherman Act and the Transportation Act. A temporary restraining order was issued on September 1 by Judge James H. Wilkerson,[20] which, after hearing, was continued on the twenty-third as a temporary injunction. On January 5, 1923, he refused to dissolve this injunction, and on July 12 he made it permanent after final hearing.[21] An appeal was taken but not pressed, probably because the strike was hopelessly broken, so that we have no review of the injunction. However, Judge Wilkerson's three long opinions are extremely useful and make it much easier to discuss his action than that of Judge Anderson.

This case presented at least three arguments for the injunction which did not exist in the coal strike of 1919.

[20] Resentment was felt by the unions at the fact that the request for this broad order of an infrequent type was made to a judge who had been appointed earlier in the year, presumably at the recommendation of the Attorney General who now appeared before him. With every confidence in the impartiality of our federal judiciary, it would be desirable if the President, in the selection and promotion of judges, were furnished definite advisers, entirely dissociated from the Department of Justice, necessarily involved as it is in litigation before these judges. See Works, *Juridical Reform* (1919), pp. 123-125.

[21] The opinions of Judge Wilkerson will be found in U.S. *v.* Ry. Employees, 283 Fed. 479; 286 Fed. 228; 290 Fed. 978. The text of the restraining order, with analysis, is given by Frankfurter and Landis, 37 *Harv. L. Rev.* 1057 n.; 1101 ff. The injunction is supported by Moorfield Storey, 32 *Yale L.J.* 99, and Prof. E. N. Durfee, 21 *Mich. L. Rev.* 90. It is adversely criticized by Prof. W. W. Cook, 32 *Yale L.J.* 166; see also Prof. A. L. Corbin, *ibid.* 157.

First, the strike was in violation of the decision of a government Labor Board. This ground was stressed by the Attorney General and the press, and played some part in the judge's opinions. The Supreme Court's decision on the powers of the Labor Board,[22] which preceded Judge Wilkerson's last decision, make this argument wholly untenable. It is significant that the United States Court of Appeals has since refused to use the injunction to remedy the previously mentioned disobedience of the Board by the Pennsylvania System, one of the carriers prominent in the shopmen's strike.[23]

Second, the interference with interstate commerce and the mails was much more direct in a railroad strike than in a coal strike, so that definite federal interests were affected which might be protected by a court of equity if the interferences enjoined could be regarded as illegal. The judge's main reliance was on this ground and the related power to enjoin violations of the Sherman Act at the suit of the Attorney General. The difficulties suggested in the discussion of the Sherman and Clayton Acts in connection with the coal strike [24] are not, however, entirely absent. For instance, every railroad strike hinders interstate transportation of freight, passengers, and mails. Can all such strikes be therefore enjoined at the suit of the Attorney General without explicit statutory authority? Or did the size of the strike introduce the essential basis for relief? And if the Sherman Act be invoked as furnishing the necessary legislation for this purpose, is a large railroad strike *per se* an unreasonable restraint of trade?

[22] See *supra,* note 18.
[23] Penn. System Board *v.* Penn. R.R., 1 Fed. (2d) 177 (C.C.A., 1924).
[24] *Supra,* p. 202.

At this point, a third argument is pertinent. The court found that this strike was accompanied by much violence and intimidation, which were not mentioned in the coal-strike injunction. Such definitely unlawful features were held to render the whole strike a conspiracy which could be enjoined as an entirety, and to allow the court to forbid not only these illegal methods but also those ordinarily considered lawful, such as strike orders to union members and all peaceful persuasion of outsiders. Blanket clauses enjoined the unions from "in any manner" interfering with the operation of interstate railroads, from attempting to prevent any persons from entering upon or continuing work, and from "in any manner directly or indirectly hindering" the operation of trains. Although revocation of the strike was not ordered, as in Judge Anderson's injunction, the effect was somewhat the same, since any member of the defendant unions actively participating in its continuance subjected himself to possible imprisonment for contempt.

A distinction must be taken between a strike which aims to accomplish its purpose by intrinsically illegal methods and may therefore be considered an indivisible conspiratory violating the Sherman Act, and a strike whose intended methods are intrinsically lawful, but during which unlawful acts by some unionists occur. To enjoin all participation in strikes of the latter type is going very far.

While the propriety of the sweeping clauses of the railway shop injunction deserve careful examination,[25] atten-

[25] See the discussion of this question in another aspect, *supra,* pages 193-195, and the detailed comparison of the Wilkerson injunction with the less sweeping Debs injunction in 37 *Harv. L. Rev.* 1057 n., 1109. The other law review references in note 21 may also be consulted.

tion here may be directed to their effect upon freedom of speech. The question is not constitutionality as with a statute, but whether there was any law to authorize the judge to do what he did. Congress had deliberately refused to declare railroad strikes illegal or to penalize disregard of a Railroad Labor Board ruling. We find the preëxisting law, constitutions, statutes, and decisions, repeatedly emphasizing a policy of open discussion of all public questions. This policy is especially important during strikes. So long as they remain a legal method for the settlement of industrial disputes, free communication among the strikers is in itself as valuable and legitimate an activity as the right of business men to correspond and confer freely with one another about contracts and sales. Interference by the government with open discussion of strike issues is also a serious injury to the public. Many strikes are ultimately decided by public opinion, and unless the people at large are kept fully enlightened by both sides of the controversy, public opinion in matters involving the living conditions of thousands of citizens and the satisfactory industrial organization of the country will be formed on biased and inadequate data.

Mr. Daugherty declared that "free speech must not be used to encourage riot or murder." This justifies the clauses of the injunction forbidding violent or threatening language, but other clauses prohibited peaceable talk. Union members were enjoined from inducing or attempting to induce any person to quit or refuse a railroad job "by . . . arguments, persuasions," from "encouraging" any person to quit or refuse a job "in any manner by letters, printed or other circulars, telegrams, telephones, word of mouth, oral persuasion or suggestion or through interviews to be published in newspapers, or otherwise in any manner whatsoever." Even more remote from violence and other recognized illegal acts was the prohibition of the union officials from "issuing any instructions, requests, public statements or suggestions in any way" to members about the conduct of the strike, or to induce anybody "to do or say anything . . . calculated to cause" anybody to quit or refuse railroad work. These clauses rendered all union discussion promoting the strike a cause for imprisonment, no matter how peaceable. They forbade any statements to press and public of the union side of the strike and the injunction controversy, for such statements necessarily encourage men to continue striking.

If the evidence of violence submitted to the court was so strong as to prove that practically all the language of the strikers would be directed toward threats and force, the injunction would be defensible in its actual operation, though much too sweepingly worded. Otherwise, all the speech clauses quoted above from the injunction seem very questionable, and would perhaps have been struck out by an appellate court.

No matter how great the national danger was, it could not warrant a judge in acting contrary to law. Justice according to law is the foundation of our liberties; when the sovereign himself, whether Stuart king or American people, comes into his courts, he shall be shown no more favor by the judge than the poorest citizen; he shall receive nothing but what the law allows him. If this emergency required new law, Congress was in session. While the law remained unaltered, it was the duty of judges to decide controversies in accordance therewith, and not to depart from it, even to save the nation from disaster. If any one is to overstep the laws for the sake of avoiding disaster, this is the task of the President and not the courts. Judges are not intended to be "soldiers putting down rebellion." [26]

In both these great strikes it is a cause for regret that no appellate review was practicable, so that the ultimate decision on difficult questions affecting thousands of persons had to be made by a single trial judge.[27] The invocation of the Sherman Act in these cases against unions gives rise to a misleading impression that they were parallel to cases against corporations. Yet contrast the injunction breaking up the Standard Oil Company— which came at the end of years of litigation, after a thorough sifting of all the facts and all the legal considerations by a succession of courts, terminating in the highest of all—with the injunction breaking up the railway shop strike which came at the very beginning of the litigation by the fiat of one judge of one of the lowest courts.

Enough, it is hoped, has been said to show that these two injunctions are questionable precedents for future controversies and do not furnish a satisfactory remedy for the undoubted evil of great strikes. If such strikes are to be forbidden, then the workmen with a grievance should be given another method of redress by the government. True, in the railway shop dispute they did have the Labor Board; but when its decisions had already

[26] Sir John MacDonell, *Historical Trials* (Oxford, 1927), p. 86.
[27] See *supra*, pp. 188-189 and note, on the desirability of a right of immediate appeal.

been flouted with impunity by a leading railroad, they naturally resented being forced to obey the Board merely because their disobedience caused greater public inconvenience. Compulsory arbitration has not been adopted by Congress, and the steps taken toward it in either the nation or the states have met with serious difficulties in the Supreme Court.[28] The situation is puzzling and highly unsatisfactory, but these temporary injunctions are only temporary expedients which furnish no adequate solution.[29] When the Department of Justice at short notice throws the power of the nation on the side of the employers, and needs only the approval of a single District Court judge to defeat the workmen, the United States government loses much of its natural advantage as an impartial arbiter of industrial controversies.

[28] After the Railroad Strike of 1894, Attorney General Olney, who had obtained the Debs injunction, was desirous of avoiding similar strikes in future, and secured the adoption by Congress of a plan for settling railroad labor disputes by arbitration, in which the unions were recognized as useful participants, and carriers were forbidden to prohibit union membership or discriminate against unionists. (The Australian experience has shown the value of unions to conciliation tribunals; see references, *supra,* p. 166, note 4.) This feature of the scheme was overthrown by Adair *v.* U.S. 208 U.S., 161 (1908), two judges dissenting. For the decisions on compulsory state arbitration, see *supra,* p. 166, note 4. A full discussion is given by S. P. Simpson, "Constitutional Limitations on Compulsory Industrial Arbitration," 38 *Harv. L. Rev.* 753 (1925).

[29] After the English general strike of 1926, Parliament authorized the Attorney General to apply for an injunction against the application of trade-union funds for a similar strike. Trade Disputes Act, 1927, § 7.

THE STATE AND ITS RIVALS [1]

In political science courses of 1905 we were handed out the hard and fast propositions that the state was sovereign, and somewhere in every state was located the center of sovereignty, the power to which all else must give way. Then followed the obvious illustration of the British Parliament, which could do anything it wanted except change a man into a woman. Some of us in a moment of rash inquisitiveness asked where this political superior existed in our own country. After an awkward pause we were assured that it consisted of Congress plus three-quarters of the states, since they alone could change the Constitution. [2] Those were the days before federal amendments chased each other like aeroplanes across the Atlantic, and we had already learned that the Constitution would probably never be altered again because of the great difficulties involved. Somehow we were not altogether satisfied to believe in a sovereign that slept like Frederick Barbarossa to awake once in a blue moon, and was, moreover, scattered in pieces across a continent. This alleged center of control seemed inadequate for a hundred million people, far less real than Tammany Hall, which was said not to be a part of our system of govern-

---

[1] A review of *Authority in the Modern State*, by Harold J. Laski, New Haven: Yale University Press, 1919. First printed in the *Harvard Law Review*, June, 1919.

[2] For a similar view, that sovereignty is in the states collectively, see Irving B. Richman, "From John Austin to John C. Hurd," 14 *Harv. L. Rev.* 353.

ment at all. We should have been much better pleased
with the explanation of John Chipman Gray: "The real
rulers of a political society are undiscoverable." [3]

The problem of the location of sovereignty within the
state was less simple than our teachers would have had
us believe, and now we begin to doubt whether sovereignty belongs to the state at all. Is it the sole ruler
of the people who dwell in the United States, or France,
or any other demarcated portion of the earth's surface?
Are there other forces operating in the same territory just
as powerful in their own spheres as the state, which cannot struggle against them without going down to almost
sure defeat? If so, those forces share the sovereignty and
leave the state only a limited control of affairs within its
borders. Such is Mr. Laski's conclusion.

To lawyers, of all men, his book, *Authority in the
Modern State,* is especially valuable, for it warns us not
to exaggerate the importance of law. From a purely legal
point of view, our teachers and John Austin, their master, may have been right. In our professional capacity as
judges and practitioners we must acknowledge the men
chosen under the Constitution as the supreme rulers of
the land and assert that the Constitution is changed solely
through the methods provided by its own terms. In that
capacity we recognize the validity of the three amendments of 1865-70 because of their formal adoption, and
ignore the fact that they merely register the result of a
four years' war, without which they would have been impossible. But just because this assumption that the law-
givers are the real rulers is an essential portion of our
professional conduct, we ought to be careful lest we re-

[3] *The Nature and Sources of the Law* (1st ed.), p. 77.

gard it as containing the whole truth. As thinkers and as citizens we must realize that there are powers behind the law-givers, not mentioned in the Constitution, which shape their acts and sometimes successfully defy them. Law is oftentimes only the formal expression of reality. Any corporation embodies the will of a group of men with a definite purpose, and that group might continue to exist even though refused recognition by the state. The Adamson Law was made, nominally by Congress, actually by unelected bodies whose representatives sat in the gallery during its passage and whom Congress rightly or wrongly chose to obey. Formerly tariffs were regulated by very different unelected bodies whose representatives did not sit in the gallery. In the days of Jethro Bass, the government of New Hampshire was in his room in the Pelican Hotel.[4] The Thirteenth Amendment was not created by Congress and the state legislatures, but by the Northern armies and the awakened conscience of a nation.

Even those who disagree with Mr. Laski and hold that the state as representative of all the people has no theoretical bounds will admit that there are practical limits beyond which it is not expedient for government to go, and will find in this book many interesting illustrations of those limits. One of the weaknesses of the study of politics in this country has been its concentration on American and English data, and even then without much consideration of the events of our own time. We have threshed over the old straw until we are sick of it. Unconsciously we have realized that the slavery question, which occupied the thought of our ablest men for forty years, has not much bearing on the problems of today.

[4] Winston Churchill, *Coniston.*

Mr. Laski's book has the great merit of freshness. He brings us a wealth of new facts from contemporary England and from the development of France during the last hundred years. Persons who are not specialists in politics and history will get most pleasure from the first chapter on recent encroachments upon the traditional irresponsibility of the state, and the last chapter, "Administrative Syndicalism in France," with its side lights on civil-service difficulties in this country. The study of Lamennais adds for most of us a new figure to the great victims of persecution. The chapter on Royer-Collard has great significance, for he faced intelligently the antinomies of order and freedom which confront us today, and Professor Freund [5] has directed attention to his scientific scrutiny of the proper limitations of freedom of speech.

As a foreign observer in our midst, the author's statements about the United States are full of interest. I shall briefly restate his theory with reference to his American illustrations.

We have long recognized in this country that certain individual interests ought to be free from legal control, which is therefore prohibited by our Bills of Rights. Fashionable as it has been to sneer at those documents in recent years, it may be that "with the great increase of state activity that is so clearly foreshadowed, there was never a time when they were so greatly needed." Principles which are the result of social experience are thereby put beyond the reach of ordinary mischance.[6] We have, however, assumed that there is nothing which

<hr/>

[5] Ernst Freund, "Debs and Free Speech," *New Republic,* May 3, 1919.
[6] Laski, *op. cit.,* 62, 101.

limits the government except these rights of individuals, ignoring the fact that the state is not the only association to which men are loyal. In his *Studies in the Problem of Sovereignty,* Mr. Laski narrated several defeats suffered by the state when it forced men to choose between it and a church in matters of the spirit. In its own sphere the church would seem to be sovereign. We have not realized this in the United States, because religion has been protected from political interference by tradition and law, but it is disclosed by the way in which the Quakers won exemption from military service during the Civil War and were accorded it as a matter of course in 1917.[7] Charitable and educational bodies should also be allowed to live their own lives, growing unfettered by legal restrictions based on the real or supposed will of dead men[8] —an interesting principle to a lawyer who is considering whether a college can abandon the sectarian requirements in its charter. On the other hand, charities ought to bear the responsibilities of an ordinary corporate enterprise, including liability for the torts of their servants. "A negligently administered charity may aim at inducting us all into the kingdom of heaven, but it is socially essential to make it careful of the means employed." The same duty of meeting its just obligations rests on the greatest association of all, the state.[9]

Thus the author, like Maitland and Gierke, regards the state as a large group, surrounded by other independent groups, which share in its sovereignty. This is a novel conception for American law, which has always failed to

[7] Page 45.
[8] Page 102. See Austin W. Scott, "Education and the Dead Hand," 34 *Harv. L. Rev.* 1 (1920).
[9] Pages 102-107.

"recognize fully the existence of social groups and group relationships," [10] especially that important group, the un-incorporated trade-union. Mr. Laski points out that the state can hold the loyalty of the unionist only until he thinks that in the given situation the union has the superior claim. He may believe that the object of a railway strike is worth the temporary industrial dislocation it causes, just as a statesman is willing to involve the country in the sacrifices of war for purposes he considers good.[11] We may not approve the workingman's choice of class welfare over public welfare, but it does impose at least a practical limitation on the power of the state.

Courts of Conciliation, as in Australia,[12] might reconcile the conflict of loyalties, but Mr. Laski proposes an entirely different scheme. He considers that producers must take a direct part in the control of production, and not merely mingle in the general mass of electors. The government can never deal adequately with the interests of the trade-unions, for it naturally represents the whole body of consumers, whose position is irreconcilable with that of the producers. The state may yield an occasional industry to the strikers to secure the public supply of necessities, as a Russian sleigh-driver flings a baby now and then to the wolves, but eventually the electorate will force the government to use its powers to keep down the high cost of living. Of course, the workingman is also a consumer, but not on a large enough scale to outweigh his interest as a producer. The higher wages to be obtained by striking are tangible and immediate; the

[10] Hoxie, *Trade Unionism in the United States*, p. 216.
[11] Pages 83, 84.
[12] See *supra*, p. 166, note 4.

lower prices to be gained if nobody strikes are too uncertain to influence him. Consequently, Mr. Laski conceives a duplex organization of society. Men will continue as individual consumers to elect the government which will supervise the supply of their needs. On the other hand, the trade-unions, representing men as producers, will choose an independent legislature and executive to regulate remuneration and working conditions. This producers' system, like the hierarchy of the Roman Catholic Church, will be outside the state. It is a functional federalism, which will derive much help from the experience of federalism in the United States. And when the interests of producers and consumers conflict, a sort of Supreme Court will decide between them.[13] The difficulties of this plan seem enormous, but there will probably be ample time to consider them before the scheme is adopted. It certainly emphasizes factors which must enter into any system that is ultimately established.

Not only is there danger that the state may become unduly centralized, but the same is true of the churches and the trade-unions. The life of Lamennais is a strong argument for federalism within the Roman Catholic Church, and it is rumored that autocracy is not wholly unknown in the American Federation of Labor. This leads the author to emphasize the freedom of the individual as against both the state and the group. The problem is evidently to find a mean between despotic unity

[13] Pages 85-89. Mr. Laski appears to have subsequently become doubtful of the feasibility of such a legislature of producers possessed of power, and would make it instead an organ of consultation, i.e., a body which the government should be compelled to consult before any policy be given statutory form. Laski, *A Grammar of Politics* (London, 1925), pp. 80-83.

and disintegration. He does not, it would seem, solve the problem, but he blocks out the factors which will determine its solution. Devices like federalism and the separation of powers help keep authority within bounds, but liberty is less a tangible substance than an atmosphere. The most carefully planned machinery of government will break down unless it is operated by men who think. "Every one who has engaged in public work is sooner or later driven to admit that the great barrier to which he finds himself opposed is indifference." "Thought is the one weapon of tried utility in a difficult and complex world." [14] Consequently, the mental qualities and methods of the electorate, the three branches of the government, the leaders of industrial groups, and the civil service, become a decisive element in political life.

Repression of thought in the electorate and the civil service will produce in the end just the kind of spirit that we want to get rid of—the revolutionary spirit. [15] The experience of France, set forth in the last chapter of the book, shows this conclusively. It is all very well to say that men ought to be loyal to the state. What do we mean by the state? After all, it comes right down to the government that we deal with, and the government comes down to the human beings that we deal with, which means those who will on occasion put us into the hands of the police. If the individuals in the legislatures and the departments of justice and on the bench do not stand for the best things men stand for—for the development of mind and spirit, and the search for truth—men begin to

[14] Pages 107-108, 188.
[15] This concluding paragraph of the review has appeared in a different form in *Freedom of Speech*, p. 375.

wonder whether, after all, that government ought to endure. We cannot love the state as a mystical unity if that unity as we actually face it prevents us from living a true human life. So, in order to make people loyal to the state, you must make the state the kind of institution that they want to be loyal to.

LIBERTY UNDER SOCIALISM [1]

SOME one has said that the difference between those eminent English sociologists, Sidney Webb and Graham Wallas, is that Webb is interested in town councils, but Wallas in town councilors. In the same way Mr. Brett perceives that the nub of Socialism is the officials. We should ask ourselves "not that conundrum so dear to philosophy, 'What is the state?' but the far more important and more easily overlooked question, 'Who is the state?' " He starts from Acton's proposition: "The end of government is liberty, not happiness, or prosperity, or power . . .; the end of government is that the private individual should not feel the pressure of public authority, and should direct his life by the influences that are within him, not around him." From this standpoint, the prevalent antithesis between conservatism and radicalism becomes unsatisfactory. On one side are the Liberals seeking Acton's freedom; on the other, those who want men controlled, whether by aristocrats or by bureaucrats. The Radicals, at least the Socialists, are merely one type of Conservatives, and it is against them that Mr. Brett seeks to rally his comrades in thought.

Some may deem this book unworthy of attention because of its lightness of touch and the absence of pro-

[1] A review of *A Defence of Liberty*, by the Hon. Oliver Brett, New York: G. P. Putnam's Sons, 1921. Reprinted from the New York *Evening Post*, April 16, 1921.

found scholarship. Thus Latin literature is set down as
"unimportant" in accordance with the author's theory
that great art is impossible without liberty. Rome may
not have produced "the Shakespeare of free England,"
but one would match Lucretius, Virgil, and Horace against
any other Elizabethan. Such broad generalizations are
characteristic defects of the stimulating conversation of a
well-read and observant man of the world, and that is
what this book is, a running comment on questions of the
day by the heir to a viscount, the grandson of an able
judge, fortunate himself in five years of association with
John Morley during his administration of India. What
it loses in solidity it gains in freshness. Socialism is for
him not a system in a row of books, but the activities of
a group of men in power, and he describes them as if he
had just been traveling in their country.

Consider, for example, the difficulties of an author in
the Socialist state, a problem which made even Bertrand
Russell hesitate to throw in his lot with Marx. How will
he fare with the bureaucrats?

The inclination of men who obtain the power to govern is to
use that power for the purpose of controlling not only the
actions but the thoughts of men. . . .

We shall be wise to ask ourselves whether the state newspapers will be anxious to print articles that conflict with its
policy or that attack its administration. It may quite possibly
be that the bureaucrat who is examining such an article will
contrive to lose it among the rabbit-warren of branches into
which he will have divided his business; or, at any rate, his
instinct will prompt him to decide that such an article is not
what the public wants. What will be the attitude of the state
publisher when confronted with a revolutionary manuscript?

Surely, it would not be surprising if he discovered in it faults of style and general lack of literary quality that would force him, most reluctantly, of course, to discard it in favor of a conservative treatise on the same subject. . . . Can we conceive an Oxford don deciding to publish the atheisms of Shelley, or the Duke of Grafton passing the letters of Junius for publication? . . . We can visualize the procedure accurately enough if we imagine the manuscript of Mr. Keynes's "Economic Consequences of the Peace" being surveyed by the myrmidons of the Coalition Government.

Now, this may not be a conclusive argument against Socialism, but it is practical comment on a real difficulty. So with the problem of the idle. The unfortunate and the stupid are not to be penalized under Socialism; will idleness also be exempt? If idleness is punished, how about the wife and children of the idle? And how will the bureaucrats distinguish idleness from stupidity? "It seems probable that if the official inspector does not like the color of my hair he will decide that I am idle and not stupid." Will he then deprive me of food until I work, or will he degrade me to a lower profession?

For these officials will be the distributors of all work. From the time the state selects a child's profession will go on "the business of filling up forms" that will be a constant occupation in the servile state. Mr. Brett lists the numerous classes of bureaucrats that will be required to pass on all the questions of life. What, for instance, is a luxury?

Could not hairpins be dispensed with if an order in council made it obligatory for women to have short hair? Shall men shave in a shop or at home? How can the number of people to be earmarked for employment in the state laundry be ascertained unless it is ascertained how many times a week the community is to change its underclothes?

And there will be no getting away from all this.

If we are not satisfied with the food at the state hotel we cannot go elsewhere, for there is nowhere else to go. If the state waiter is rude to us, we shall be as powerless to mend his manners as we are the manners of a telephone operator.

It is true that poverty gives the workman very little freedom of demand now, and Mr. Brett insists that Liberalism must give him more. But that a thing is bad now is no reason for Socialism, which would make it perpetual and universal. The workman now is the victim of vast economic forces; under Socialism he will be the victim of a visible bureaucracy, which would greatly increase his sense of tyranny. Socialists assume that human beings who dislike being ordered around by people who are better born or richer than themselves are going to relish being ordered about by people who are cleverer than they are. It is the illusion of the schoolmaster, which generations of schoolboys have failed to dispel. The nation which objected to the taxation of tea by George III in the eighteenth century and the monopoly of kerosene by Mr. Rockefeller in the nineteenth does not welcome with delight the prohibition of beer in the twentieth century, even though it is imposed by elective officials.

If these charges are not true, if officials are to be so perfect that such faults can be counted out of our political calculations, then also governments will have become needless, for "when the governors are perfect, the governed will be perfect also."

It must not be thought, however, that the author views the existing situation with complacent satisfaction. Liberalism must fight capitalism as well as Socialism. "The appeal that Socialism makes is that it alone is genuinely and sincerely determined to oppose the obstruction that capital makes to human progress." He points to the growing distrust of our democratic institutions and the overwhelming sensation of futility which is the nemesis of the organized party system. He attacks the secret juntas which control politics on both sides of the Atlantic, in England by the power to dispose of the vast funds that the sales of peerages and knighthoods produce, in America through excessive campaign contributions. And he puts his finger on unemployment as the open sore of our economic system. Although suspicious of Socialism because it removes the incentive of hunger and may have to tolerate idleness, he calls capitalism to account "the moment it is selfish enough to refuse security against hunger to those who are not idle." Most institutions have fallen, not because they were tyrannical, but because they were incompetent. The French aristocracy was far less oppressive in 1789 than a century before, but it had been unable to avert national bankruptcy. Men will stand much from a successful superior, but little when he accomplishes nothing despite his superior station. Unemployment is the bankruptcy of capitalism, and those of us who share Mr. Brett's qualms about the bureaucrats must bestir ourselves.

This tract for the times, sprinkled with such witty

phrases as "In the American melting pot the temperature is always at boiling point," ought to be read, for the personality of the public official is the greatest problem not merely of Socialism but of the state today with its multifarious control over human work and pleasures.

MILL TODAY [1]

THE problem of what rules of conduct should be imposed by law and the pressure of public opinion to limit individual independence was declared by Mill in his *Liberty* to be the principal question in human affairs. His solution drew a sharp line between "self-regarding acts," which affect only the individual himself, and acts affecting others. A man should not be compelled to act or to abstain for his own physical, mental, or moral well-being, but only if his conduct is calculated to produce evil to some one else.

The subsequent advance of science has demonstrated the need for revision of Mill's classic distinction between these two types of acts, in at least two important ways. First, Mill himself admitted that his distinction applied only to human beings in the maturity of their faculties, and that children must be protected against their own action. Now, we know that a very large number of adults have the mental capacity of children. Still others of normal ability are forced by economic pressure to choose against their own best interests. The existence of these large classes of dependents constitutes a much greater factor in determining the desirability of state supervision of "self-regarding acts" than Mill supposed. Shall the possibility that feeble-minded men will be stirred to assassination by bitter attacks on officials prevent normal citizens from hearing or reading such attacks? Shall adults

[1] Reprinted from part of a review in the New York *Evening Post*, Oct. 1, 1921.

be allowed to witness motion-picture plays which are un-
suited for minors, although children are sure to be present; or shall the whole audience be subjected to the standard of a ten-year-old child?

Secondly, the scope of "self-regarding acts" has been
immensely narrowed by the germ theory of disease and
the increasing complexity of modern life. What can be
more personal than constant failure to brush one's teeth?
Yet if several decayed molars result, poor health lessens
the individual's power to support his family, and his dis-
qualification for military service weakens the nation's
fighting strength. Other perplexing problems which have
become acute in recent years are military conscription,
prohibition of intoxicants, sabbatarian legislation, compulsory vaccination, control of drug addicts, suppression
of tobacco, sterilization of the feeble-minded, removal of
tuberculous persons to sanitariums, removal of children
from the custody of unwise parents, physical examination
before marriage.

The truth is that very few acts are wholly self-regarding, but some affect our fellow citizens much less than
others. Mill's rigid distinction is thus transformed into a
question of degree. Is the probability of injury to others
enough to offset the disadvantages of state interference,
such as the likelihood that it will prove futile, the expense
and annoyance of governmental spying, the weakening of
individual initiative, and self-reliance? The difficulties of
the problem of political freedom lie in its application.
Each concrete situation must be decided by a careful
weighing of all the conflicting factors. Mill's great strength
lies in his examination of many such situations and in his
powerful presentation of the benefits to society from unfettered individual thought and action.

THE BRITISH EMPIRE [1]

THE title of Mr. Jenks's book, *The Government of the British Empire*, arouses hopes which are not realized. There is very little in it about the British Empire or even the British Isles, outside England. One can learn nothing here about such vital colonial matters as the right of a British subject, e.g. a Hindoo, to possess full citizenship everywhere in the Empire; the legal status of the blacks in South Africa; the inclusion of natives in Indian councils; the unfortified frontier of Canada; colonial demands to share in Imperial foreign policy; the Australian Monroe Doctrine; the veto power of colonial governors and their liability to civil action for official misconduct; the relations of the various federal governments to their states or provinces. Under this last head we should like to read of the problem of McCulloch *v.* Maryland in Australia; the inability of the Privy Council to review Australian decisions on constitutional law unless allowed to do so by the Australian High Courts; or the extent to which the Canadian government exercises its veto power over provincial legislation. Much is said of English political parties, nothing of the French Canadian Nationalists, the Labor party in Australia, or Sinn Fein. Out of thirty-eight pages on courts, only half a page is devoted to industrial tribunals in the Dominions.

[1] A review of *The Government of the British Empire*, by Edward Jenks, Boston, 1918. First printed in the *Harvard Law Review*, April, 1919.

Yet the book is valuable as a storehouse of information about English government, gathered with much effort to secure accuracy and to include the most recent developments, of which it would be very inconvenient to learn elsewhere. For example, the terms of the 1917 franchise act are given with considerable fullness. This is the book to answer those troublesome questions which continually recur to the casual reader of English political novels and articles. What does the Lord Privy Seal do? How is a budget introduced? What is the function of the various English courts, ancient and modern?

There are occasional interesting discussions of constitutional and political principles. For example, it is questioned whether the old two-party system unfits the House of Commons for a proper handling of the problems of Empire. "Secret diplomacy" is felt to be necessary in a modified form. "Crises which, if handled confidentially, can be discreetly averted, are apt to become distinctly more unmanageable when they are discussed in public with the aid of an excited press, bent on arousing the passions of its readers." The sanest proposition, in Mr. Jenks's opinion, is a joint legislative committee on foreign relations, to which all international negotiations should be continually reported. (This frequent use of fear of the press as a check on popular control of government will perhaps one day suggest the treatment of newspapers as educational institutions instead of money-making enterprises.)

There are some features of the English Constitution, when spread out in its details, which transport us into the realms of Gilbert and Sullivan. Chapter I is devoted to "The King-Emperor," who "stands at the head of the

British Empire," and to his extensive powers over army, police, courts, legislation, foreign policy. But the last paragraph warns us against the natural impression "that the British Empire is an autocracy." All that has gone before is only make-believe, and the King-Emperor does not really rule the lives of his subjects by his personal likes and dislikes. Chapter II, "The Constitutional Monarchy," will make him safe for democracy. The curious outsider who wonders why this official exists at all is told of the immense "influence of the Royal Family in matters of religion, morality, benevolence, fashion, and even in art and literature." Passages in *Joan and Peter* spring to mind, and Max Beerbohm's cartoon of "Mr. Tennyson reading 'In Memoriam' to his Queen." And besides, says Mr. Jenks, "it is possible that the majority of the people, even of the United Kingdom . . . believe that the government of the Empire is carried on by the King personally." In other words, if he did not exist, it would be necessary to invent him.

It is suggested that the King-Emperor has three true political rights. The first is, to be informed by a daily letter from the Prime Minister of the public proceedings of Parliament and the secret discussions in the Cabinet. It is clear that this right has no effect in making the sovereign indispensable; if he were abolished, nobody would need the information and the Prime Minister's time would be freer. The second right is, to warn his ministers privately out of the lessons of his political experience, which is continuous, unlike theirs. The value of this right depends upon the certainty that the King-Emperor will be a man of political sagacity. Is inheritance the best method to secure that result? The third right is, to refuse to act on the advice of his ministers in certain rare cases. Thus he can refuse to appoint an unworthy man to office or to swamp the House of Lords with newly created peers. Mr. Jenks also thinks that he can refuse to dissolve Parliament under certain circumstances, but the citation of precedents is needed on this point. A possible fourth right is not mentioned, that of deciding between two candidates from the majority party for the office of Prime Minister. On the whole, the case for continuing the monarchy in England, as presented in this book, does not appear strong.

The book is as full of survivals and exceptions as a Latin grammar. Crown colonies are under the Colonial office, but Ascension Island is under the Admiralty. The inferior clergy are still summoned to Parliament, but they never come. Indeed an Anglican or Roman Catholic clergyman cannot sit in the House of Commons, but he can sit in the House of Lords as a matter of course. Scotch and Irish peers elect some of their number to represent them there. The unlucky Scotch lord who loses the election cannot even run for the House of Commons, but an Irish peer can. Every exercise of the royal authority until recently was required by statute to have three seals before the Great Seal, each imposed by a separate official, who should be entitled to charge a fee for his share in the process. "A cynical observer might say that the last provision afforded the most powerful guarantee that the statute would be obeyed." A member of Parliament cannot resign, but gets appointed Bailiff of the Three Hundreds of Chiltern, and automatically ceases to be a member; then he resigns as Bailiff. County courts have nothing to do with counties.

The Archbishop of Canterbury is a member of the Board of Trade. He is a Primate of All England, while his brother of York is only Primate of England. When a bishop dies, the cathedral chapter receive a letter from the Crown giving them leave to elect his successor. Unfortunately for the chapter a second letter follows close, containing the name of A, the Crown candidate. It is true that B's name is also added in this letter, to keep up the appearance of a free choice. But if the chapter elected B, they would be punished with all the terrors of a *praemunire*.

All these provisions of the British Constitution seem like papers stuck into pigeonholes at random, with the hope of systematic filing on a day that never comes. But let us be humble, and think of the Electoral College. What should we do if Democratic electors voted for the Republican candidate?

We may mention some discussions of minor details which interest an American reader:

(1) The Canadian government pays the Leader of the Opposition a salary out of the national revenue, because of the value to the country of systematic independent criticism. (2) Under the budget system, proposals for the expenditure of money can come only from the Administration; River and Harbor Bills are impossible. (3) When higher customs duties are proposed, no opportunity is given to importers to remove goods from bond before the taxes are enacted; the higher rate is levied at once, and if the proposed increase does not become law, the excess is repaid to the importers. (4) The Postmaster General, although a business rather than a political official, is necessarily a member of Parliament, because "persistent

questions in Parliament are one of the best means of
bringing about reforms in a department which, by the
very nature of its business, tends toward routine." Over
there he must explain if he abandons pneumatic tubes
because they do not pay, and then institutes an aerial
mail service. (5) Each university in the United Kingdom
is now represented in Parliament, and a college graduate
can vote for a University member as well as for his local
member. This use of an occupational as well as a geo-
graphical basis for representation is capable of wide extension. Trades-unions, bar associations, medical societies,
railroad presidents, might each choose members of Congress. (6) Certain sinecure offices exist in the Cabinet,
to which it is usual to appoint men whose advice is desired, but who do not wish to undertake definite depart-
mental work. We needed an office like the Chancellor of
the Duchy of Lancaster for Colonel House.

WOODROW WILSON [1]

WILLIAM ALLEN WHITE has been so prominent in the American Progressive movement that high expectations were aroused when he wrote the life of one who, with the possible exception of Roosevelt, was the foremost national leader of our time. Unfortunately, serious obstacles prevented him from answering two of the most important questions which the reader asks about Wilson.

First, what was Wilson really like as a man? The greatest biographies grow out of the intimate personal acquaintance of the writer with his subject. We are told from day to day what he did and said, what he thought of men and affairs and the universe. Mr. White knew Wilson only through a few brief interviews. Other biographers, though lacking personal acquaintance, have been able to picture the mental and emotional development of the man in his letters. Mr. White, while he has evidently had access to some of these, was not authorized to reprint them. They were reserved for the life by Ray Stannard Baker. These two great gaps, caused by want of personal knowledge and of correspondence, are imperfectly filled by the valuable information which the author painstakingly gathered from Wilson's friends and associates.

The second question has to do with the development of

[1] A review of *Woodrow Wilson: The Man, His Times, and His Task,* by William Allen White. Houghton Mifflin Company.
First printed in the *Nation,* Aug. 5, 1925.

Wilson's political ideas. Together with Disraeli, Wilson is one of the few men who set forth their political views in their writings before they engaged in active politics. Like Disraeli, Wilson's performance differed very widely from his program. When and why did he change? Mr. White's own political experience might have enabled him to picture the growth of Wilson's political views, but he fails to do so. He dismisses his books as mostly college texts. This is not an adequate description of *Congressional Government*, which is a picture of a political system in action that takes its place beside Bryce's *American Commonwealth* and the *English Constitution* of Wilson's favorite, Bagehot. A fascinating study might be made of the contrast between the views of the Presidency set forth in this book and Wilson's conduct in office. Somewhere in his letters and conversation and state papers, the material must exist which would enable us to trace the change.

Much more could have been done to fix Wilson's place in the Progressive movement, with which the biographer was actively familiar. Mr. White's statement that Wilson was at first unfriendly or indifferent to the movement probably has some basis in fact, but it still rests too much on conjecture. How do we know, for instance, that Wilson was "quite oblivious of the tumult in the East and the turmoil in the hinterland"? There must be notes of his lectures at Wesleyan and Princeton which would give concrete information on the matter. Mr. White's best contribution to this question is his emphasis on the Princeton controversy as turning Wilson's attention to the undue influence of great wealth upon matters of national importance, and his narrative of Wilson's relation to the Democratic machine when he became candidate for Governor of New Jersey. At this point the biographer's knowledge of practical politics enables him to say much of distinct value.

Although the subtitle holds forth promise of an account of Wilson's "times," little is said about this; much less than was to be expected from a close neighbor of Populism and Mr. Bryan. The best contribution is a single phrase, the chapter-heading on the 1916 election: "Our First National Liberal Victory." Unfortunately, as in most discussions of Wilson, the war overshadows in this book his achievements for American liberalism. The fifteen months between his first inauguration and August 1, 1914, deserve a much more intensive study than they have ever received. For a record of progressive legislation his first term may compare with Gladstone's first administration. Even after the war begins domestic questions ought to receive attention from a biographer—for instance, the controversial Adamson law. And adequate study would treat failures in liberalism as well as successes. Why, for instance, did a man whose whole training should have led him to value brains in politics consent to the haphazard selection of ambassadors? Was this owing solely to Bryan? How far did Wilson's dependence on the Democratic machine in the South force him to abandon his liberal program?

Such a friendly man as Mr. White is frequently shocked by Wilson's inability to make and keep friends. It must be said that the universal denunciation of him on this point loses some of its force when we remember the friends of his successor.

A material fact bearing on Wilson's character, a fact

concerning which Mr. White gives us little information, is his health. Even while he was at Princeton it was rumored that he took two hours' rest in the middle of each day. May it not be that a limited physical vigor caused him to dismiss persons and topics abruptly, in much the same manner as a hospital nurse unceremoniously sends out a visitor when the patient shows signs of fatigue? Wilson may have disregarded customary courtesies because he felt forced to save his strength for matters for which he thought it imperatively needed. If he had possessed the inexhaustible vitality of Roosevelt he might have put forth just the little energy required here and there to prevent subsequent disasters. Any one familiar with invalids will comprehend these sudden and irritable refusals to think or act further in a given direction. Mr. White hints at this explanation and shrewdly recognizes that Wilson's strength could have been much economized if he had not been unwilling to delegate important tasks to able subordinates—a fault wholly alien to the genial Kansan.

For all its merits of friendliness and insight, we lay down the book with the feeling that the story has not yet been told. This man was far more than "a shy, middle-aged gentleman." He cannot be explained by Mr. White's constant attempt to balance his Scotch maternal ancestry against his Irish forebears. Those of us who were aroused by Wilson in 1912 and 1916, as never before or since, are waiting impatiently to learn more of his mind and soul. We have waited through years of detraction; we have read, and heard praised without limit, all that was written against him by Walter H. Page, generously open to the contagion of English war-time fever, of whom it has been said that he was an excellent ambassador but that he was sometimes a little uncertain which country he represented; a man who, though an honor to America and a warm-hearted friend of Wilson, remained throughout wholly incapable of understanding the imperialism of all the warring nations, the temper of our West which did not want war, and the President's endeavors to build up a nation-wide desire for a permanent international settlement. Until we have Wilson's letters,[2] the best answer to such attacks is found in his state papers, of which Mr. White makes too little use, and which even after the lapse of years revive in us the deep emotions of the day they were written. No biography can give us this man so well as the paragraph in the address of January 22, 1917, which begins: "They [the terms of a lasting peace] imply, first of all, that it must be a peace without victory." That the speaker of these sentences should have been content with the Treaty of Versailles is one more, and the greatest, problem in the life of Wilson for which we still await the answer.

[2] Two volumes of *Wilson's Life and Letters*, by Ray Stannard Baker, have now been published, and the New York *Herald Tribune* is printing the remaining portion, which will contain Wilson's letters while President.

JOHN MARSHALL [1]

ALL those who have made the delightful journey through Beveridge's four volumes will be glad to compare his estimate of the mind and work of the Chief Justice with that of a distinguished student and teacher of political science. Despite the great merits of the longer biography, its uninterrupted eulogies occasionally give the impression that the former Senator from Indiana is placing before a national convention "that peerless statesman, John Marshall of Virginia," as a Presidential candidate. Professor Corwin supplements Beveridge's accounts of the historical backgrounds of Marshall's various important decisions by furnishing a critical judgment upon their legal significance and devoting much attention to the subsequent development of Marshall's constitutional principles. His comment on the Dartmouth College case is a good sample: [2]

Perhaps, however, it will be argued that the real mischief of the decision has consisted in its effect upon the state legislatures themselves, the idea being that large business interests, when offered the opportunity of obtaining irrepealable charters, have frequently found it worth their while to assail frail legislative virtue with irresistible temptation. . . . Yet, what is to be said of that other not uncommon incident of legislative

[1] A review of *John Marshall and the Constitution*, by Edward S. Corwin. Chronicles of America Series. New Haven: Yale University Press. First printed in the *New Republic*, Feb. 15, 1922.
[2] Page 169.

245

history, the legislative "strike," whereby corporations not protected by irrepealable charters are blandly confronted with the alternative of having their franchises mutilated or of paying handsomely for their immunity? So the issue seems to resolve itself into a question of taste regarding two species of legislative "honesty." Does one prefer that species which, in the words of the late Speaker Reed, manifests itself in "staying bought," or that species which flowers in legislative blackmail? The truth of the matter is that Marshall's decision has been condemned . . . for evils which have been experienced quite as fully in other countries which never heard of the "obligation of contracts" clause.

Corwin is not always so favorable. He stigmatizes Marshall's conduct of the Burr trial as "the one serious blemish in his judicial record," though extenuated by Jefferson's vindictiveness. Of the opinion directing Burr's acquittal, which Beveridge terms "a state paper of first importance," Corwin says, "Reputation is a great magician in transmuting heresy into accepted teaching." Only an expert in the law of treason can adjudicate this dispute, and the Burr trial will furnish an interesting passage in that unwritten treatise on the American law of treason, insurrection, and sedition, which ought soon to be called into existence by the great bulk of recent legislation and prosecutions against opposition to government. One wishes that Corwin had ventured a more decided opinion about Burr's guilt. He certainly does not share Beveridge's confident belief in his innocence. Did Burr himself know what he intended, or did he wander along the rivers, like Micawber, waiting for something to turn up?

One conclusion in this part of Corwin's book is questionable. Marshall held that it was not enough for the government to prove by two witnesses the occurrence of the supposedly treasonable assemblage on Blennerhassett's Island; since Burr was not there himself, it must also produce two witnesses to establish the fact that he ordered the assemblage or conspired with others to bring it about. Corwin, after stating that the common law did not require such strong proof and that the logical result of Marshall's view is to prevent the procurer of treason from being a traitor unless he personally participates in an act of war, continues: [3]

Such a result is monstrous, and what is more, it has not been found possible to adhere to it in practice. In recent legislation necessitated by the Great War, Congress has restored the old common law view of treason but has avoided the constitutional difficulty by labeling the offence "Espionage." Indeed, the Espionage Act of June 15, 1917, scraps Marshall's opinion pretty completely.

Marshall's opinion is not on the ash-heap yet. He was not guarding us against legislative extension of the criminal law, but against a different and very real danger, the excesses of judges. English judges had stretched Parliament's definition of treason so as to send men to death for conduct which was of moderate danger to the state or which was proved by testimony too weak for the severity of the punishment. Therefore, he insisted that our Constitution prevented judges from treating such conduct and such testimony as constituting the crime of treason, punishable by death and forfeiture of property. He did not hold that it prevented Congress from punishing this

[3] Page 110.

less serious or less solidly proved conduct as a different kind of crime. Indeed, in an earlier opinion,[4] he expressly stated the contrary:

It is therefore more safe as well as more consonant to the principles of our Constitution, that the crime of treason should not be extended by construction to doubtful cases; and that crimes not clearly within the constitutional definition should receive such punishment as the legislature in its wisdom may provide.

Congress did not wait until 1917 to do this. During the Civil War it made incitement of insurrection punishable by ten years' imprisonment, and conspiracy to overthrow the government of the United States by six years' imprisonment.[5] The conspiracy section of the Espionage Act, to which Corwin refers, punishes the slighter offenses of conspiracy to obstruct enlistment, etc., through speeches and publications, by imprisonment for twenty years.

Has not the value gone out of Marshall's opinion since Congress has now allowed the courts to convict for such conduct as Burr was charged with, without two witnesses? No; because the new offenses are not punishable, like treason, by forfeiture and death. Regardless of the correctness of his decision on the technical point, his rigidity in the Burr trial set the precedent for a strict construction of treason, which even in the excitement of the late war was always preserved in trials for that crime. The attitude of judges in the few and abortive treason prosecutions of recent years is in marked contrast to the loose interpretation which they gave to the Espionage Act

---

[4] *Ex parte* Bollman, 4 Cranch 127 (1807).
[5] U.S. Criminal Code, §§ 4 and 6.

and to the broad construction of treason by the House of
Representatives in the Berger case. It may be conjectured
that except for Marshall's firmness, many opponents of
the late war would have been tried for treason under the
old English precedents and convicted, and that death
sentences would have been inflicted by the judges who
made such generous use of the maximum penalty of the
Espionage Act.

One may also take issue with Professor Corwin's comment upon McCulloch *v.* Maryland,[6] that the Supreme
Court in construing state legislation looks at the facts,
i.e. its substantial effect in operation, and invalidates the
law if the legislative power is abused; but that in construing congressional legislation it is more liberal and
follows Marshall's "bolder method," holding that "where
power exists to any degree or for any purpose, it exists
to every degree and for every purpose." Does not any
difference in result arise from the fact that Congress has
no powers but those expressly given, whereas state legislatures have all powers except those expressly taken away,
so that the inquiry as to state legislation is usually focused upon the alleged limitation, and with federal legislation upon the question whether the power exists? In
the comparatively few cases which involve limitations
imposed by the Constitution on powers granted to Congress, is the court more favorable to Congress than when
it construes limitations upon the states? Would "due
process of law" be applied more gingerly to invalidate a
statute forbidding employers to discharge workmen for

[6] 4 Wheaton 316 (1819); see Corwin, 143. Corwin's view, that an
express Congressional power is unrestricted in scope, could hardly be
maintained since the overthrow of the Child Labor Tax, in 259 U.S.
20 (1922), three years after his book appeared.

joining a union, if it were federal legislation under the Fifth Amendment than if it were state legislation under the Fourteenth Amendment? [7]

It is interesting that J. B. Thayer also made a distinction in the attitude of the Supreme Court toward Congress and the legislatures, but very different from Professor Corwin's. Thayer held that the court should be very slow to invalidate acts of Congress, because it was a coördinate branch of the government, but could have a much freer scope with state legislatures, because they are inferior bodies. Both Corwin's and Thayer's distinctions may be questioned. First, such discrimination seems unneutral in a tribunal established to settle burning controversies between the nation and a sovereign state. Second, it seems inconceivable that any group of judges could consciously keep two inconsistent theories of constitutional interpretation operating side by side without falling into hopeless confusion.

Similar problems of the relation between nation and states have arisen in Australia, where their Supreme Court has followed McCulloch v. Maryland and held that Victoria could not levy an income tax on the salary of a postmaster employed by the Commonwealth.[8] One would very much like to have Corwin's opinion of the arguments against this phase of Marshall's decision advanced by Justice Higgins, formerly head of the Court of Con-

[7] Compare Adair v. U.S., 208 U.S. 161 (1908), with Coppage v. Kansas, 236 U.S. 1 (1915); Adkins v. Children's Hospital, 261 U.S. 525 (1923), with Murphy v. Sardell, 269 U.S. 530 (1925), federal and state minimum-wage laws.

[8] Deakin v. Webb, 1 Comm. L. Rep. 585 (1904); but this has been overruled by Amalgamated Soc. of Engineers v. Adelaide S.S. Co., 28 Comm. L. Rep. 129 (1920), which in the converse situation to McCulloch v. Maryland held a state trading concern to be within the operation of a federal compulsory arbitration statute.

ciliation,[9] that a tax which rests as lightly on a federal salary as on similar income from other sources is valid, and that it is time enough to raise the proposition that the power to tax is the power to destroy when obstruction of a federal agency is actually threatened in a concrete situation. Marshall's decision has undoubtedly landed us in many difficulties. It has led logically to the converse proposition that the United States cannot tax state instrumentalities, such as the income from state or municipal bonds, and thus brought about the present exodus of capital into such securities when it is badly needed in private enterprise, with a resultant haphazard distribution of the burdens of war taxation. A further complication is created by the embarkation of the federal government into merchant shipping and the states into liquor, banking, and grain elevators. If Marshall's reasoning applies, each sovereignty is able to withdraw large amounts of hitherto taxable business out of the reach of the other sovereignty. Realizing this danger, the Supreme Court refused to allow the liquor business in South Carolina to escape the internal revenue officers when it was taken over by the state dispensaries.[10] Will it similarly hold that coupons from North Dakota bonds issued to take over grain elevators are subject to the federal income tax? And can they be distinguished from bonds issued by New York City for its water business? No opinion is ventured, except that we are in a tangle. Similarly, Marshall's decision in Brown v. Maryland [11] that goods arriving in a state from outside were exempt from state taxa-

[9] "McCulloch v. Maryland in Australia," 18 *Harv. L. Rev.* 559.
[10] South Carolina v. U.S., 199 U.S. 437 (1905).
[11] 12 Wheaton 419 (1827).

tion or regulation so long as they remained in the original package, paralyzed the efforts of dry states to keep liquor out, and forced prohibition to become a national issue.

Corwin gives a helpful explanation of this absolutistic conception of national powers in fields where some scope for local action was practically desirable: [12]

The Constitution was established under the sway of the idea of the balance of power. . . . The nation and the states were regarded as competitive forces, and a condition of tension between them was thought to be not only normal but desirable. The modern point of view is very different. Local differences have to a great extent disappeared, and that general interest which is the same for all the states is an ever deepening one. The idea of the competition of the states with the nation is yielding to that of their coöperation in public service.

Although our present governmental machinery is satisfactory to secure this coöperation between a state and the nation, a serious and little-discussed difficulty is the absence of machinery to enable the states to coöperate with one another. Nothing in the Constitution prevents Massachusetts from taxing New Jersey bonds, though the United States cannot. This typifies the odd situation of forty-eight partially sovereign states regulating economic forces whose natural operation disregards state lines. The inability of the six New England states to adopt a uniform railroad policy; the obstacles to interstate rendition of deserting husbands; the want of reciprocity between states as to automobile licenses; the duplication and triplication of state inheritance taxes on the same securities, when justice and a healthy attitude toward fresh capital

[12] Page 229.

require the levy of a single tax, which should be distributed among the states concerned in a ratio roughly based on their respective interests; the conflicting decisions of state courts on commercial matters, even in their interpretation of the same section of a Uniform Law: all these problems of increasing gravity may have to be met by some new form of control from Washington, unless happily they can be solved by agreement among the states themselves, perhaps under the little-used clause of the Constitution which permits compacts between the states when Congress consents.[13] Even though Marshall's doctrine of national supremacy went far at times, perhaps it was unavoidable in order to reduce to a minimum the possibility of similar frictions between state and nation.

Such are a few of the problems in our system of government which are raised by Marshall's career.

[13] See further discussion by the author, 33 *Yale L.J.* 727; Frankfurter & Landis, "The Compact Clause of the Constitution—a Study in Interstate Adjustments," 34 *ibid.* 685 (1925).

ECONOMIC INTERPRETATION OF JUDGES [1]

LONG years ago, in the time of the Progressives, political discussion was focused on the problem: What is the proper task of judges in carrying on the work of a modern democracy? Those of us who think that the advocates of the recall of judges and of decisions were on the wrong scent must at least admit that they illustrated the proposition of John Stuart Mill, that the free expression of error is valuable because it puts truth on its mettle and forces it to justify itself to the public by strong arguments instead of resting content with antique and flabby reasoning. The controversy over the origin and merits of judicial review of legislation bade fair to produce a thorough reëxamination from a twentieth-century point of view of the questions: What does a judge do? What ought he to do? How shall he be chosen? How long shall he be left undisturbed in his office? There was a popular overhauling of these questions in speeches, newspaper editorials, and ten-cent magazines, and the publication of scholarly investigations by Beard, Corwin, and Mc-Laughlin. But before the problem of the judicial function was completely solved, the outbreak of the European

[1] Reprinted from the *New Republic*, June 7, 1922, with some changes. On the general problem of judicial method, *The Nature of the Judicial Process* (1922), by Benjamin N. Cardozo, now Chief Justice of the New York Court of Appeals, should be read.

254

war and the collapse of progressivism caused its importance to be forgotten.

New life has now been given to these issues by the
publication of Senator Beveridge's widely read biography
of our greatest judge. Study of the part which Marshall
played in American economic and political development
inevitably throws light on the work of judges in general.
Moreover, those who regard a judge as really a political
official, who consequently ought to be elected, controlled,
and removed by the people at large, point to Beveridge's
frequent praise, not so much of Marshall's legal ability,
as of his statesmanship. It is repeatedly stated that he
deliberately made use of small cases to establish his own
views of what was good for the nation. We are told that
the dispute in Marbury v. Madison had become "of no
consequence whatever to any one" as a concrete matter,
when Marshall used it to establish the power to declare
acts of Congress unconstitutional, a step "which for
courage, statesmanlike foresight, and, indeed, for perfectly calculated audacity, has few parallels in judicial
history"; that his decisions on international law illustrate
not only his legal knowledge, but "his broad conceptions
of some of the fundamentals of American statesmanship
in foreign affairs"; that in McCulloch v. Maryland he
rebuked disunionists and the Virginia Republican machine. Beveridge describes Fletcher v. Peck as a trumped-
up case, which a weaker man would have refused to decide, but thinks it one of the firmest proofs of Marshall's
greatness that he considered it necessary for the nation's
highest court to lay down plainly the law of public contract. Still more startling is Beveridge's opinion that

Johnson, a Republican justice, would have differed out-right from Marshall in this case, had not the disposition that Marshall made of it been ardently desired by the Republican leaders, Jefferson and Madison.[2]

Even if we regard with considerable doubt this presentation of judges as using controversies before them to carry out definite party policies, we must reckon with the sober judgment of Corwin, that Marshall refused "to regard his office merely as a judicial tribunal; it was a platform from which to promulgate sound constitutional principles." [3] Is the Chief Justice of the United States not merely the arbiter of disputes according to settled law, but in fact a statesman, creating national policies? If so, should not he be responsive to the popular will like the Lord Chancellor of England? And the same question exists, with slightly less importance, with respect to all other judges, federal and state.

Certainly, the views just quoted from Beveridge and Corwin are far from the orthodox theory of the judge's part in the development of law, that he applies already existing rules to the facts before him, or if a new rule is necessary he evolves it from existing rules by the application of rigid logic. This theory makes his operations as impersonal as those of an adding machine. The facts press the buttons, the cogs revolve, out comes the answer. Only one right answer is possible, but if the judge's mind is of an inferior make, a cog occasionally slips and the wrong result gets printed. However, the quality of the additions is not affected by the fact that the machine has been set in the city or the country, among rich or poor,

[2] Beveridge, III, pp. 125, 132, 593; IV, pp. 121, 304.
[3] Corwin, *John Marshall and the Constitution*, p. 122.

scholars or men of action. Advocates of this theory resent even the suggestion that Marshall's decisions were influenced by his early contact with Washington and his experiences of state incompetency in and after the Revolution.

At the opposite pole is the theory of Gustavus Myers' *History of the Supreme Court*, that a judge is a loaded roulette-wheel, which always makes the banker come out ahead. He describes Marshall and his associates on the bench as engaged in a ceaseless practice of "You scratch my back and I'll scratch yours," each justice virtuously abstaining from participation in the decision of cases affecting his own pocket-book in the confident expectation that the rest of the Court would stand by him in return for similar favors when their cases came up. The holocaust of corruption which he paints makes one suspect that Mr. Myers got his two books mixed up, and carried over into the Supreme Court too many impressions gathered in his researches into the history of Tammany Hall.

Others (and in part this is Mr. Myers' view), without charging a judge with corruption, lay great emphasis on his unconscious class bias as the main explanation of his legal doctrines. It is evident that as soon as we reject the adding-machine theory and admit that those doctrines depend on something besides strict logic, the question of what the additional factors are becomes very important. If a judge is only a political official, statesman perhaps, who makes deliberate choice of policies, the way is readily open for supporters of the economic interpretation of history to insist that his choices are largely attributable to financial motives and class attitude. Thus the reviewer of

Beveridge in the *New Republic* [4] thinks that "perhaps the decisive influence" in determining Marshall's mind toward nationalism was "his own economic interests," and that the fact that the Constitution of 1787 was calculated to protect Marshall's ownership of one thousand acres of land in Fauquier county under the Fairfax title, because it would prevent Virginia from disregarding treaty rights, "no doubt was influential in inclining Marshall to support" that Constitution in the Virginia Convention of 1788.

In view of the low value of frontier land and the number of forcible arguments of public advantage stated by Marshall to support his vote, it seems rash to assume that because his private profit might have swayed his opinion on a matter which obviously affected thousands of persons on whose behalf he knew he was deliberating, therefore it did sway him. As well assume that a man's insistence that exemption from Panama tolls for American shipping is a breach of a treaty, arises from his ownership of a few transcontinental railway shares, which may suffer from marine competition. That the desire to obtain necessities and luxuries for one's self and family, and the craving for the power which comes with wealth, are elements in the formation of character and opinions, is conceded. Furthermore, the accumulation of a large number of instances where differences of political views coincide with differences in economic status, as Beard proposes in his *Economic Interpretation of the American Constitution*, may show that economic motives must have guided

[4] Review by B. B. Kendrick, *New Republic*, April 6, 1921; correspondence between Professor Kendrick and Charles H. Burr, *ibid.*, May 4, 1921.

the action of enough unspecified men in a mass to decide the action of the mass. It is a very different matter to pick out a particular man in that mass and feel sure that economic motives explain his action. In the same way, life-insurance tables show how long the average man of thirty may expect to live, but not the actual longevity of Mr. Richard Roe, aged thirty.

The statement that the decisive influence upon the legal principles of any judge is economic is a generalization which, to be sound, requires, first, the elimination of his logical powers of reasoning and of negative data which indicate the presence of non-economic motives of greater strength than the economic motives; and second, the careful verification of affirmative data which indicate the operation of economic motives. For instance, in Marshall's case, the reviewer already quoted says, "As a practicing attorney in Richmond his largest fees are coming from the members of those very commercial classes who, with the land speculators, were most influential in the support of the new government." Is it so certain that his clients were mainly of this type? This could be tested by an examination of all Marshall's cases in the Virginia Court of Appeals (listed at the close of Beveridge, Vol. II). An inquiry into ten cases argued in 1793 and ten in 1797 shows four cases of family disputes over the division of a decedent's property, one case on behalf of a sheriff, one defense of a prosecution for assault and battery. No class conflict here! Two land-title disputes turn on technical points of law. Four cases on behalf of creditors look more promising for the economic interpretation; but one is against the grantee of a fraudulent conveyance, another to collect a debt from an English tobacco-buyer, another by a son-in-law against his father-in-law for a marriage portion, and the fourth to foreclose a mortgage on slaves. And in eight cases, Marshall's clients were debtors, the very class which suffered from the Constitution as interpreted by him. The only client from "the commercial classes" is the tobacco-seller! Although a complete investigation of all the cases appealed—and his poorer clients would be less likely to appeal—may not conform to these twenty,[5] it may be surmised, and is indicated by Beveridge's anecdotes, that Marshall's clients were well scattered through the social scale, and at any rate that he had no chance to become biased from constantly representing the rich against the poor.

The trouble with the economic interpretation of the conduct of an individual is that it is a *vaticinium post eventum,* which, knowing the result, is able to seize upon the particular economic factors which seem to justify that result. If the result had been exactly the opposite, very likely other economic factors could have been found to justify that. For instance, suppose the general attitudes of Marshall and Jefferson had been reversed. Whatever the influence of a thousand frontier acres on Marshall, what more natural than that Jefferson, who inherited

----

[5] Subsequent investigation indicates that these twenty cases (the first ten listed by Beveridge from 1 Call's Reports and the first ten from 1 Washington's Reports) fairly represent the kinds of clients Marshall had. An examination of the remaining forty-six cases listed from Call's Reports shows six argued for creditors, eleven for debtors, and such miscellaneous clients as a jailer, a sheriff, a slanderer, a man who wanted to build a mill, a soldier who had lost his pay certificate, boatmen who had helped salvage a wreck, the owner of a ship seized by the state, the whole group of Virginia successors to the Fairfax title on the Northern Neck (many of them pioneers), and William and Mary College. Family and land disputes are very frequent.

6,900 acres nearer civilization and bought 3,000 more, should be a conservative, that as an eldest son he should oppose the abolition of primogeniture whereas he actually secured it, that the founder of the University of Virginia should applaud the Dartmouth College case which safeguarded the wishes of donors, that the widely traveled internationalist should despise state lines? And John Marshall, born poor on a farm where thorns were used for buttons, married on small earnings, who spent years in paying off indebtedness to British creditors, who had frequent cases against wealthy men, so that their iniquities may have become clear to him, who had many debtors as his clients, who saw Europe under conditions which gave him good cause to hate all foreigners, who never went north after his military campaigns, how plain indeed the reasons why he became the champion of southern localism, the narrow interpreter of treaty obligations, and the partisan of agrarian debtors against urban and European capitalists!

All these explanations of the judicial task are too simple. A judge is not a calculating-machine, but a human being, subject to the subtle influence of heredity and environment, especially the surroundings and mental training of his first twenty-five years. And he cannot get outside of himself to do his thinking. His product is, therefore, bound to be affected by these influences. All the more need to recognize this frankly, so that he may lessen the risk of unjust decisions by allowing for the effect of large means or other personal factors upon his reasoning processes and thereby reduce their operation to a minimum, just as the astronomer learns to estimate the habitual lapse of time between the appearance of a star and his visual reaction to its light, and corrects his observations accordingly.

On the other hand, even if we reject the adding-machine theory and conclude that a judge's political or economic views play some part in the making of law, this does not mean that he should be selected on the basis of those views, as if he made law like a legislator or carried out policies like a Cabinet officer. The legislator initiates measures or votes on them solely according to his own views of policy or those of his supporters. The judge must wait until a controversy comes before him, and then must decide it, not by unrestricted considerations of policy or according to party welfare, but by rules of law. It is true that he sometimes has to work out new rules, and that even in the application of statutes his decision as to what they mean adds something to them which in a sense was not there before, but in all this his scope is limited by the preëxisting law. No one has stated this better than the judge who has been most quick to recognize social and economic aspects in law, Justice Holmes:

We do not forget the continuous process of developing the law that goes on through the courts, in the form of deduction, or deny that in a clear case it might be possible even to break away from a line of decisions in favor of some rule generally admitted to be based upon a deeper insight into the present wants of society. But the improvements made by the courts are made, almost invariably, by very slow degrees and by very short steps. Their general duty is not to change but to work out the principles already sanctioned by the practice of the past. No one supposes that a judge is at liberty to decide with sole reference even to his strongest convictions of policy and right. His duty in general is to develop the principles which he finds, with such consistency as he may be able to attain.[6]

I recognize without hesitation that judges do and must legislate, but they can do so only interstitially; they are confined from molar to molecular motions.[7]

This being so, the most important factor determining the quality of a judge's output is not his economic or social doctrine, but his legal power. By this I do not mean his knowledge of law conceived as a body of static rules, the way a football referee knows the rules of the game. The game of life cannot be played under conditions which remain constant from year to year, and law must change with life. Legal power includes comprehension of the principles of law evolved out of past experience, and in addition the training and ability to distinguish rules workable today from the unworkable, to discard outworn conceptions, to refuse to employ time-honored words without finding exactly what they mean. The principles of the past, after being thus clarified, are used and gradually extended to solve the complex problems of the judge's own time. If a whole court without this understanding of the law were installed in order to carry out a radical program which they heartily endorsed, they would accomplish very little. Their efforts to make a great leap forward would be futile for want of a solid jumping-off place, and they would be too confused to know whether in the end they were going backward or ahead. The ultimate tangled result would furnish no sound body of prin-

[6] Stack *v.* R.R., 177 Mass. 155, 158 (1900).
[7] Dissent in So. Pac. Co. *v.* Jensen, 244 U.S. 205, 221 (1917).

ciples to guide either subsequent judges or ordinary citizens anxious to conduct daily transactions in such a way as to be safeguarded by law.

All the talk about Marshall as a great statesman has obscured the fact that he based all his opinions on the words of the Constitution. He understood the law which he was applying. This, of course, meant more than knowing the clauses of the Constitution by heart. A judge interpreting a contract construes its words in the light of its purpose, and the more he knows of business, the better he understands the contract. So Marshall read the words of the Constitution so as to carry out the framers' purpose of founding a nation. Another man might have understood that purpose differently, but it is noteworthy that while for most of his régime a majority of his associates had been taken from the opposite political party, enough of these supported him to make his view the view of the Court in every constitutional decision but two. And in those two as in all the other constitutional cases where Marshall's court divided, the split did not at all coincide with party lines.[8] This indicates that the part which political views play is after all very small. And so probably with a judge's personal economic views. The so-called radical opinions of Justice Holmes proceed from a man

[8] The two constitutional cases in which Marshall was in the minority were: Houston v. Moore, 5 Wheat. 1 (1820), in which he agreed with the dissenting opinion written by Story, nominally at least a Democrat, and the majority opinion by Washington, a Federalist, was supported by three Democrats; Ogden v. Saunders, 12 Wheat. 213 (1827), in which Marshall, Story, and Duvall, a Democrat, dissented, and Washington with three Democrats formed the majority. Similar disregard of party lines (even if Story be called a Federalist) appears in the fifteen other constitutional cases in Marshall's time where the judges were divided in their views, though not always dissenting: U.S. v. Fisher, 2 Cranch 358; Fletcher v. Peck, 6 Cranch 87; Dartmouth College v. Woodward, 4 Wheat. 518; Gibbons v. Ogden, 9 Wheat. 1;

who expresses a conservative view-point off the bench, in his letter on Economic Elements.[9] There is, indeed, a non-legal element in his making of law, as with Marshall. Holmes interprets a statute or common-law principle in the light of its purpose, and understands that purpose because of his open-minded comprehension of the human activities which law serves only to regulate. So Lord Mansfield created modern business law because he understood business as well as law. Legal power is much; it is not all; but the important residuum in the equipment of a great judge is not, I believe, the possession of this or that political or economic or social view, but the desire to understand human life as well as embalmed legal experience.

The problem of the judiciary is, therefore, not the selection and easy removal of judges on a political or class basis, but the question, what methods will make it easier to place men of this legal and ultra-legal power on the bench, and after they are there will enable them to keep in continuous fruitful contact with the changing social background out of which controversies arise.

Osborn v. Bank of U.S., 9 Wheat. 738; Bank of U.S. v. Planters' Bank, 9 Wheat. 904; Brown v. Maryland, 12 Wheat. 419; Weston v. Charleston, 2 Pet. 449; Craig v. Missouri, 4 Pet. 410; Cherokee Nation v. Ga., 5 Pet. 1; Worcester v. Ga., 6 Pet. 515; Martin v. Hunter's Lessee, 1 Wheat. 304; U.S. v. Smith, 5 Wheat. 153; Mason v. Haile, 12 Wheat. 370; Satterlee v. Mathewson, 2 Pet. 380. In deciding what cases are constitutional, I have relied upon the *Writings of John Marshall upon the Federal Constitution*, Boston, 1839.
    [9] Holmes, *Collected Legal Papers*, New York, 1920, p. 279.

INDEX

NOTE. Only the most important judicial decisions are indexed; prosecutions are indexed by the name of the accused.

CONFESSIONS, admissibility of, 89-98; relation to self-incrimination, 95-98; false, 96.
CONNECTICUT, blasphemy prosecution, 111 *n.*
CONSCRIPTION, military, 8, 42, 57, 204.
CONSPIRACY, 122, 123.
CONSTITUTION. See various topics, e.g., SPEECH, FREEDOM OF; also UNITED STATES CONSTITUTION, and the names of states.
CONSOLIDATION COAL CO., 177.
CONTEMPT, for violation of injunction, 82, 187, 188; effect of *habeas corpus,* 77 *n.,* 78 *n.;* criticism of judicial decisions, x.
COOK, W. W., 188 *n.,* 189 *n.,* 203 *n.,* 210 *n.*
COOLIDGE, Calvin, 10, 30, 133.
CORBIN, A. L., 210 *n.*
CORONADO, case, 6, 186 *n.,* 202 *n.*
CORRISTON, Chief of Police, 90.
CORWIN, E. S., 245-253, 254, 256.
COUTTS, E., 84, 85.
CRANE, Judge, 102 *n.*
CRIMES, use of injunctions against, 80-88, 187, 205.
CRIMINAL ANARCHY. See NEW YORK; MASSACHUSETTS.
CRIMINAL SYNDICALISM. See SYNDICALISM.
CROMWELL, Oliver, 147.
CROTHERS, Samuel M., 115 *n.*
CROWLEY, Superintendent of Boston Police, 139, 152.
CURLEY, Mayor of Boston, 115 *n.,* 116, 144.
CUTTEN, G. B., 19.

DARTMOUTH COLLEGE, case, 245, 246, 261.
DARWIN, 4, 31, 34.
DAUGHERTY, H. M., Attorney General, 209, 213.
DAVIS, Elmer, 138 *n.*
DAVIS, Jerome, 173 *n.*
DAVIS, prosecutions, 150 *n.*
DAVISON, Archibald, 18.
DEBS, E. V., 133, 153, 200, 201, 216 *n.,* 219 *n.*

Decameron, 135 *n.*
DEFAMATION, calling man anarchist, 101 *n.;* injunctions of, 70 *n.,* 71 *n.*
DENBY, Edwin, 10.
DEPORTATIONS, x, 69, 121, 148 *n.*
DEVINE, E. T., 172.
DISBARMENT, of radical lawyers, x.
DISRAELI, 241.
DODD, E. M., 48.
DREYFUS, Alfred, 36.
DRURY, H. B., 164.
DUE PROCESS OF LAW. See UNITED STATES CONSTITUTION.
DURFEE, E. N., 210 *n.*

EDUCATION, 3-32; knowledge as problems, 3-21; biographical illustrations, 4-7; difficulty of current problems, 8, 9, 31 *ff.;* method of inquiry in colleges, 9-14; adult education, 14-17; alumni control of colleges, 17-21; academic freedom, 19-21, 26-29, 32-39, 146, 147; purpose of colleges, 22-39; false or exaggerated aims, 22-27; real aim, 9, 21, 27-39; research, 4-7, 9-14, 25, 26; legislative control of education, 33-35, 62-73, 99 *n.,* 103; teaching of evolution, 33, 34; see EVOLUTION; of history, 9-14, 34 *ff.* See COLLEGES; SCHOOLS.
EINSTEIN, 5, 6, 20.
ELDON, Lord, 185, 205.
ELIOT, C. W., 17.
ELLIOTT, Howard, 20, 21.
ENGELS, 107.
ENGLAND, allows comment on failure of accused to take stand, 97. See GREAT BRITAIN, BRITISH EMPIRE.
EQUITY, overstraining courts of, 87, 88, 205-207. See INJUNCTIONS; CONTEMPT.
ESPIONAGE ACT, 40, 41, 42, 43, 44, 47, 53, 65, 74, 103, 104, 105, 133, 204, 247-249; mail provisions, 55 *ff.;* repeal of 1918 amendment, x.

INDEX

EURIPIDES, 38.
EVARTS, W. M., 148 *n.*
EVIDENCE, rules of, 86. See
  CONFESSIONS; SELF-INCRIMI-
  NATION; WITNESSES.
EVOLUTION, laws against, 33,
  99 *n.,* 106, 147; work of
  Darwin, 4.

FANEUIL HALL, 149.
FASCISM. See ITALY.
FERGUSON, I. E., 101 *n.*
FISKE, prosecution, 128, 129, 130.
FLEXNER, Abraham, 24.
FOLEY, District Attorney, 139.
"FORCE AND VIOLENCE," legisla-
  tion punishing advocacy of,
  63 *ff.,* 75 *ff.,* 101 *ff.,* 108-110,
  119, 121.
FOSTER, W. Z., 164.
FRANCE, 220, 223, 224; press law,
  60; compulsory examination of
  accused in, 97; law of meet-
  ings, 156. See FRENCH REVO-
  LUTION.
FRANKFURTER, Felix, 210 *n.,*
  212 *n.,* 253 *n.*
FRANKLIN, 13, 135.
FRAUD ORDERS, of post-office,
  59 *n.,* 60 *n.*
FREEDOM, American conception
  of, 16; *v.* efficiency, 58, 87, 88;
  under Socialism, 226-231; Mill's
  views, 232, 233. See ASSEMBLY;
  CENSORSHIP; SPEECH.
FRENCH REVOLUTION, 11, 146,
  230; effect in England, 38, 39,
  105, 205.
FREUND, Ernst, 220.
FREY, John P., 183-189.
FROST, Robert, 107.
FULLER, Governor, 152, 153.

GARDINER, A. G., 155 *n.*
GARRISON, W. L., xi, 162.
GARY, E. H., 163, 165.
GIERKE, 221.
GILBERT *v.* MINNESOTA, 40-54,
  99 *n.*
GITLOW, Benjamin, prosecution
  of, 49, 51, 62 *n.,* 99-107, 117,
  118, 123, 127.

GLADSTONE, W. E., 242.
GLYN, Elinor, 135 *n.*
GRAY, J. C., 218.
GREAT BRITAIN, government of,
  234-239; control of Ministers
  by Parliament, 10, 237-239;
  effect of schools on government, 23; effect of French
  Revolution, 38, 39, 105, 205;
  free speech in, 104, 105, 107;
  censorship of plays, 141; Hyde
  Park, 154, 155; labor injunctions, 186 *n.,* 216 *n.*
GREENBAUM, Judge, 67.
GREGORY, T. W., Attorney General, 44, 49.

HALE, Swinburne, 69 *n.*
HALLS, PUBLIC, control of,
  116, 143-150. See ASSEMBLY,
  BOSTON.
HAMMOND, John Hays, 172.
HAPGOOD, Powers, 152, 159 *n.*
HARDING, W. G., 16, 133, 242.
HART, H. H., 91.
HART, SCHAFFNER & MARX, 165.
Harvard Law Review, 127 *n.*
HARVARD UNIVERSITY, 17, 18, 23,
  142.
HAYS, W., Postmaster General,
  61 *n.*
HIGGINS, Chief Justice, 166, 250.
HISCOCK, Chief Justice, 102 *n.*
HISTORY, teaching of, 9-14, 34-36.
HOLMES, Justice, 46, 47, 57, 60 *n.,*
  99 *n.,* 102, 105, 106, 107, 122,
  124, 191, 195, 262-265.
HOLT, Arthur E., 172 *n.*
HOOKER, Richard, 170.
HOUSE, E. M., 239.
HOWELL, Clark, 172.
HOXIE, R. F., 222.
HUDSON, M. O., 203 *n.*
HUGHES, C. E., 11, 155.
HUNT, E. E., 172.
HUNT, Governor, 133.
HYDE PARK, 154, 155.

ILLINOIS, sedition law, 133.
IMMIGRATION, x.
INDEX LIBRORUM PROHIBITORUM,
  30.

UNITED STATES COAL COMMIS-
SION, 172-182, 190.
UNITED STATES CONSTITUTION,
162; compared with British,
238, 239, 256; sovereignty,
217 ff.; separation of powers,
10, 11; appearance of cabinet
members before Congress, 10,
11, 238, 239; need of ministers
without portfolio, 239; Electoral College, 107, 238; relation
between nation and states, 249-
253, in war, 40-54; interstate
agreements, 252, 253; powers
of Congress, 249; taxation,
249-253; child labor, 202 n.,
249; minimum wage, 250 n.; interstate commerce, 202, 208-
215, see SHERMAN ANTI-TRUST
LAW; injunctions of strikes by
government, 200-215; compulsory arbitration, 166 n., 216 n.,
249, 250; contracts clause, 245,
246; treason clause, 131 n., 246-
249; "privileges and immunities" clause, 50.
Bill of Rights, 220; First
Amendment, 99 n.; origin, 124,
125; federal sedition law in
peace, 129, 130, 131 n.; religious
freedom, 112; confessions and
self-incrimination, 94-98; Civil
War amendments, 218, 219;
Fourteenth Amendment, 249,
250; and state sedition statutes,
49-52, 99 n., 103-107, 117, 120-
132; application to schools, 33,
67 ff., 99 n., 103, 104; right of
assembly, 150; relation of Fourteenth Amendment to First,
102 n.; Fourteenth Amendment
and police power, 67-69, 122;
and right to hearing, 71, 72;
and vague statutes, 121; and
inequality of classification, 121;
Eighteenth Amendment, 132,
229.
UNITED STATES STEEL CORPORA-
TION, 163-171.
UNITED STATES SUPREME COURT,
Gilbert v. Minnesota, 40-54;
Milwaukee Leader case, 55-

61; Leach v. Carlile, 59 n.,
60 n.; Wan case, 89-98; school
cases, 99 n.; Gitlow case, 99-
107; syndicalism cases, 117-
133; power to review state
criminal cases, 129; on compulsory arbitration, 166 n.,
216 n., 249, 250; on injunctions,
191, 193; under Marshall, 245-
264; divisions not on party
lines, 264; dissenting opinions,
107. See UNITED STATES CON-
STITUTION; JUDGES.
UNIVERSITIES. See COLLEGES;
EDUCATION; SCHOOLS; also
names of various institutions.
UNTERMYER, Samuel, 66.

VANZETTI. See SACCO AND VAN-
ZETTI.
VIENNA, 144.
VIRGINIA, revolutionary sedition
statute, 41; Marshall's cases in,
259, 260.

WALLAS, Graham, 17, 37, 38, 226.
WALLING, W. E., 166 n.
WALPOLE, Spencer, 155 n.
WALWORTH, Chancellor, 191.
WAN, Z. S., prosecution for
murder, 89-98.
WAR, state sedition statutes, 40-
54; post-office and pacifist
newspapers, 55-61; injunctions
against interference with,
203 ff.; legal duration of,
203 n.; policies, 16; Wilson in,
244; treason, 246-249. See
ESPIONAGE ACT.
WASHINGTON, G., 11, 13, 257.
WATCH AND WARD SOCIETY, 136-
139.
WEBB, Sidney, 226.
WELLESLEY COLLEGE, 117.
WELLINGTON, 23.
WELLS, H. G., 7, 236.
WEST VIRGINIA, coal towns,
176 ff.; coal-strike injunctions,
190 n., 196, 197.
WHIPPING, 111.
WHIPPLE, L. E., 111 n., 158.
WHITE, Chief Justice, 46, 47, 57.